THE DRESSMAKING BOOK

Books by Adele P. Margolis

THE DRESSMAKING BOOK

THE COMPLETE BOOK OF TAILORING

HOW TO DESIGN YOUR OWN DRESS PATTERNS

PATTERN WISE

THE DRESSMAKING BOOK

BOOK

A Simplified Guide for Beginners

ADELE P. MARGOLIS

DOUBLEDAY & COMPANY, INC., GARDEN CITY, NEW YORK

1967

Dear Linda:

This book is for you.
You must admit this is going to
great lengths to tempt you
to learn to sew.

               Your loving mother

Dear Mother,

Well, you've tried everything else to get me to sew. Dedicating a book to me must surely be the final step in the conspiracy between you and Dame Fashion. And who knows? Maybe, at long last, I have come to terms with my impatient nature and am ready to be led by the hand (as you so skillfully manage in this latest book) through what used to seem to me an interminable process—dressmaking. If I seem to wax a bit nostalgic in this brief note to you, it is because, as I read your rough draft manuscript, vignettes kept coming to mind. Like the time when I came home from school the very first day of first grade feeling utterly frustrated because they didn't teach me how to read right then and there. A clear and early indication of my need to see immediate results! Or that great chest of drawers I used to love to rummage through because it held masses of patterns, treasures of cloth, and that fabulous button box. Do reassure me that fingering those things wasn't merely a desire for possessions but a genuine love of color and texture as well as a little girl's sense of femininity and fashion. And my more recent abortive attempt at making a terrycloth beach robe. Now that I've read your piece on fabric selection I find that there are good reasons for the demise of the whole project—what beginner starts out on such loopy fabric which isn't meant to hold shape anyhow? I shall always remember vividly the day I took you all around Boston, and then to my favorite boutique in Cambridge, looking for a shirtwaist dress (which you hadn't had time to make) to wear traveling across the country. You were, I thought then, totally irrational. What's so special about fitting a shirtwaist dress? You and your darts! Remember all those salesladies we exasperated, all those dresses we didn't buy?

So now you've done it. Now I am beginning to understand. You have asked me to read this manuscript not so much from the point of view of my professional training as an editor but as a beginning sewer. Beginning sewer I am about to become. I've actually learned something about planning, selecting, layout, cutting, sewing, and fitting. I've gone along and followed all the little exercises you suggest here. I've even taken the old sewing machine you gave me years ago and had it completely overhauled. I'll have to get rid of the old rusty pins you keep complaining about, and I may even buy a thimble (perhaps more for your grandmotherly duties as a sewer of patches on young boys' articles) in my burst of enthusiasm. I am about to join the forty million "do-it-yourself" home sewers—and how I have scoffed at the "do-it-yourselfers."

The fact is that I am tired of clipping pictures of high fashion ensembles and fantasying about how, if I save for six months *very* hard, I might be able to buy one. And I'm tired of seeing rows and rows of the same dress on a rack in all sizes and colors which has the virtue of being priced right for everyone. I don't want to look like everyone. I want to look like me!

If a mother's duty is, among other things, to educate her child, you've done it again! *Well,* I might add. I know that your readers (many of them understand mother-daughter relationships, I'm certain) will share my spontaneous enthusiasm and realize that this "bouquet" to you from your progeny is no small tribute. I am no "Bertha-the-sewing-machine-girl" type. My goal is fashion; for putting it literally at my fingertips, I say lovingly

Thank you,

LINDA

CONTENTS

Hold That Line!   **212**
Back to backing: an insurance for the subtle shape of fashion —
how to cut the backing — how to mark and stitch it in sheer and
very lightweight fabrics, in lightweight to mediumweight fabrics,
in heavy fabrics and crisp backings — how to join the backing
to the outer fabric — how to underline a garment with fullness

That All-Important Lining   **216**
Lining used as a coverup in a fully lined dress — the staying
power of lining: to prevent "bagging" — lining used as a stay
in a dress

Thinking in the Round   **218**
Sewer turned sculptor — think form, work form, preserve form

No Exit?   **219**
Zip — and you're in — or out! — the easiest, fastest, most beautiful way to set a zipper: by hand — how to set and stitch the
regulation-zippered closing, the underarm dress zipper, the slot-
zippered closing

Happy Ending — the Hem   **224**
Adopt or adapt a fashionable length — settle the fabric and set
the hem — hem finishes: bound, French dressmaker's, edge-
stitched, slip-stitched, double-fold, rolled, whipped, catch-
stitched, "give-'em-the-works" treatment

Make a Skirt   **228**
A pretty skirt that fits well is worth its weight in fabric — plan
for making the skirt

The Waistband   **229**
Classic vs. unorthodox approach — grain makes the difference
— to determine the length and width of on-grain and bias waistbands — extension or underlay closing — interface or not, as you
prefer — locate the waistline — an easy method for attaching the
waistband to the skirt — how to make a topstitched waistband
— how to make an inside waistband

PART I

SO YOU WANT TO SEW!

Why Not?

So you want to sew! And why not?

Openly or secretly, what woman has not yearned to make herself as attractive as possible? Consciously or unconsciously, what woman has not sought some means of expressing her creative talents? And, what woman doesn't love to feel she has made a great saving on some item, be it fur coat or bargain-basement trinket? Where but in home sewing can she achieve all three—beauty, creativity, economy?

Add to this the lure of today's magnificent fabrics, the availability of high style in a range of patterns, the perfection of the new sewing machines which can do just about everything (well, almost)—and the inducement to sew is irresistible. No wonder so many women and girls are turning their hands to home sewing.

All you need to know to learn to sew

Sewing is an art. It would be less than truthful to suggest that any art is just one great, instant fun-fest. But if you know what you are handling and you understand the reasoning behind it, even a difficult procedure will seem easier.

Many a veteran sewer has learned most of what she knows from the instruction sheet that comes with a pattern. This is the hard way! Most pattern instructions are written with the assumption that sewers have some background knowledge or that they will know where to find the elementary information which because of space limitations cannot possibly be included in the pattern directions. That's why books are written on the subject. This one will provide the reader with all the information needed to learn to sew.

Despite the mystery the professionals always make of their trade, sewing skills can be readily learned. You don't need to be "born that way" or be initiated into some secret order before you can practice the craft. Anyone can learn to sew.

When the ABC's of sewing techniques are mastered sufficiently to make them a secondary consideration, the sewer can then concentrate on fashion. If the struggle with technique is constant, the art of sewing as well as the joy in it are both lost. However, interest and enthusiasm are equally vital. Where motivation exists, one can always find a way to solve a technical problem. Without motivation, the struggle to master technique becomes merely a dull exercise in character building.

Vintage stitching and a switch in time

When I was a little girl (many long years ago), I learned to sew by making yards and yards of sample stitches and seams. Then on to inspiring projects like bean bags, button bags, and pencil cases. Practical problems like mending and aprons. Miles of fine hemming on huck towels. For "kicks" at home—dozens of doilies, pillow covers, and bureau runners. And, for what the teacher's manual termed a "fitting climax for the pupil's training," a graduation dress celebrating the completion of the eighth grade. (I still remember mine—a smashing little number of white batiste with yards of ready-made rosebud trimming around the neck and sleeves. Never mind if it was somewhat soiled after a year's fondling and hand construction. It was proudly worn in the processional.)

It is possible that there are still those who place sewing skills first and then, at long last, reward the learner (assuming she has survived the ordeal and the boredom) with the thrill of making her first real garment. But in the main, this type of teaching has gone out of fashion along with whalebone corsets.

Rx for the use of this book

You could read this book through like a novel or stash it away on your reference shelf along with the dictionary and assorted magazine clippings and recipes. But you'll have a heap more fun if you make something pretty as you follow the text. Some of you will start timidly. Others plunge right in. It doesn't matter so long as you get started. So—sew!

SEE HOW IT RUNS!

You can do it all by hand but really there is no need to be quite so spartan (or so archaic) about it. Happily, the machine age has conferred its benefits upon the sewer along with the rest of humanity. This does not mean that you can exchange your hands for a set of push buttons. Fine hand-sewing is still essential for fine results but the sewing machine is the basis for present-day clothing construction.

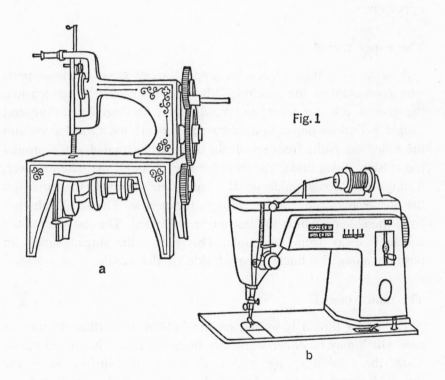

Fig. 1

a

b

Whether it looked like this (Fig. 1a) or looks like this (Fig. 1b), in principle the sewing machine has not changed since its invention, though many exciting features have been added.

This is how it works: two threads, the upper one coming from a spool, the lower one from a bobbin or shuttle interlock in the center of the fabric to form a stitch (Fig. 2).

To do this the threads must be placed in such position as to facilitate an easy flow while the machine is in operation.

All home sewing machines have this in common: the upper thread must be laced through a number of operating parts, the bobbin or shuttle must be wound and set, the tension disks and the pressure bar adjusted for the fabric used, the needle threaded, the bobbin thread drawn to the surface.

The method for doing all this is described in the instruction book which comes with your machine on purchase. Keep this handy for reference. Most companies also give some instruction in the operation of their sewing machines. It is well to avail yourself of this opportunity.

The upper thread

A series of guides places the upper thread close to those parts which accomplish the stitching—the spool pin, the upper tension, the thread take-up lever, the needle bar, the needle. In general (slight variations depend on make and model) the thread travels in the following path: from spool pin through the thread guide around the tension disks, under the thread guide, through the take-up lever, through the thread guide on the face plate, through the guide on the needle bar, and, finally, through the needle. The needle threads from the side on which the last guide is located. The flat side of the needle is away from the guide. This places the thread snugly in position along the finely grooved side of the needle.

The under thread

The under thread is wound on the bobbin or shuttle, set into its case which may be either stationary or removable. The thread passes under the tension spring, and is drawn to the surface when the threaded upper needle is forced down through the small hole in the throat plate, looping the upper thread around the under thread.

The sewing machine mechanism is a fascinating one which you might be interested in investigating at another time. Our concern as home sewers is with those parts which deal with the passage of fabric through the machine. There are five of these: the tension disk and spring, the stitch regulator, the presser foot, the feed dog, and the presser bar. Locate these on your machine from the diagram in your sewing machine manual.

The tension regulator

In order to form a strong, perfect stitch and a seam free of pucker, the pull on both the upper and lower threads must be

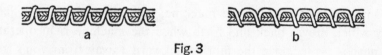

Fig. 2

equal. When this is so, the threads lock in the center of the material (Fig. 2). If the upper tension is tighter, the thread lies along the upper surface of the cloth while loops appear on the under surface (Fig. 3a). If the lower tension is tighter, the thread lies along the under surface, while loops appear above (Fig. 3b).

a   b

Fig. 3

Make a test. Cut two strips of fabric about 4″ by 8″. Place one over the other and stitch down the middle. If the tension is right the stitches will look the same on both sides of the material. If the upper tension needs adjustment, turn the tension nut which controls the disks. In the newer machines, numbers on the disk indicate the degree of tension; you simply dial to what you want. If the lower tension needs adjustment, use a small screw driver (this generally comes with the machine) to turn the screw which controls the spring on the bobbin case. Sometimes even though the tensions are balanced, a slight adjustment must be made to accommodate to the weight and texture of the material being used. For instance, knit fabric requires a looser tension because of its stretch quality.

The stitch regulator

A seam should be strong enough to last the life of the garment. Strength depends on the size and the number of stitches to the inch. The smaller the stitch (the greater the number to the inch) the stronger the seam. The larger the stitch (the fewer the number to the inch) the weaker the seam. The size of the stitch is governed by (1) the kind of fabric used, and (2) the function of the stitching. For instance:

  1. a sheer or filmy fabric like chiffon or organdy takes a small stitch while a heavy material like denim or drapery fabric takes a larger one.

  2. a basting stitch must be large enough to be seen readily and easily removed; a reinforcing stitch must be strong, therefore small.

If your machine doesn't have a stitch regulator, try this. Mark off one inch on a scrap of test fabric, stitch, count the stitches within the marking (see chart on page 59). Adjust as necessary.

The presser foot and the feed dog

On the throat plate of the machine, you will find a small, jagged part which moves back and forth when the machine is in operation. Its purpose is to move the fabric backward (away from you) so the needle will be ready to come down in the proper place for the next stitch. The length of this backward stroke depends on the size of the stitch. If the stitch is small, the feed dog moves a short distance; if the stitch is large, it moves a large distance. The feed dog feeds the fabric into the machine at a rate you determine by setting the length of the stitch.

Immediately above the feed dog is the presser foot. The presser foot holds the fabric in place so it can be fed into the machine. If the presser foot were not there, the fabric would be lifted up from the throat plate each time the needle lifted, forcing the machine to stitch in place rather than move the fabric backward smoothly. The presser foot must always be *down* before stitching begins.

Just the right amount of pressure is necessary to hold the fabric while it is being moved along. Too little makes it difficult for the feed dog to feed the material backward; too much pressure may leave a deep well along the seam line of the fabric or a seam imprint.

In general, light pressure is used for lightweight fabrics, medium pressure for mediumweight fabrics, heavy pressure for heavy fabrics.

There are these exceptions: if the fabric is very thick or has a pile like velvet, less pressure brings the presser foot closer to the surface and prevents either crushing the fabric or producing a well along the seam line. Less pressure is required when stitching around curves than on a straight line.

Often when the pressure is too great, the presser foot has a tendency to force the upper layer of the fabric toward you as the feed dog moves the under layer away from you. This stretches the top layer of cloth so that what started out as two equal lengths ends up with the top layer longer than the under layer. When the pressure is correct, both layers remain equal.

To regulate the pressure, turn the screw at the top of the presser bar, raising it or lowering it as desired. In some of the newer machines pressure is controlled by a dial rather than a screw.

Test your machine before you sew each fabric

Using a sample of your fabric, stitch two thicknesses together. Check the tension, the size of the stitch, and the pressure. Make whatever adjustments are indicated.

PRACTICE STITCHING FOR THE "I CAN'T SEW A STRAIGHT LINE, MYSELF" CONTINGENT

By this time you must certainly be anxious to try out that wonderful new machine which you have just acquired, be it ancient treadle or the very last word in new models.

Those of you who drive a car will recognize some of the same problems in handling your sewing machine: starting and stopping at a given signal, the relation of the pressure applied to the pedal and the speed, steering, maneuvering curves, turning corners, judging distances, hands and feet in position for co-ordinated action. The following exercises are designed to give you some practice in all of these elements so that you will get the "feel" of your machine.

Dry run

Trace the following charts (Figs. 4 to 8) to unlined paper. Leave your machine unthreaded.

1. Seat yourself comfortably—chair of proper height and in proper position, light directed on the stitching area, foot in position to operate the pedal, knee control, or treadle.

2. Raise the presser foot by lifting the lever.

3. Slip a chart under the presser foot. Place it so that most of it is to the left. This is the way in which you will later place your fabric in the machine. As you can easily see, the space on the right is too small for large sections of a garment while stitching. Set the paper so that the line of stitching will be directed toward you at a right angle.

4. Turn the balance wheel slowly with your right hand until the needle is brought down into the paper at the starting point.

5. Lower the presser foot.

6. Place your hands in position to guide the paper—left hand behind the presser foot, right hand forward. (Reverse, if this is more comfortable.) Keep your fingers away from all movable parts, particularly the needle. The idea is to get the needle through the paper and ultimately through the fabric, not your finger.

7. Start the machine by turning the balance wheel with your right hand while applying pressure to the pedal, knee control, or treadle.

8. Stitch slowly and evenly. Learn how much pressure is needed to produce the speed you want.

9. Slow down as you approach the end of your line of stitching and get ready to "brake" your machine.

10. Stop the machine at the stopping point. Turn the balance wheel until the thread take-up lever is all the way up. Raise the presser foot.

Starting and stopping

In this exercise (Fig. 4), it is more important that you learn to start and stop at the given points than to stitch a straight line, though it would be fine if you could do both.

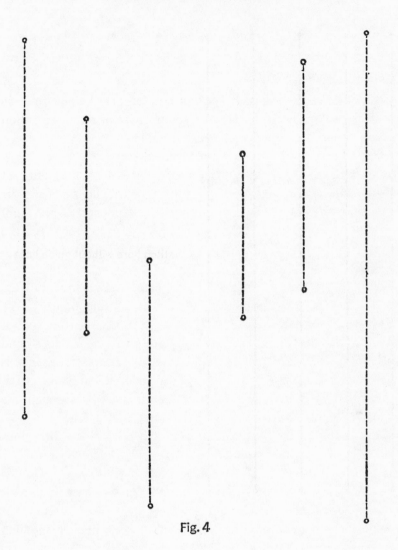

Fig. 4

A few practice exercises—straight lines

Stitch along these lines (Fig. 5). Ruled notebook paper or a shorthand book is excellent for this purpose. Stay on the track. Stitch slowly at first. Increase speed as you grow more confident.

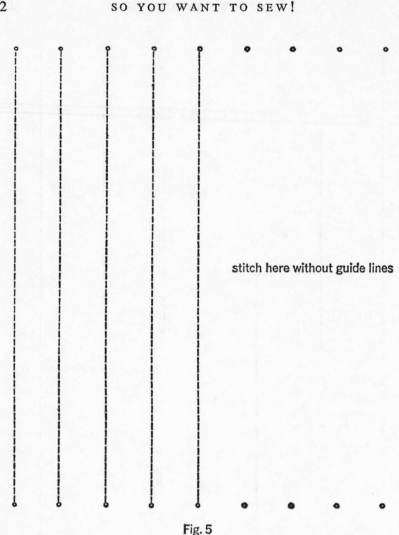

stitch here without guide lines

Fig. 5

Do the same thing in the unmarked space at the right, keeping the rows an even distance apart and as straight as you can.

Place a piece of paper in the machine and "stitch a seam" along the one edge. A seam really joins two pieces of fabric—we're pretending, of course. The standard seam allowance (that is, the amount of fabric between the seam line and the cut edge) on most patterns is ⅝". It is hard for beginning sewers to judge this distance by eye. Give yourself some help in any of the following ways.

1. Mark the seam line on paper or fabric ⅝″ in from the cut edge.

2. Use a "stitch guide" (an attachment for the sewing machine) set for this distance.

3. Mark the distance on the throat plate with masking tape, Scotch tape, or nail polish. The newer machines have seam allowance guides marked on them.

Turning corners

Fig. 6a

1. Bring the needle in the paper at the start of the stitching-point *1*.

2. Lower the presser foot.

3. Stitch along the line until you come to the corner.

4. Stop the stitching with the needle in the paper.

5. Lift the presser foot.

6. Pivot on the needle.

7. Lower the presser foot.

8. Repeat until the stitching is completed to point *2*.

9. Make a second row of stitching outside the first row and an even distance from it. Use your presser foot as a guide by placing the right prong on the previous line of stitching and keeping it in this position as the stitching proceeds.

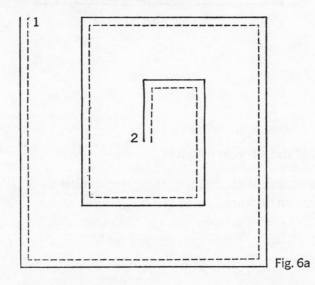

Fig. 6a

Fig. 6b
   1. Stitch the outside square.
   2. Stitch the center lines.
   3. Stitch the diagonal lines.
Make very sure that all lines cross *exactly* at the center.

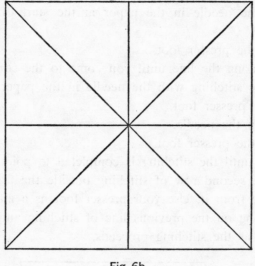

Fig. 6b

Change the size of your stitch

Practice straight-line stitching using large stitches, small stitches, and in-between stitches.

Circular stitching

Make a continuous line of circular stitching. Start at the outside (1) and stitch toward the center (2). Slow up for the smaller curves. Turn the paper as you stitch. Keep on the track.

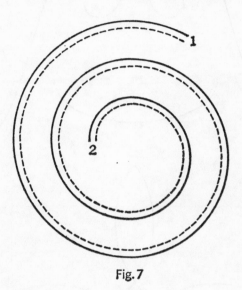

Fig. 7

Make a second row of stitching starting at the center (2) and stitching toward the outside (1). Use the presser foot as a guide for keeping the stitching an even distance from the original stitching. Try this:

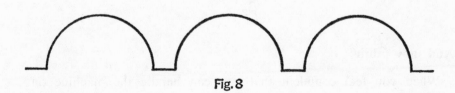

Fig. 8

And these arabesques just for fun! (Like floating through the air with the greatest of ease.)

Fig. 9

And now fabric!

When you feel confident that you can handle the machine on paper for straight lines, corners, and curves, thread the machine and try these same exercises using scraps of firm fabric in place of paper.

In the beginning striped or checked material or any visible line in the weave is a help in learning to follow a straight line while stitching. When your eye is trained to judge distances, dispense with these "crutches."

Note how the feed dog moves the fabric along without your assistance. You don't need to pull the fabric through. Use your hands merely as guides.

Practice stitching until you get the feel of the passage of the cloth through the machine and until you can control the direction of the line of stitching with ease and freedom.

FABRICS AND FIBERS

Having decided, for one reason and another, that he needed clothing, ingenious man looked about him and found the sources—both plant and animal—which could give him fibers from which to make cloth. These were (and still are) wool, silk, cotton, flax, jute, and hemp. The first four have had the most persistent use—wool for warmth, silk for luxury, cotton for low cost, linen for versatility.

In recent years there has been an astonishing growth of man-made fibers with truly remarkable qualities which have revolutionized the textile industry. At first there was considerable contention between those with unswerving loyalties to the "pure" fibers and those who sang the praises (to the tune of multi-million-dollar advertising campaigns) of the "synthetic" ones. It seems hopeless for the "pures" to hold the line against change. It seems equally hopeless for the "man-mades" to dismiss a heritage that is so deeply rooted in our culture. The current trend is a very sensible solution: to combine and blend the best features of both to create new fabrics wonderfully suited to contemporary living.

Facts about fabrics

Regardless of the source of the fiber—natural or man-made—several strands of it are twisted into yarns which in turn are woven or knitted into cloth.

In principle, weaving is exactly the same today as when man

first discovered that reeds and grasses could be strengthened by interlacing a set of lengthwise yarns (warp) with a set of crosswise yarns (woof, weft, filler). What was once a slow hand operation on a small loom is now mechanically and speedily done on a huge loom. The chief advances in weaving have been in separating or lifting groups of lengthwise yarns in a pattern so a filling yarn can be shot through with one motion of a shuttle.

It is possible that a haphazard or random weaving of the yarns may have produced a satisfactory cloth. But, being sensitive to design and rhythm, early weavers found it more satisfying to thread the yarns over and under in a planned pattern. The resulting cloth was more pleasing and more decorative. These simple basic weaves are still used today—the plain weave (Fig. 10a), the twill weave (Fig. 10b), the satin weave (Fig. 10c).

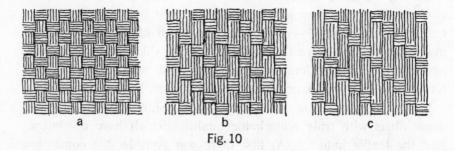

Fig. 10

An enormous variety of fabric is derived from these woven patterns by using various fibers (silk, wool, linen, cotton, synthetics), various kinds of yarns (thick, thin, tightly twisted, loosely twisted, looped, slubbed, etc.), various colors, and endless combinations of all of these.

Basic weaves

The *plain weave* is non-directional. It has no right or wrong side unless finished or printed so. In a solid color this weave is the easiest to use. It is highly *recommended* for beginning sewers.

In the *twill weave,* either the warp or filling thread is interlaced in such a way that it progresses one or more spaces to the right or left. This produces a diagonal line called a "wale." Twills *do* have a right and wrong side. If the wale goes up to the right on the right side, it will go up to the left on the wrong side. *Diagonal* weaves are difficult to handle. They limit the choice of style and require complex and judicious cutting—definitely *not recommended* for beginners.

The *satin weave,* like the twill, is a diagonal weave except that the "float" (any yarn that goes over two or more yarns) is longer. Though this gives a beautiful luster and smooth feel to the fabric, floats may snag or break. Fabrics of this weave call for directional cutting and special handling in sewing and pressing. It is wise for *beginning sewers* to *avoid them.*

In the *velvet weave* an extra yarn is woven through the cloth at right angles to it and the pile is cut through the middle (Fig. 11). Save these pile fabrics for *future projects.*

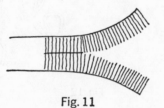

Fig. 11

A number of *novelty weaves* are derived from these basic weaves but they are not generally used for clothing fabric.

The "hang" of it

When the loom is set for weaving, the warp yarns (lengthwise) are laid first. These must bear the stress of separating and lifting, so they are pulled taut. Since they must also bear the weight of the filler threads (crosswise) they are usually tougher. This construction makes the warp threads straighter, stronger, and less apt to stretch than the filler threads. Because this is so, most fabrics are meant to hang with the lengthwise of the goods. For some fabrics it makes little difference whether they are used vertically or horizontally. Sometimes they are more attractive on the crosswise grain.

All yarns, whether crosswise or lengthwise, are called the grain of the fabric. The warp threads are the lengthwise grain; the filler threads, the crosswise grain. In your patterns you will find these grains referred to as the "straight of goods." Patterns are placed on fabric with strict observance of the straight of goods. This assures that the garment will hang as the designer intended it.

Basic knits

The *loop* is the principal unit of knitted fabric. When the series of loops runs horizontally (Fig. 12a) the fabric is called a filling knit. When the loops run vertically, the fabric is called a warp knit (Fig. 12b).

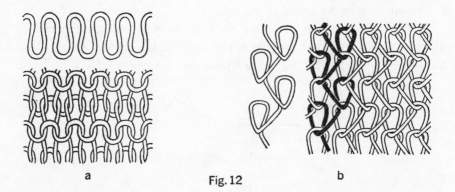

a   Fig. 12   b

In *filling knits,* the crosswise yarns are interlocked in a chain of stitches. When the chain is broken, the fabric "runs" or "ladders." You will recognize this as the knit of stockings and handmade sweaters. Cutting into such knits requires great care to avoid "running." In filling knits there is generally a right and wrong side. They are usually made on a circular machine and come to the consumer as tubular fabric.

In a *warp knit,* the yarn follows a zigzag path, forming a loop each time it changes direction. These loops interlock with adjoining loops, following a similar zigzag path (Fig. 12b). Warp knits are knitted flat. They stretch less, are firmer and stronger than filling knits. Because they don't run or snag, they can be cut like woven cloth. (Tricot is a warp knit.)

Double knits are made on a rib knitting machine. Two sets of needles produce the same stitches on both sides, as if the two layers of similar fabric were knitted together. They are knitted flat, have the stability of woven cloth, and are treated as such.

Knits are high fashion these days but perhaps you had better save them for a time when you are somewhat more experienced.

FACTS ABOUT FIBERS

To protect the consumer, Congress has enacted laws to require the labeling of the fiber content of fabric. Somewhere—stamped on the fabric or noted on a tag which accompanies the bolt of material —there will be a statement as to the fiber content (Fig. 13).

CONTENTS

____% Acetate   ____% Linen
____% Arnel   ____% Metallic
____% Bemberg   ____% Nylon
____% Cotton   ____% Rayon
____% Cupro   ____% Silk
____% Dacron   ____% Viscose
____% Fiberglas ____% Wool
____% Fortisan   ____% ....
____% Goat Hair ____% ....
____% Jute   ____% ....

QUALITY CONTROL

FINE FABRICS
SINCE 1897

Fig. 13

Wool is the fiber taken mostly from the fleece of sheep or lamb. Sometimes other specialty fibers are also classified as wool: camel's hair, vicuna, cashmere, mohair, angora, alpaca, and fur blends.

If the fabric is labeled "wool" it means it is made of new or virgin wool which has never been used before.

"Reprocessed wool" is wool that has been reclaimed from woolen fabric which has never been used before (clippings or scraps from clothing factories).

"Reused wool" is wool that has been reclaimed from woolen fabric which has been used before (old clothing, blankets, etc.).

Silk comes from the cocoon of the silkworm in long filaments, very thin but very strong.

"Cultivated silk" comes from domesticated silkworms. The filaments are fine and even (taffeta, satin, peau de soie, crepe).

"Wild, tussah, or raw silk" come from wild silkworms. These fibers are coarse and non-uniform, dry to the touch, both light- and heavyweight. Sometimes they have sheen but usually the color is matte or dull.

"Douppioni silk" is made of filaments from cocoons which have grown together making uneven nubs at irregular intervals (quality shantung, pesante, other slubbed fabrics).

"Waste silk" is the tangled mass of silk called noils, taken from the outside of cocoons or from damaged cocoons. Noils are fuzzy and dull, with irregular slubs, somewhat similar to douppioni (less expensive shantungs, spun silk, and rough-textured silks).

Like woolens, silks require labeling. When the fabric is made of silk fiber only, it is labeled "pure dye," "pure dye silk," "silk," "all silk," or "pure silk." Any metallic weighting, any loading or adulterating material, must be stated and the percentage noted.

Cotton is made of the soft, white, hairy fiber that grows on the seeds of the cotton plant. The cotton fibers are cleaned, then separated and straightened by carding. Combing after carding makes the fibers lie parallel. Combed cottons are high-quality fabrics. So are the long "staples" (long fibers). The finest of these are Sea Island, pima, and Egyptian.

Cotton has been subjected to a number of treatments and special finishes all of which it takes very well. Cotton can be made resistant to wrinkles, shrinkage, flame, mildew, spots, stains, and perspiration. It lends itself successfully to anticurl, glazed, permanent, water-repellent, and colorfast finishes. "Mercerization" adds luster and more absorbency.

The manufacturers who treat cotton fabrics to any or all of the above finishes are not only happy to comply with the government order to label them so; they proclaim their virtues in impressive advertising.

Linen is made of the fibrous material in the stem of the flax plant. Its fibers are long, strong, smooth, and pliable and vary so in size—from very coarse to very fine—that a great variety of fabrics can be produced from them.

Linen, too, requires labeling. "Linen," "pure linen," or "pure flax" means that the fabric is made entirely of linen fiber. The characteristic linen weave (plain weave) is often copied in inexpensive fabrics of rayon, nylon, or spun silk to make them resemble linen. Look for the label. It protects you.

There are literally hundreds of new *man-made fibers*. So many, in fact, that it is hard even for people in the textile business to keep up with all of them.

The methods for making synthetics chemically vary considerably. In general, the production involves these stages:

1. Some basic material is transformed into a liquid.
2. The liquid is drawn out into fine streams.
3. The liquid streams are changed into solid filaments.
4. The solid filaments (fibers) are combined to make yarns.

The yarns are woven or knitted into cloth in exactly the same way as the natural fibers. As with the natural fibers, the content of synthetic fibers is also noted on the tag which accompanies the fabric.

"THE RESPONSIVE EYE"

The beauty of fabrics makes dreamers—and collectors—of us all. This fascination with fabric is as symptomatic of the beginning as of the experienced sewer, though the addiction does increase with time. Many a hoard of precious fabric grows old along with its proud owner before she can bring herself to betray its promise by cutting into its splendor. However lovely the resulting dress, it is often an anticlimax.

Beauty by design

The beauty of fabric does not just happen. It is literally by design. The textile designer exploits those elements of color and pattern to which the eye so enthusiastically responds. The sewer, too, is concerned with these elements. They determine the choice and use of a particular fabric.

Color

The fiber, the type of dye, and the method by which it is applied determine the color and the degree of color fastness of a fabric. Dyes are supplied in the following ways.

Stock-dyed: the fibers are dyed before they are made into yarn.

Spun-dyed: dye is added to the solution from which man-made fibers are spun into yarn.

Yarn-dyed: the yarns are dyed before they are made into cloth.

Piece-dyed: the dye is applied to the cloth after it has been woven or knitted.

Cross-dyed: the same dye applied to one fabric composed of two different fibers produces two different colors, each fiber taking the same dye differently.

Dye penetrates fiber or yarn better than cloth.

Stock-dyed, yarn-dyed, or spun-dyed fabrics have more permanent colors than piece-dyed fabrics.

Pattern

Printing a design on cloth is very like dyeing. Rather than the color being applied to the whole cloth, it is applied only to certain planned areas. Even the same dyes are used except that a liquid form is used in the dye bath and a paste is used for printing.

In the long history of textile production, there have been many and varied methods of printing cloth. The two most used today are roller printing and screen printing.

Roller printing accounts by far for the greatest yardage. Actually, it is not profitable except on a huge scale. In turn, it is this vast production which makes it possible to offer so many attractive materials so inexpensively.

Screen printing is a hand-printing operation, done in small yardages by skilled and carefully trained teams. This makes hand-screened fabrics more individual, more experimental, more exclusive, and therefore more expensive.

Repeats. In every patterned fabric (woven as well as printed) there is a place in the design where a unit starts all over again. This is known as a *repeat*. (Obviously it would be impossible for the designer to conceive of, and the manufacturer to produce, one design as long as the projected yardage of cloth.)

In roller printing, the artist's design is transferred to a roller which prints the repeat over and over again. In screen printing, the artist's design is transferred to a screen which is moved along by hand. One repeat at a time is printed. In both roller printing and screen printing each color in the repeat is done separately in perfect register with the other colors. Modern printing machines can print as many as 16 colors at the rate of 200 yards a minute! Repeats are arranged in a planned, formal, regular pattern. The overall effect of a design is the result of this repetition.

The artist must plan his design so cleverly that the repeats join each other inconspicuously and harmoniously. Sometimes the designer is so ingenious and the design flows so smoothly from one repeat to the other that it is very difficult to discern the joining. However, it is very important to the sewer to find just where the unit begins and ends. To utilize fabric in the most pleasing fashion, the *repeats must be matched.* (You've no doubt run into this same problem when you've had drapes or slipcovers made. You know what a disjointed look can result if the repeats don't match.) Each repeat is made up of a motif (or motifs) which may be non-directional (Fig. 14a) or directional (Fig. 14b).

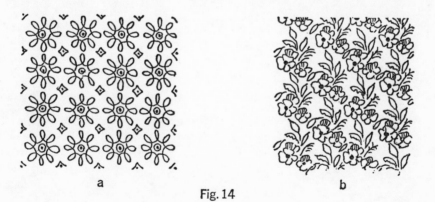

a   Fig. 14   b

If the design of your fabric is like that in Fig. 14a, it makes no difference how you hold it. The design is the same all the way around. Your pattern could be placed in any direction. If, however, your fabric is like that in Fig. 14b, the movement of the motifs is all in one direction. All pattern pieces must be placed going in the same direction. You certainly wouldn't want half a dress with flowers standing on their heads!

When buying your fabric

1. Find the repeats. (Stripes and plaids have repeats as well as florals and geometrics.)

2. Study your pattern for the number of sections which must match as they join.

3. Note the direction of the motifs.

4. Determine the amount of yardage depending on the size of the repeats, the direction of the motifs, and the number of sections which need matching.

PART II

GET READY!

AS EXCITING AS THE FABRIC THAT MAKES IT

A dress is a dress is a dress—but it is only as exciting as the fabric that makes it. And there are plenty of exciting fabrics today even among the inexpensive ones.

You may not want to put a great deal of money into your first few ventures. On the other hand, why work on something you wouldn't be proud to wear? Suppose, by some good fortune, your dress should turn out to be a surprising success. Wouldn't you be sorry that all that time and effort didn't go into something good?

When you have made several successful garments, move right up to quality fabrics. Don't remain fearfully pegged to innocuous ones. What if you do make a mistake or even spoil something? It's only fabric! Think how much you have learned! Besides, there's always more fabric, often even prettier than what you've botched. It is much more important that right from the start you develop a sense of freedom and boldness in your approach to sewing.

Here is a good guide: if you don't enjoy the material while you are working on it, you probably won't enjoy wearing it. Chances are you may not even want to finish it. On the other hand, you will discover what a delight it is to work on something that is a joy to look at and a pleasure to handle.

Made for each other

The first creative step in sewing is selecting a fabric that best interprets the style. Some fabrics are better able to do this than others. The designer refers to this as "hand." He means the feel of the fabric—its quality of smoothness or roughness, its softness or stiffness, its flexibility or drapability, its "dryness" or luxuriousness.

At one time, certain fabrics were always used for particular types of dresses. A shirtwaist dress was always cotton; an evening dress was always silk. This isn't true today! There are no rules! A shirtwaist dress can very effectively be made of satin; an evening dress of cotton. Witness the famous little Mainbocher pink-checked gingham evening dress—high fashion, noteworthy, and costly. Or Sybil Connolly's dream dresses of Irish linen.

An unusual use of fabric may give an unexpected charm to a dress. There is a whole crop of avant-garde boutique shops across the country whose success is the featuring of offbeat fashions in fascinating innovations of drapery fabric, bed ticking, burlap, etc. This takes a very special touch. Be imaginative and courageous in your choice of fabric *but* do strive for a fashionable rather than a freakish look.

Choosing your fabric is an exercise in your ability to visualize the effect of the material on the style, and vice versa. This may be a little hard to judge at the very beginning of your sewing career but it is one of the most challenging and satisfying aspects of home sewing.

Beginner's choice

There are lovely solid colors—clear, sharp, joyous, or soft, pastel, dreamy—in plain weaves and smooth surfaces which make charming dresses. They are easy to handle and permit a wide choice of style lines in your patterns.

A bright, bold, bizarre print is fun for a shift dress, either short or at-home length.

Also good choices: small all-over prints with non-directional motifs or prints with such complete coverage that an overall effect can be retained although motifs are not matched.

If your first project is a skimmer or shift dress, choose a fabric with some "body" to it so that it will hold its shape without understructure. Ditto for a princess-line dress or an A-line skirt.

If the design has a pressed pleat, choose a firm, close weave which takes a pleat well. Unpressed pleats are best in soft material.

Gathers, shirring, smocking, or draping call for soft fabrics which can fall in graceful folds.

Consult the back of the pattern envelope for suggested fabrics. You may depart from these suggestions only if substitute fabrics are of similar character.

Cotton is the easiest fiber to sew and makes the least expensive material for beginning explorations. Silk is the most difficult. A mediumweight, smooth wool handles well but requires special pressing techniques. Most synthetic fibers present some difficulty in stitching, sewing, and pressing.

In the beginning, every fabric will appear to present some problem to you. Many by their very structures present more difficulties than others. Even experienced sewers hesitate to get involved with the following materials: plaids, stripes, checks, and units which need matching, one-way designs, diagonals, either very sheer or very heavy material, very stiff or very stretchy cloth, naps, piles, puckered, or blistered fabrics. Beginners would do well to avoid these.

Don't skimp! Buy sufficient fabric. If anything, buy a little more than is called for in the pattern. This will allow enough yardage for straightening the grain (page 94), preshrinking when necessary (page 96), making any necessary alterations in the pattern (page 81), and (heaven forbid!) correcting any mistakes.

Before making a final choice of fabric read "The Pattern, Structural Diagram" (page 40).

Above all, do remember that the recipe for a memorable dress is simple lines, exquisite workmanship, flawless fit, and *beautiful fabric* that is the inspiration for it all.

HIGH STYLE IN AN ENVELOPE

By ear, by eye, by golly

There is a folklore that tells of sewers who by some very special talent are able to take scissors in hand, cut out a garment, whip it up, and presto—an exact replica of what one has in mind. Like many a myth there may be some element of truth in the tale. Undoubtedly some dressmakers—amateur or professional—are so familiar with the shape of a sleeve or a neckline or a collar that they can cut from memory. For most of us sewers this free-for-all method of cutting is undependable if not downright disastrous. We depend, and rightly so, on patterns for cutting into valued material. These may be individually designed and developed by the sewer. What is more likely, they may be selected from those commercially available.

By pattern

There are six major pattern companies in the home sewing field: Simplicity, McCall's, Advance, Vogue, Butterick, and Spadea. You will find attractive patterns, equally good and equally reliable, made by all of them. They offer a wide selection of styles of various degrees of complexity, in a range of figure types and sizes. There are plenty to choose from. You will find complete catalogs of each pattern company in department stores and fabric specialty shops. Current pattern books are available by subscription. The Spadea patterns appear in many newspapers across the country.

All of the pattern companies offer simple patterns for beginners. Simplicity's entire line is easy to make. McCall's has "Easy" patterns, Butterick has "Quick 'n' Easy," Advance has "Sew-easy," and Vogue has "Easy-to-make." Avoid the "Instant" patterns. They sound terribly appealing but they give very little experience in layout and cutting. Save them for "quickies" sandwiched between your learning projects.

As you grow more proficient and more confident, you will undoubtedly be lured by the big-name designer patterns which most companies feature. Spadea's entire line is its International and American Designer Series. The most difficult and the most exciting of the designer patterns are the Vogue Paris Original Models.

Beginner's choice

One way to test simplicity is to note the number of pattern pieces in the style. You will find this somewhere on the pattern envelope—either by actual number or by a little diagram showing the layout. Just remember, the fewer the pattern pieces, the fewer the headaches.

TRY THIS FOR SIZE

Pattern sizes vs. ready-to-wear

Wouldn't it be great if you could try on a pattern for size as you do a dress when you buy it?

The truth is, you really must try the dress on; there is such anarchy in sizing in the ready-to-wear industry. One can hardly blame the manufacturers. After all, who is going to change to a new set of measurements or even share his with a competitor if he has made a fortune with those peculiarly his own?

There is also the small matter of snob appeal. When you pay $400 and upwards for a dress, the manufacturer can certainly afford to throw in a little flattery as well. This makes it possible for you to squeeze into a size ten in an exclusive salon when you just about make it in a bargain-basement size fourteen.

Once you've worked out your size in a commercial pattern, however, you can depend on a certain uniformity of size whatever the pattern company, whatever the style, and whether it be dress, coat, or suit.

It takes a little doing, though, to determine your pattern size. There are several considerations: your body measurements, your figure type, the amount of ease* and the design.

Take a few body measurements

Wear the foundation garments you plan to wear with the dress you are making. The best measurements are taken over a slip. Using a tape measure, measure your bust around the fullest part. This is a snug but not tight measurement. Measure your waist comfortably. Next, tie a string around your waist to define it. Measure your hips around the fullest part. Note how far this is below the waistline string at center front, center back, and side.

Now, bend your head forward. Locate the prominent bone at which your head is hinged. Raise your head; straighten up. Have someone measure the distance between this socket-bone and the string at your waist.

Consult the measurement charts below to compare your measurements with those on the chart. (These charts are also found in the complete pattern catalogs.)

The standard measurement charts are based on statistics issued by the U. S. Government. They have been adopted by most of the

---

* Ease—an amount added to body measurements in length and width to allow for body movements and comfort in wearing. See page 39 for details.

pattern companies as the basis of their sizing and their figure types. The exception is the Spadea Company whose designer measurements appear in the chart on page 36.

Revised Measurement Chart for All Pattern Companies

Approved by the Measurement Standard Committee of the Pattern Industry

Select your size by the bust measurements on this revised chart. That size is your correct size for all patterns. These are actual body measurements, not garment measurements.

Misses	10	12	14	16	18	20
If bust is	31	32	34	36	38	40
Waist	24	25	26	28	30	32
Hip	33	34	36	38	40	42
Back waist length	15¾	16	16¼	16½	16¾	17

Junior misses	9	11	13	15	17
If bust is	30½	31½	33	35	37
Waist	23½	24½	25½	27	28½
Hip	32½	33½	35	37	39
Back waist length	15	15¼	15½	15¾	16

Teens	8	10	12	14	16
If bust is	29	30	32	34	36
Waist	23	24	25	26	28
Hip	31	32	34	36	38
Back waist length	14½	14¾	15	15¼	15½

Children	½	1	2	3	4	5	6
If chest is	19	20	21	22	23	23½	24
Waist	19	19½	20	20½	21	21½	22
Hip						25	26
Back waist length							10½

Girls	7	8	10	12	14		
If bust is	25	26	28	30	32		
Waist	22½	23	24	25	26		
Hip	27	28	30	32½	35		
Back waist length	11	11½	12¼	13	13¾		

Sub-teens	8s	10s	12s	14s			
If bust is	28	29	31	33			
Waist	23	24	25	26			
Hip	31	32	34	36			
Back waist length	13½	13¾	14	14¼			

Women	40	42	44	46	48	50	
If bust is	42	44	46	48	50	52	
Waist	34	36	38½	41	43½	46	
Hip	44	46	48	50	52	54	
Back waist length	17⅛	17¼	17⅜	17½	17⅝	17¾	

Half-sizes	12½	14½	16½	18½	20½	22½	24½
If bust is	33	35	37	39	41	43	45
Waist	27	29	31	33	35	37½	40
Hip	37	39	41	43	45	47	49
Back waist length	15¼	15½	15¾	16	16¼	16½	16¾

SKIRTS, SLACKS, AND SHORTS

Teens		8	10	12	14	16			
Waist		23	24	25	26	28			
Hip		31	32	34	36	38			

Junior misses		9	11	13	15	17			
Waist		23½	24½	25½	27	28½			
Hip		32½	33½	35	37	39			

Misses & women	10	12	14	16	18	20	40	42	44	46
Waist	24	25	26	28	30	32	34	36	38½	41
Hip	33	34	36	38	40	42	44	46	48	50

BOYS' AND MEN'S CLOTHING

Boys	1	2	3	4	5	6	8	10	12	14	16
Chest	20	21	22	23	23½	24	26	28	30	32	34
Waist	19½	20	20½	21	21½	22	23	24	25½	27	29
Hip					24	25	27	29	31	33	35
Neck-base girth						11½	12	12½	13	13½	14

Men										
Chest	32	34	36	38	40	42	44	46	48	50
Waist	28	30	32	34	36	38	40	42	44	46
Neck-base girth	13½	14	14½	15	15½	16	16½	17	17½	18
Shirt-sleeve length	33	33	33	33	34	34	34	35	35	35

Spadea's Ready-to-wear Size Charts

Regular sizing

Sizes	6	8	10	12	14	16	18	20
Bust	32	33	34	35	36½	38	40	42
Waist	22	23	24	25	26½	28	30	32
Hip (5″ below waistline)	33	34	35	36	37½	39	41	43
Length (nape of neck to waist)	16	16¼	16½	16¾	17	17¼	17½	17¾

For mature figures

Sizes	14	16	18	20	40	42	44
Bust	36½	38	40	42	44	46	48
Waist	27½	29	31	33	35	37	38
Hip (5″ below waistline)	37½	39	41	43	45	47	49
Length (nape of neck to waist)	17	17¼	17½	17¾	18	18¼	18½

For diminutives (short figures, 5'5" and under)

Sizes	8	10	12	14	16	18	20
Bust	33	34	35	36½	38	40	42
Waist	24	25	26	27½	29	31	33
Hip (5" below waistline)	34	35	36	37½	39	41	43
Length (nape of neck to waist)	15¾	16	16¼	16½	16¾	17	17¼

For tall girls

Sizes	8	10	12	14	16	18	20
Bust	33	34	35	36½	38	40	42
Waist	23	24	25	26½	28	30	32
Hip (5" below waistline)	34	35	36	37½	39	41	43
Length (nape of neck to waist)	17	17¼	17½	17¾	18	18¼	18½

For half-sizes

Sizes	12½	14½	16½	18½	20½	22½
Bust	35½	37½	39½	41½	43½	45½
Waist	27½	29½	31½	33½	35½	37½
Hip (5" below waistline)	35½	37½	39½	41½	43½	45½
Length (nape of neck to waist)	15¾	16	16¼	16½	16¾	17

For junior sizes

Sizes	5	7	9	11	13	15	17
Bust	31½	32½	33½	34½	36	37½	39
Waist	21½	22½	23½	24½	26	27½	29
Hip (5" below waistline)	32½	33½	34½	35½	37	38½	40
Length (nape of neck to waist)	15½	15¾	16	16¼	16½	16¾	17

Coats (capes, stoles, aprons)

Sizes	Small	Medium	Large
Bust	33–34	35–36½	38–40
Waist (used if garment has waistline)	23–24	25–26½	28–30
Hip (5" below waistline)	34–35	36–37½	39–41

Locate your figure type

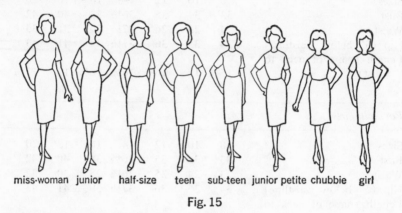

miss-woman junior half-size teen sub-teen junior petite chubbie girl

Fig. 15

You may know from your buying experience whether your size is a misses, women's, junior, half-size, teen, sub-teen, junior petite, chubbie, or girl's. The widest selection of patterns and styles is in the misses and women's sizes. If you are another figure type you may in time be able to buy these patterns and alter them to suit your figure requirements. At the beginning you will save yourself a good deal of time and trouble (not to mention frustration) if you confine your pattern selection to your figure type in the correct size.

If your measurements correspond to those on the chart, you are not only lucky, you are downright rare. There is nothing more unusual than the mythical "standard" figure. Practically no one is a perfect size. Most of us vary in some respects. Fortunately, patterns can be adjusted for most of these variations.

Read through the entire chart until you locate a set of measurements most nearly like your own—say, three of the four measurements. Since the bodice is the most difficult to fit, size is usually determined by the bust measurement. A method advocated by experienced saleswomen is the following: if you are 5'5" or under, choose a pattern one size smaller than your bust measurement would indicate; if you are tall or large-bosomed, choose the size indicated by the bust measurement. As a general rule, you will require a larger size in a pattern than you do in ready-to-wear. There is also this to consider: if a design has much fullness, you may be able to get away with a smaller size; if it is very fitted, you may need a larger size. If you are a borderline size—somewhere between two sizes—choose the smaller size and grade it up. Should the discrepancy between the bodice and hips be very great—say, a difference of more than one size—buy two patterns, one for the bodice and the other for the skirt.

As you look through the pattern books, you will notice that not all styles come in all sizes. Each style is designed for a specific size. What would be delightful on a junior miss might look ridiculous on a half-size.

Easy does it

If you were to construct your garments merely on body measurements, you would undoubtedly look very glamorous but you would hardly be able to move about your normal, daily tasks. Most garments have an extra amount of fabric over and above body measurements for wearability. This additional room is called ease. The amount of ease necessary, desirable, or preferable depends on: the function of the garment (you need a lot more ease in sportswear than you do in evening clothes), the design of the garment (some styles have a great deal more fullness than others), your personal preference (you may feel self-conscious in a tight-fitting dress or you may not want to wear any other kind).

The minimum amount of ease necessary in a fitted dress is 3" for the bust, ½" for the waist, 2" for the hips. You may prefer more or less. Here is one way to tell: try on a favorite dress, pinch out the excess fabric until the dress fits tight against the body, measure the amount of fabric in the "pinch."

The pattern you buy has the ease built right into it; you do not need to add any if the pattern is the right size. The one problem with the amount of ease in a pattern is its unpredictability. While the pattern companies all start with the same basic body measurements, they have different policies in regard to ease, some adding more, others less. (All of them add more than the minimum amount indicated above.)

Right size only

Beginners often make the mistake of buying patterns that are too large for them. This is understandable. They are fearful of cutting the garment too small without a chance for remedying the error. They feel safer with a larger one that can be taken in. But this is not the solution. Every pattern piece is scaled according to size. If you make a change in one, every corresponding piece needs similar adjustment. Too often, it is the shaping of the garment as well as its size that is affected.

Having gone to such lengths to determine your size, insist on getting it when you shop. Stores which carry patterns stock only a few in each size because of space limitations. It is possible they may not have your size on hand. The temptation is great to get what they do have at the urging of the sales person. Don't settle for anything but the right size. Altering to fit is too difficult, particularly at the start of your sewing career. If the right size is not available, order it.

Experiment and a little experience will tell you what size pattern is best for you.

THE PATTERN, STRUCTURAL DIAGRAM

A house, a bridge, a piece of furniture, a dress—all start with the designer's conception. This may be a dream or an actual design. But each needs a structural diagram to provide a working plan for its realization. A dress pattern is to the sewer what a blueprint is to an architect or a cabinet maker.

A pattern is generally made of paper. It is flat. It contains many symbols. If you follow their meaning and direction, you can convert this flat pattern (later a flat length of cloth) into a three-dimensional form which will fit the contours of the body.

You've had some experience with this kind of magic when as a child you made this little Easter basket from this pattern (Fig. 16a) or this lantern from the pattern in Fig. 16b.

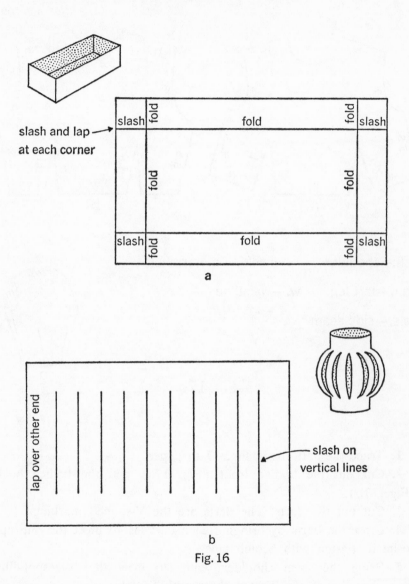

Fig. 16

A dress pattern achieves exactly the same three-dimensional quality by means of its *darts and seams*.

Trace and try

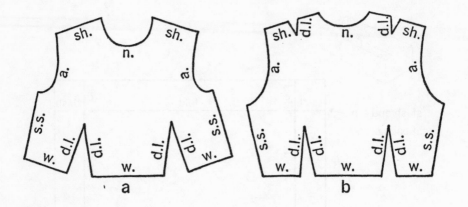

sh.—shoulder   n.—neck   a.—armhole

d.l.—dart leg   w.—waistline

s.s.—side seam

Fig. 17

1. Trace the patterns in Fig. 17 to paper.

2. Cut out the bodice front (Fig. 17a) and the bodice back (Fig. 17b).

3. Cut out the darts. The darts are the V-shaped markings.

4. Close the darts by bringing each dart leg to meet the one opposite it. Fasten with Scotch tape.

5. Bring the front shoulder seams to meet the corresponding back shoulder seams. Fasten them with Scotch tape.

6. Bring the front side seams to meet the corresponding back side seams. Fasten them in the same way (Fig. 17c).

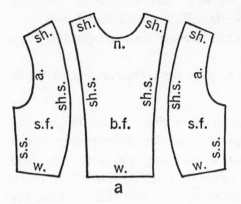

a

sh.—shoulder

sh.s.—shaping seam

s.s.—side seam

b.f.—bodice front

s.f.—side front

b.b.—bodice back

s.b.—side back

n.—neck

a.—armhole

w.—waist

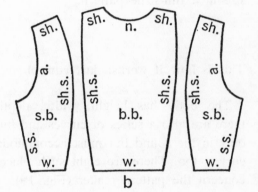

b

c

Fig. 18

1. Trace the patterns in Fig. 18.

2. Cut out the bodice front (Fig. 18a) and the bodice back (Fig. 18b).

3. Bring the seam lines of the side front sections to meet the seam lines of the center front section. Fasten with Scotch tape.

4. Bring the seam lines of the side back sections to meet the seam lines of the center back section. Fasten with Scotch tape.

5. Bring the front shoulder seams to meet the corresponding back shoulder seams. Fasten.

6. Bring the front side seams to meet the corresponding back side seams. Fasten (Fig. 18c).

Magic? No. It is the shaping darts in Fig. 17 and the shaping seams in Fig. 18 that have converted the flat paper pattern into a three-dimensional form. Were you to cut a length of cloth from these patterns and join the darts and seams by stitching instead of taping, you would produce a real garment—doll size in this instance, life size in a full-scale pattern.

This is how it works: dart control

The body has height, width, depth. Within these dimensions there are also a series of curves and bulges. A garment must fit not only in the round but must accommodate to all of these secondary curves, too. There are eight such places in a woman's body which concern the pattern maker (Fig. 19).

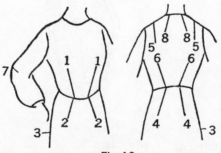

Fig. 19

(1) bust, (2) abdomen, (3) side hip, (4) buttocks, (5) upper shoulder blades, (6) lower shoulder blades, (7) elbow, (8) dowager's hump (back of neck).

When you come to think of it, these are the places where you find darts and seams in your clothing (Fig. 20).

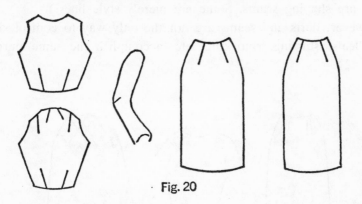

Fig. 20

So, of course, you will find them in corresponding places in the pattern (Fig. 21).

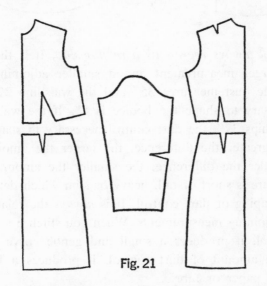

Fig. 21

Darts and shaping seams are clever devices which allow enough material to cover the body where it is fullest while at the same time providing a means of taking in the excess fabric in adjoining smaller areas. This principle is called dart control and it is the basis of all flat patterns.

The most usual and the simplest form in which the dart control appears is in the darts. The darts in Fig. 17 are called control darts. The shaping seams in Fig. 18 are called control seams. (Not all seams are shaping seams. Some are merely style lines.)

However, darts and seams are not the only way to control shaping. Pleats, shirring, smocking, etc. accomplish the same purpose (Fig. 22).

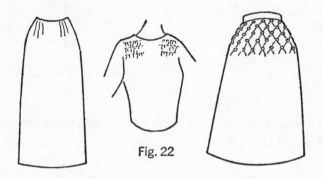

Fig. 22

Dart control always represents a relationship. It is the difference between a larger measurement and a smaller adjoining one. For instance, if the bust measures 35″ and the waistline 27″, the dart control necessary to shape the bodice is 8″. If the waist measures 27″ and the hips 37″, the dart control necessary to shape the skirt is 10″. The greater the difference, the larger the amount of control; the smaller the difference, the smaller the amount. It is not whether a figure is short or tall, heavy or slim which determines the amount of shaping or dart control. It is *always* the relationship between two adjoining measurements. When you stitch a small amount of dart control, it produces a small and gentle curve. When you stitch a large amount of dart control, it produces a large bulge. Try this with paper or fabric.

Dart control—a very personal matter

The moral is clear: if your pattern has too much dart control for you, it will create large bulges where you don't have them. If you have ample proportions and use a pattern that does not have enough dart control for you, the garment will not have enough shaping for you.

To be effective, the dart control *must* be located in the area where the high point of any curve occurs. A bust dart must head for the high point of the bust; a back skirt dart must head for the fullest part of the buttocks. If the dart control is not properly placed, it will release the fullness where it isn't needed and span the body in an area where it is needed. To make clothes that fit well, it is very important that the dart control be placed *where it is needed* and *in just the amount that is needed*.

Can you now understand why dart control is the key to good fit? Try on some of your "store-bought" clothes. Examine the darts and shaping seams. Are they right for you? Would a change in position or amount of dart control make the garment fit better?

An art to a dart

The placement of darts and seams affects not only the shaping and fit of the garment; it also affects the use of fabric. Any dart or seam when stitched interrupts the continuity of the fabric design. Therefore, you must use those which do so with the least disturbing effect.

To minimize distortion to the fabric, a large dart may be divided into several smaller ones (Fig. 23).

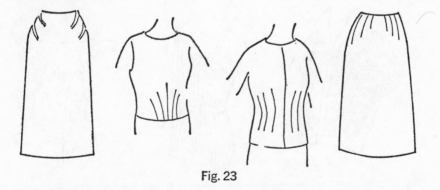

Fig. 23

When you use a solid-color fabric of plain weave, you have great freedom in the choice of pattern since it doesn't matter where the darts and seams are placed. When you use a figured material, either stripes, checks, plaids, a vertical, horizontal, or diagonal weave, or a spaced print of either large or small motifs, the placement of the darts matters very much, indeed.

A pleasing use of darts and control seams

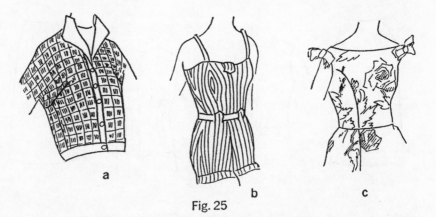

Fig. 24

Fig. 24a—Straight darts balanced on the straight lines of checks, stripes, or plaids.

Fig. 24b—Dart control used ingeniously on striped fabric to create design interest.

Fig. 24c—Control seams provide opportunity to use grain for design purposes.

Unpleasant breaks in the continuity of the fabric design (Fig. 25).

Fig. 25

Fig. 25a—French underarm dart makes it impossible to match the checks.

Fig. 25b—Control seam on a striped fabric produces exaggerated effect of questionable taste.

Fig. 25c—A beautiful floral design mutilated by a control seam. (Like deliberately breaking a beautiful vase.) There is an art to a dart!

THE PATTERN ENVELOPE — WHAT'S IN IT FOR YOU?

Patterns galore: pick one

Shifts, skimmers (or whatever they happen to be called in the fashion copy of your locale) are very popular today. They have probably encouraged more women to sew than any other known fashion. They seem so possible! And they are! In beautiful colors or exotic prints they make excellent first projects for beginners.

Park yourself at some pattern counter with all those wondrous catalogs or prop yourself up comfortably at home with one of the many pattern books available to home sewers and let yourself in for that great moment—the selection of a pattern.

This is a tempting world of fashion you have just entered. Everything can be yours for the doing. No frustrating price tags. Page after page of enormously appealing styles. Your excitement mounts. You are ready to buy half a dozen patterns—no matter that they look more intricate than you can handle at the present. BUT—hold yourself in check. All that comes later. For your first efforts limit yourself to a simple, collarless, sleeveless, straight or slightly flared skimmer dress or jumper. Plan to wear it belted or unbelted, semi-fitted or unfitted. Or, if you have more need for it, choose a sleeveless, collarless overblouse.

Having made your selection, note the name of the pattern company and the number of the pattern. Be sure to get it in the right size.

You are on your way!

Whether you pay 50¢ or $3.50 for the pattern, you are getting a great bargain. Much know-how is packaged in that compact little envelope. What does it offer you?

A pattern, like Gaul, is divided into three parts: the envelope, the pattern itself, and an instruction sheet.

The pattern envelope contains much important information which you really should examine carefully before you buy your pattern. In most places, patterns are not returnable. You must be quite sure this is exactly what you want.

Being the simplest of patterns, your present one will contain a minimum amount of the following information. In your future choices of more complex patterns, this information will be very important and very meaningful. You should know what to look for and what to expect.

The front of the envelope contains the following information:

1. The name of the pattern company, the pattern number, the size, and often the figure type.

2. Either a picture or a sketch showing how the completed garment will look. Sometimes there are several sketches showing different versions of the same design. These can be made by lengthening or shortening the pattern, omitting or including certain of the pattern pieces, for instance: a dress can be made sleeveless or with sleeves, with or without the collar, street or evening length; if it is a two-piece dress, the bodice and skirt may be shown of contrasting colors; if it is a design that can be successfully made up in a print, a stripe, or a plaid, one of the sketches will show this; if the dress has a jacket, both views will be shown.

From a construction point of view, the sketches are perhaps even more important. They show the placement of the darts and seams (we've seen how important these can be in co-ordinating the fabric with the pattern), the exact position of any pleats or other fullness, the number, placement, and relative size of the buttons, or if any other type of fastening is used, how the collar falls, where the pockets and flaps are placed, whether there is any trimming, the kind of belt suggested, and any other of the myriad style details which make up the design you have chosen.

3. Some label is present which characterizes this particular pattern as different from all others. It may state: Paris Original, Special Design, Designed exclusively by ———; or, it may say: Proportioned Pattern, Easy-to-Sew, etc. Whatever label that, in the pattern company's opinion, makes this pattern unique is prominently displayed.

5608

SUB-TEEN
Size 12S
Bust 31

A "HOW-TO-SEW" PATTERN

Including a tissue lesson-chart on "How to use stitching techniques"

Simplicity Printed Pattern **50c** IN CANADA **60c**

12 SIZES...3 PATTERN TYPES

SIMPLE-TO-SEW

AVAILABLE IN
SUB-TEEN: 8s-10s-12s-14s   TEEN: 10t-12t-14t-16t
MISS: 12-14-16-18

Fig. 26a

4. Also included: the price of the pattern; some measurement—most often the bust measurement, since this is the guide most frequently used for choosing size; sometimes the hip measurement, too.

The back of the envelope contains this information:

1. A line sketch of the back of the garment in its several views. Often this line sketch is easier to read than the illustration on the front, particularly if that happens to be a fashion photograph, which can be vague or misleading.

2. There is always some description of the design. For instance:

One-piece dress has shirt-style bodice with an Italian collar, set-in sleeves, and side zipper closing. There are soft pleats at waistline of full skirt, with a concealed opening at the left side. Belt may be self-fabric or purchased. View 1—¾-length sleeves are finished with buttoned sleeve bands. View 2—short sleeves roll up to form cuffs.

The information about the concealed opening and the rolled-up sleeves is vital. One could be unaware of the former and very mistaken about the latter.

Two-piece dress. Easy-fitting overblouse has bias front with cowl neckline. Short sleeve and sleeveless. Slightly gathered skirt joined to hip yoke.

Without this description, the sketch on the front could just as easily have been thought a one-piece dress with a hip length bodice. This information may make the difference in your entire approach to the design, the fabric, or the color.

Often there is not only a description but editorial comment:

Straight from Paris—brought from Balenciaga's showroom. The yoke front and patch pockets, placed at the new level, offset the two rows of buttons beautifully and give this design perfect balance. The back interest is typical of Balenciaga in that it has a low-placed martingale topping soft pleats. The pleats have a beautiful swing to them and are wonderful in motion. This pattern is carefully cut to keep all the subtle shaping of the original.

Now confess, aren't you just panting to get started on this? You see how important these descriptions can be.

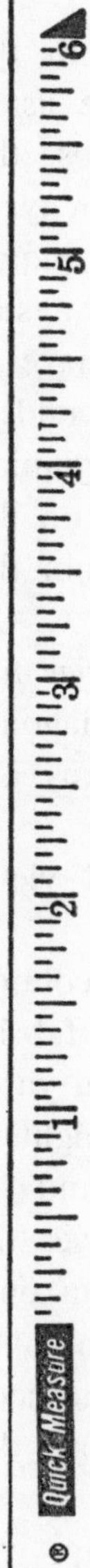

1
2
3
4
5
6
Quick Measure

5608

A PATTERN FROM SIMPLICITY'S "HOW-TO-SEW" SERIES

Extra fabric required for matching plaids, stripes, one-way design fabrics.
Use nap yardage and nap layout for one-way design.
This garment is not suitable for diagonal fabrics.

	SUB-TEENS				TEENS				MISSES				
Fabric required Sizes	8s	10s	12s	14s	10t	12t	14t	16t	12	14	16	18	
Blouse Even lengthwise striped or plain fabric													
35″, 36″ without nap	1¾	1¾	1⅞	1⅞	1¾	1⅞	1⅞	2⅛	1⅞	1⅞	2¼	2⅜	Yds.
41″, 42″ ″ ″	1½	1⅝	1⅝	1¾	1⅝	1¾	1¾	1¾	1¾	1¾	1⅞	2	″
44″, 45″ ″ ″	1¼	1¼	1½	1½	1½	1½	1½	1⅝	1½	1⅝	1¾	1⅞	″
Jumper or Dress													
35″, 36″ with or without nap	2¼	2⅜	2⅜	2½	2½	2⅝	2⅝	3	2⅝	3	3⅛	3⅛	″
44″, 45″ with nap	1⅝	1¾	2⅛	2⅛	2¼	2¼	2¼	2⅜	2⅜	2⅜	2½	2⅝	″
44″, 45″ without nap	1⅝	1⅝	1¾	1⅞	1¾	1¾	2	2⅛	1⅞	2¼	2¼	2⅜	″
54″ — ″ ″	1⅜	1½	1½	1½	1½	1½	1⅝	1¾	1⅝	1⅝	1⅞	1⅞	″
60″ — ″ ″	1¼	1¼	1½	1½	1¼	1½	1⅝	1⅝	1⅝	1⅝	1⅝	1⅝	″
Width of lower edge of jumper or dress	40¾	42	44¼	46½	42¾	45	47¼	49½	46	48	50	52	Ins.

Ribbon for blouse bow — ¾ yard of ½″ width (optional).

STANDARD BODY MEASUREMENTS	8s	10s	12s	14s	10t	12t	14t	16t	12	14	16	18	
Bust	28	29	31	33	30	32	34	36	32	34	36	38	Ins.
Waist	23	24	25	26	24	25	26	28	25	26	28	30	″
Hip	31	32	34	36	32	34	36	38	34	36	38	40	″
Back length — neck base to waist	13½	13¾	14	14¼	14¾	15	15¼	15½	16	16¼	16½	16¾	″
Finished back length of blouse	19¼	19½	19¾	20	21	21¼	21½	21¾	22¼	22½	22¾	23	″
Finished back length of jumper or dress	35	36	37	38	38½	39½	40¼	41	41½	42	42½	43	″

Sewing notions — Thread for each garment. Blouse: One ¼″ button. Jumper or Dress: Bias seam binding (opt.), neck type zipper; 20″ for sizes 8s thru 14s, 22″ for sizes 10t thru 16t and sizes 12 thru 18.

JUMPER OR DRESS AND BLOUSE IN SUB-TEENS', TEENS AND MISSES' SIZES: Simple-to-Sew. (INCLUDING TISSUE LESSON-CHART . . . "How to use stitching techniques.") Blouse has a collar, opening in center front seam and kimono sleeves with roll up cuffs. Ribbon bow is optional. The A line jumper or dress has a U shaped neckline, back zipper closing and optional patch pockets.

Suggested fabric types — Cottons, blends; stretch fabrics. Linen. Synthetics, blends; shantung. Jumper also in cotton suede, velveteen, corduroy, looped mohair, wools; blends; tweeds, double knits.

Printed in U. S. A.
© 1964 Simplicity Pattern Co. Inc., 200 Madison Avenue, New York 16, N. Y.
In Canada: Dominion Simplicity Pattern Ltd., 120 Mack Ave., Scarborough, Ont.
In Great Britain: Simplicity Patterns Ltd., 52-56 Osnaburgh Street, London, N. W. 1, England.

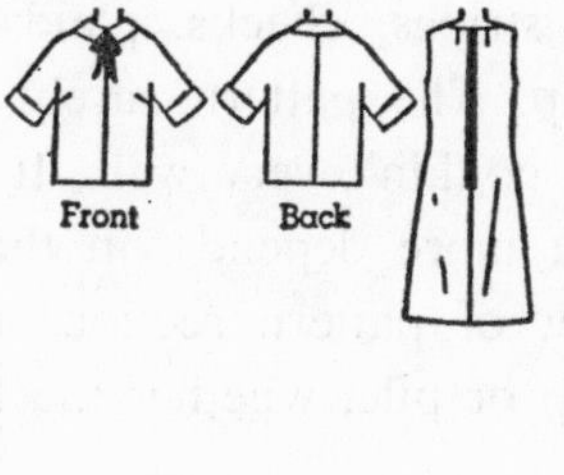

Front
Back

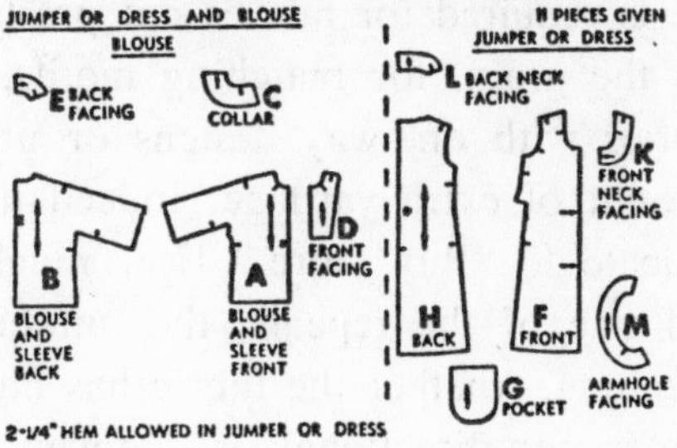

JUMPER OR DRESS AND BLOUSE
BLOUSE
E BACK FACING
C COLLAR
B BLOUSE AND SLEEVE BACK
A BLOUSE AND SLEEVE FRONT
D FRONT FACING
11 PIECES GIVEN
JUMPER OR DRESS
L BACK NECK FACING
K FRONT NECK FACING
H BACK
F FRONT
M ARMHOLE FACING
G POCKET
2-1/4" HEM ALLOWED IN JUMPER OR DRESS

Fig. 26b

3. Often the number of pieces in the pattern is stated. (Remember, the fewer the pieces, the fewer the headaches.) Or instead, there may be a diagram showing each pattern piece. You can count the number yourself.

4. A very important body of information is contained in the section on Suggested Fabrics. It is well to study this. Those listed best carry out the lines of the dress. While you may not choose the exact material suggested, you would be wise to choose a similar type. A dress envisioned in matte jersey would be impossible in pique; one designed for a light wool would be perfectly awful in a stiff ottoman. An unorthodox use of fabric (if that is what you have in mind) requires a thorough knowledge of interfacings and underlinings to achieve the effect that a particular fabric cannot. Beginning sewers would do well to be guided by the fabric suggestions on the envelope. These fabrics have been judged best able to sustain the lines of the design without elaborate sub-structure.

Perhaps even more important is the caution on what fabrics *not* to use. If the pattern says "Not suitable for stripes, plaids, diagonal weaves, naps or piles," you can be sure this is so. Patterns are tested before issued to ascertain the effect on these fabrics.

5. A chart gives the yardages necessary for the several views in those sizes in which the pattern is cut.

6. Find the view you wish to make, run a pencil down the column which shows your size until you come to the width of your fabric. Draw a circle around the amount. Don't forget that additional yardage is required for fabrics not preshrunk or sponged, for straightening the grain, for matching motifs, stripes, checks, plaids, and for fabrics with one-way designs or nap. The pattern rarely gives the amount of extra yardage. Indeed it couldn't very well. It can only indicate to "Buy more." How much more depends on the number and size of the repeats, the number of pattern sections that need matching, whether the fabric has nap or pile, whether the fabric design is non-directional or one-way.

7. Somewhere on the back of the envelope or on the flap, you will find an abbreviated body measurement chart. You may need this for reference. The pattern will also state the width at the sweep of the skirt and the length of the garment at center back when completed. Check these measurements against some article of clothing which you think fits you well and compare. You will then be able to decide whether some changes are indicated to bring this design more to your liking.

8. There is also a list of additional materials and findings necessary for this design: yardage of interfacing, lining, underlining; the number and size of buttons, length of zipper, seam binding, thread, buttonhole twist, shoulder pads, boning, belt, grosgrain ribbon, snaps, hooks and eyes, or anything else necessary to finish the garment.

Make a shopping list of all the items which you will need to make the garment. This can be done from all the information on the back of the pattern envelope.

Take the tissue pattern and the direction sheet out of the envelope. Set the pattern aside for the time being. Let us examine the instruction sheet first.

The instruction sheet

1. Examine the diagram which shows each pattern piece with its identifying name, number, or letter.

2. Look at the layout charts for the various widths of material in their several views and sizes.

3. Read the general information on stitching and pressing. This is, of necessity, meager because space is so limited in a pattern. To give all the necessary information, one would have to enclose a book like this one. Most pattern companies assume some background in sewing techniques.

4. Skim through the step-by-step directions for making this particular garment. Here is a language new to you. Before long you will learn this sewing vocabulary. You will then be able to read and interpret the directions. While the directions are not always adequate or clear, many a fine sewer has learned much of what she knows from the instruction sheet. We shall be working more with the instruction sheet as we proceed with our projects. But set it aside for the present. Also set aside the pattern, itself. While you are making your shopping list for fabric and findings, this is a good time to add the following tools which you must have to begin your sewing.

THE TOOLS OF THE TRADE

The proper tools make any job easier. Ask any man if this isn't true. Women are apt to ignore the fact. If you want to learn to do a professional-looking job in sewing, then get the tools with which a professional job is done.

Many of the needed supplies are already part of your home equipment. Some will be new to you. Aside from your larger purchases—sewing machine and iron—you will not be spending a great deal of money even if you splurge on all the equipment suggested. The cost will be made up many times over by the amount you save by making your own clothes.

1. Any *sewing machine* in good working order, new or used, either portable or table model. A simple machine without all the fancy gadgets is all that is required. You might even consider renting a machine for the period in which you are exploring your interest and ability in sewing. If you discover that you really enjoy it and plan to continue, you may want to invest in one of the many new wonderful models.

2. *A good cutting surface* is essential. Any one of these will do: a dining-room table (protected, of course), a metal folding-table, one of those fine folding cutting boards commercially available that has the advantage of being easy to store. In a pinch, a floor will do. A bed will *not* do; it is not firm enough.

3. *Scissors and shears* which are used only for fabric and thread. There is a difference between scissors and shears. The handles of *scissors* are the same size (Fig. 27a). *Shears* have one handle larger than the other (Fig. 27b). They may be larger or smaller than scissors. *Shears with bent handles* are used by professionals (Fig. 27c). They are easier to slide along the table.

A 3" pair of scissors is good for clipping and trimming seams. A 7" pair of scissors is a good all-around tool. When you graduate to cutting heavier fabrics, you will need shears. (There are shears for left-handed sewers, too.) Needless to say, points and edges should be kept sharp.

Use an old pair of scissors just for cutting paper. Pinking (Fig. 27d)

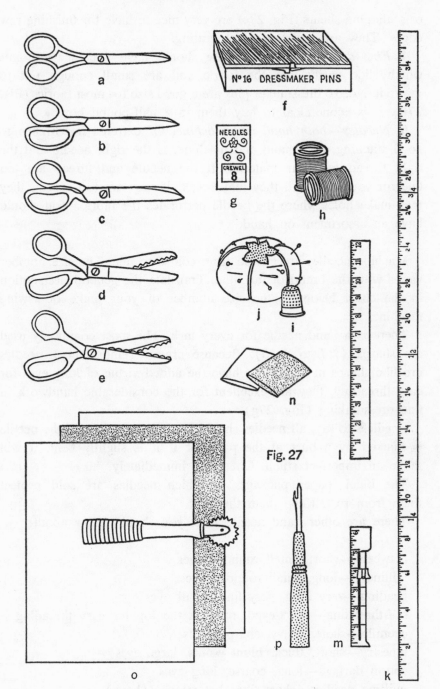

Fig. 27

or scalloping shears (Fig. 27e) are very nice to have for finishing raw edges. They are never used for cutting.

4. *Fine dressmaker pins.* These should have fine, sharp points which slide easily into the fabric and are small enough not to injure it. No. 16 dressmaker pins are a good size for most fabrics (Fig. 27f). It is economical to buy them in a half-pound box.

5. *Needles—both hand and machine.* Of extreme importance to good stitching, both hand and machine, is the right needle and the right thread for your material. If the needle and thread are too fine for your material, they may break; if they are too coarse, they may make holes where the needle perforates the fabric. You should have an assortment on hand.

Machine needles are graded from coarse to fine. The size number varies with the brand of machine. Translate the general designation in the chart below to the size number of your make of sewing machine.

There is a hand needle for every task. The most commonly used are sharps (#7 to #10). Because crewel (embroidery) needles are like sharps in length but have the added virtue of long eyes for easy threading, they are excellent for the considerable handwork in fine dressmaking (Fig. 27g).

Needless to say, all needles should have sharp points. If the needle is marred by a burr at the point or if it is slightly bent, it will make an imperfect stitch. Change it immediately.

The black paper packages in which needles are sold protect them from rust. Keep them there.

There are other hand needles that you should know about:

betweens—short, small rounded eyes
milliner's—long, small rounded eyes
beading—very long, very fine, small eyes
self-threading—calyx-eyed, open at the top for easy threading
chenille—short, heavy, sharp points
tapestry—short, thick, blunt points, large eyes
cotton darners—long, coarse, long eyes
quilting needles—short like "betweens" (above)

A guide to help you in selecting the proper needle, thread and stitch

Type of fabric	Machine Needle	Hand Needle	Machine Stitch per inch	Thread
Fine very sheer—net, chiffon	finest	10, 11, 12	16–18	silk—A mercerized cotton—70
sheer—organdy, lawn	fine	9	14–16	silk—A mercerized cotton—70
Medium light- weight chambray, gingham, crepe, taffeta	fine	8, 9	10–12	silk—A mercerized cotton—60, 70
Medium muslin, linen, chintz, velveteen, mediumweight silk fabric	medium	7, 8	10–12	silk—A mercerized cotton—50, 60
Medium heavy terry cloth, huck, denim	medium coarse	6	10	heavy duty cotton—30, 36, 40
Coarse heavy—dungaree, ticking, upholstery fabric	coarse	4, 5	8	heavy duty— 16, 20, 24
very heavy—duck, canvas	coarsest	3, 4	6	heavy duty— 8, 10, 12

upholstery needles—large and curved
mattress needles—double-pointed
glover's needles (three-cornered points for work with fur or leather)

6. *Thread* should match the characteristics of the fabric in elasticity and strength. This means using the same fiber in the thread as in the material (Fig. 27h).

cotton thread for cotton fabrics; they are both vegetable fibers
silk thread for silk and wool fabrics: they are both animal fibers
synthetic thread for man-made fabrics: they are both chemically produced

7. *A thimble* (Fig. 27i) makes hand sewing much easier. It should fit the middle finger of the hand comfortably. Someone has wisely said, "It takes longer to wear a hole in the thimble than in a finger."

8. *A pincushion* (Fig. 27j) is handy for needles and pins. There are some small cushions which are mounted on wristbands and are convenient as well as time-saving.

9. *Some measuring tools* are absolutely essential for the accuracy which marks fine dressmaking. You will need a yardstick, a sturdy, non-stretchable tape measure, a 12" or 18" ruler marked off in ⅛", a 6" gauge for measuring small distances (Figs. 27k, l, m).

10. Pattern markings are transferred to the fabric with the following materials:

Tailor's chalk in assorted colors. The chalky kind which rubs off easily is preferable to the waxy kind which spreads when the garment is ironed and needs cleaning fluid to remove it (Fig. 27n).

Dressmaker's carbon paper. This is a carbon especially for fabrics. A package contains sheets of assorted colors and sizes. Use a *blunt tracing wheel* with it (Fig. 27o).

Basting thread in assorted colors to contrast with the color of the cloth.

11. *Stitch ripper.* If it doesn't spare you the heartache of ripping, at least it makes the task easier (Fig. 27p).

12. *Skirt marker.* The safest and most accurate way to mark your hem is with an adjustable rule mounted on a stand. It uses pins rather than chalk, which has a tendency to mar some fabrics.

13. *A full-length mirror*—a must for checking fit. A triple mirror is even better if you can manage to get one and have the courage to face it.

14. *A steam-and-dry iron* with heat controls.

15. A sturdy, well-padded *ironing board* of good working height.

A great part of your sewing equipment is used for pressing. You will find a complete discussion of this in the section titled "Press as You Sew," page 180.

A place of your own

Last, but by no means least, find or make some little place for all your patterns, fabrics, and sewing equipment. Just some spot you can call your own and where you can shut the door on that whole, vast pile of precious stuff.

SHAPES AND SYMBOLS—HOW TO "READ" THE PATTERN

Open the pattern and smooth each piece flat. You can see right off that it is full of secret little messages for you. Sometimes these come to you in printed directions, sometimes in symbols, and sometimes it is the shape of the pattern piece, itself, which has special meaning.

Generally an identifying name is printed right on the pattern so that you can readily see just which part of the pattern it is—dress front, dress back, front facing, back facing, armhole facing, and so on. If there is no name printed on the pattern, it will have another kind of identification, either a letter—A, B, C, D—or a number—1, 2, 3, 4. In that event, you must consult the pattern diagram on the instruction sheet to find out what the letter or number stands for. Often the pattern will have a letter or number in addition to the printed name. This indicates the order in which the pattern pieces are used.

Every pattern includes a diagram showing all the pattern pieces and their symbols. The pieces are placed in the position in which they will be worn—that is, neck to hem. (It is always vital to know which end of your pattern is up.) Place your pattern in a similar position. Be guided by the shape of the pattern, the position of the printing on it, and the notches (those small V-shaped wedges on the perimeter of the pattern).

Let us examine the pattern pieces for the skimmer dress, jumper, or overblouse suggested as your first venture (or adventure, if you

will). Find the pattern for the dress front (Fig. 28a), the dress
back (Fig. 28b), the front and back facings (Fig. 28c), and the
armhole facings—front and back (Fig. 28d). It is possible that the
pattern may have a combined neck and armhole facing that looks
like this (Fig. 28e). Many sleeveless and collarless patterns do.

The pattern for the overblouse will be just like this. The only difference will be the length.

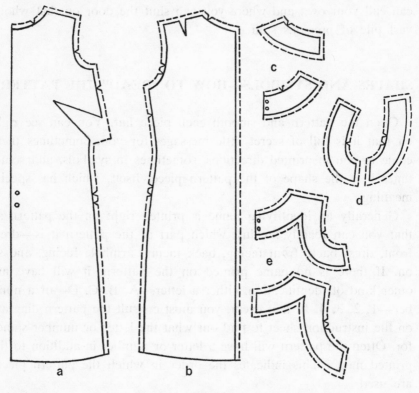

Fig. 28

Patterns generally come to you in halves, i.e., half a front, half
a back, etc. If you place half a front on a fold of fabric, you will
have the complete front when it is opened out. If you place half a
back on a double thickness of fabric and cut around all sides, you
will have two half-backs. Wherever possible, cut two of a kind or one
complete unit on a fold. This makes cutting easier, faster, and more
balanced (right and left are cut alike). It also saves space and tissue, both in the envelope and on your cutting table. It precludes

your tangling with yards of pattern tissue and fabric when it comes to laying out your pattern. It costs the pattern company less to produce half a pattern, thereby passing on the saving to you.

There are some exceptions to this general rule: a bias-cut garment or an asymmetric style—both of which require complete patterns; a small section of a pattern which can more advantageously be cut in one piece, such as a facing or a waistband.

Examine your pattern to see whether it says "Cut one," "Cut two," or "Cut on a fold."

"Reading" the pattern

Place the front and back dress or overblouse patterns side by side so the side seams are toward each other and the center front and center back are on the outside (Fig. 28). Starting at the top of the pattern, trace with your finger:

1. the neckline (it may look unfamiliar to you in this form; remember it is half a neckline)

2. the shoulder (there is often a dart located on the back shoulder)

3. the armhole (when the two halves—front and back—are stitched together at the shoulder and side seams, the resulting shape is an oval)

4. the side (the front side may be interrupted by a dart; it may shape in slightly at the waistline)

5. the center front and center back (note whether these are to be placed on a fold of fabric or are to be cut as two pieces with seam allowance all around them)

6. the hem (sometimes the amount of the hem is stated, for instance, "2½" hem allowed"; sometimes the fold line of the hem is indicated and you must determine the amount by measuring from the fold line to the edge of the pattern)

Place the front neck facing over the dress front so the neckline, shoulder, and center front match. This is how it will be used in your garment. Trace the facing with your finger:

1. center front   3. shoulder

2. neckline   4. outside edge

Do the same with the back neck facing.

Place the front armhole facing over the front armhole of the dress, matching shoulder, armhole, side, and outside edge. This is the way it will be used on your garment. Do the same with the back facing.

When you are ready to make your skirt and your shirtwaist dress, refer to this page. Identify and trace each pattern piece.

The skirt

Place the skirt front and skirt back patterns side by side so the sides face each other and the center front and center back are toward the outside (Fig. 29).

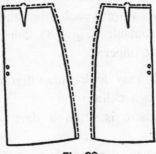

Fig. 29

Trace with your finger the waistline, the sides, the center front, the center back, the hem.

The shirtwaist dress

Place all the pattern sections of the shirtwaist dress as suggested in Fig. 30.

Trace with your finger:

1. the sleeve cap and the sleeve underarm seam
2. the neck edge of the collar and the outer edge of the collar
3. the bodice extension (the width between the center front and the finished outside edge)

Now trace these sections of the dress which will be joined:

4. the bodice waistline and the skirt waistline, front and back
5. the bodice opening extension and its facing

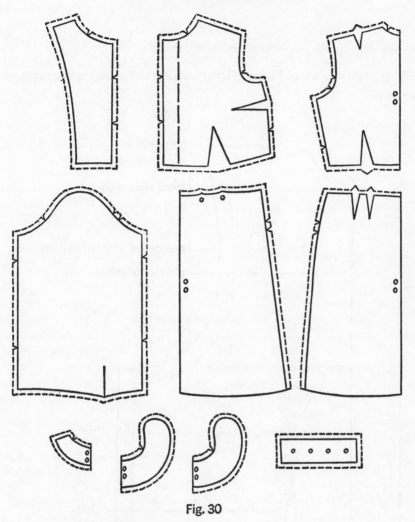

Fig. 30

6. the collar and collar facing
7. the collar neckline and the dress neckline, front and back
8. the front armhole and the front sleeve cap
9. the back armhole and the back sleeve cap

Today you've done the tracing with your finger. As time goes on and you grow more experienced, you will do the tracing with your mind's eye, until all the characteristic shapes of neckline, shoulder, armhole, sleeve cap, collars, skirts, or whatever become as familiar to you as the ABC's.

Decode the message—construction symbols

To paraphrase an old song, "Every little symbol has a meaning of its own."

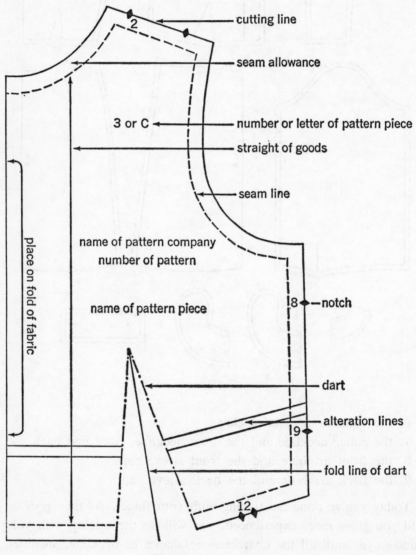

Fig. 31

The heavy outside line is the cutting line. When you place the pattern on the material, this is the line you will follow for cutting. If your pattern has a margin of paper beyond the cutting line, cut it away before you begin your work. Otherwise you may be confused by assuming the extra tissue to be seam allowance. Except for very sheer material, it is easier to cut beside the pattern than through it.

In from the cutting line you will find the *seam line*. This is the line that, matched to a corresponding seam line, is stitched to produce the garment. It may appear as a light line, a broken line, or a line of perforations.

The space between the seam line and the cutting line is called the *seam allowance*. In most patterns and in most places on the pattern the seam allowance is ⅝". However, there are some patterns and some places on them that call for less. Using your gauge, spot-check the amount of seam allowance in your pattern.

In the seam allowance or directly on the cutting line, you will find a little triangular (Fig. 32a) or diamond-shaped (Fig. 32b) symbol. This is called a *notch*.

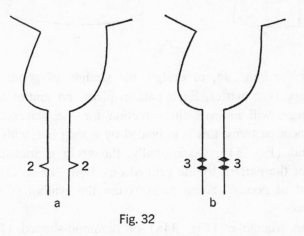

Fig. 32

Wherever you see a notch, you know that another part of the pattern with a similar notch joins this edge. Notches make the assembling of a garment quicker and easier. If they weren't there you would have to figure out this huge jigsaw puzzle from the shape of the pattern pieces. Notches are often numbered in the sequence for matching.

A fold of fabric may be indicated by a printed direction, "Place on fold of fabric," a bracket with the printed direction (Fig. 31), or by two or three medium-sized perforations.

Often there is the additional admonition, "Do not cut on this line."

The designer plans to use the "hang" of the fabric as part of his design. For most styles this is a natural or lengthwise "hang." The pattern is placed on the lengthwise grain or *straight of goods* (Fig. 33a). For design interest, a striped fabric may be placed on the crosswise grain of the goods (Fig. 33b). If a designer wants the cling of a bias fit, he places the straight of goods on the bias (Fig. 33c).

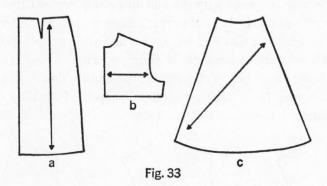

Fig. 33

Whether for hang, fit, or design, the straight of goods is an extremely important matter. Each pattern piece, no matter how small or how large, will indicate the direction for the placement of the grain. In most patterns, this is indicated by a long line with an arrow at each end (Fig. 31). Occasionally, the grain is indicated along one edge of the pattern by the printed direction, "Place this edge on the straight of goods." Some patterns use the symbol of two large perforations.

The long triangular (Fig. 34a) or diamond-shaped (Fig. 34b) areas on the pattern indicate *darts*. These, when stitched, give the garment its shape. The solid line through the middle of a dart is a fold line. Since all darts must be folded before they can be pinned, basted, and stitched, this is a useful marking, particularly for beginners. If your pattern doesn't have a fold line you can easily put one in. Draw a line through the center of the dart from the dart point

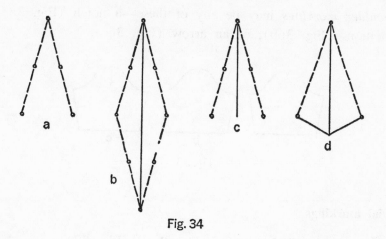

Fig. 34

to the base (Fig. 34c). The little jog that you see at the end of a dart (Fig. 34d) provides enough material to stitch the dart into a seam.

Since there must be some way of getting into a garment, the pattern provides some form of closing. The easiest for a beginner to handle is a *zippered closing*. Examine your pattern for a seam that says "Leave open above notch" or "Stitch to." The part of the seam that is left open will be the place where the zipper is inserted.

All patterns show some place where they may be *lengthened or shortened*. If the pattern piece is shaped, this is done within the pattern (Fig. 35a). If the pattern piece is straight, the lengthening or shortening may be done at the bottom (Fig. 35b).

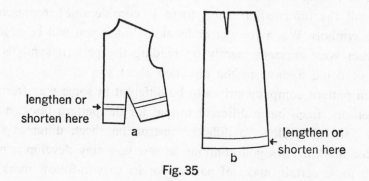

lengthen or
shorten here

lengthen or
shorten here

Fig. 35

Shoulder markings may be any of these—a notch (Fig. 36a), perforations (Fig. 36b), or an arrow (Fig. 36c).

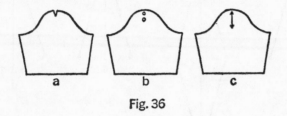

Fig. 36

Special markings

Whenever you find markings like these (Fig. 37)

Fig. 37

you will have to consult the step-by-step directions for their special meaning in a particular pattern.

When you get into more complex patterns you will find markings for the many style and construction details—center front, buttonhole placement, extension folds, dart tucks, pleats, gathers, and so on. The symbols for all of these are made up of perforations, arrows, notches, lines, printed directions. To understand them, you must "read" them in conjuction with the step-by-step directions.

The first thing to do whenever you open out a pattern is to "read" it for all the information (and there is considerable) represented by the symbols. When you get really skilled at it you will be able to construct your garment merely by reading the pattern symbols instead of being a slave to the direction sheet.

Each pattern company strives to be different in some way from its competitors. Each has a different format for the pattern book, a different pattern envelope, a different instruction sheet, different symbols for marking. As you continue to sew you may develop a preference for a certain make of pattern for its easy-to-follow markings and instructions as well as for its styles.

THE PROOF IS IN THE FITTING

Of what use to you is the most beautiful garment in the world if it doesn't fit well? No amount of high style or painstaking workmanship can disguise the sorry fact of a dress or blouse that does not fit properly. This is equally true whether you buy your clothes or make them.

One size but different figures

Simply because it is the most practical way to accommodate the millions of buyers of both ready-made clothes and of patterns, these are sold in standard sizes. The truth, however, is that practically no one is a perfect standard size. Figures, even of the same size, vary in many, small ways. They are no more alike than thumbprints. All of the figures in Fig. 38 use the same size.

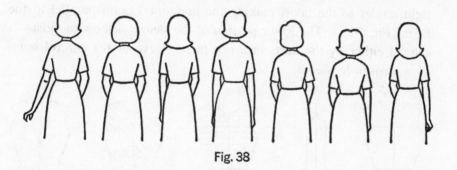

Fig. 38

Were these gals to turn around and face you, the differences in their figures would be even more striking.

All that you are saying when you say they are the same size is that it is THE size that most nearly meets their needs. Many women settle for this. As long as they can squeeze into the skirt of a dress, what difference does it make if the armhole seam of a set-in sleeve looks like a dropped shoulder or if the neckline sags a bit, or the darts are all in the wrong places? The truth of the matter is, many women don't know what constitutes good fit.

This is how a well-fitting garment should look

General impression

The garment looks graceful, balanced, proportioned to your figure. There are no wrinkles, creases, bulges, poufs, bagginess; no strain, pulling, or "busting out." It is neither too big nor too tight in its entirety or in part. The bodice, skirt, and sleeves are neither too short nor too long.

The grain of the fabric

The straight grain of the center front and center back is at right angles to the floor. The horizontal grain is parallel to the floor (Fig. 39a). Use any prominent or discernible line in weave or print as a guide (Fig. 39c). In dressmaking, the center front and center back are always marked with guide basting on grain to help in fitting (Figs. 39d and e).

The vertical grain of the upper portion of the sleeve hangs at right angles to the floor, making the horizontal grain parallel to the floor (Fig. 39b). The lower portion of the sleeve—elbow to wrist—is shaped either by the darts in a one-piece sleeve or the control seam of a two-piece sleeve.

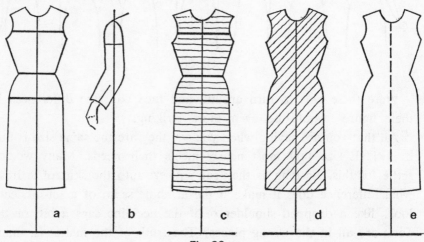

a   b   c   d   e

Fig. 39

Ease

The ease should be sufficient for freedom of movement. For general use, you should be able to walk, sit, bend, move your arm forward or upward with ease. Don't test your garment as if you were trying out for a track team. You don't have to run a half-mile course or throw a shot-put. Cocktail and evening dresses when fitted need less ease; active sportswear needs more ease.

Shaping darts and seams

The darts must head toward the high point of the curve to be shaped, and stop just short of this point. The dart control must be large enough to provide the necessary shaping but not so large that bulges are created where you don't have any. Whenever you see a pouf of fabric at the end of a dart, there is too much dart control for you. Shaping seams should pass over the high point of the curve or no more than 1" either side of it unless there is supplementary shaping provided by additional darts. (See Fig. 95, page 136.)

The silhouette seams

The silhouette seams are placed as follows:

The shoulder seam lies along the crest of the shoulder slightly forward of the trapezius muscle, from the hollow at the base of the neck to the shoulder bone. Some schools of thought say this seam should be 1" behind the lobe of the ear.

The neckline lies smoothly without gaping or straining whether it be at the base of the neck (about where a single strand of pearls is generally worn), raised, or lowered. If there is a collar to the dress, it fits smoothly around the neckline.

The armhole seam starts from any point on the shoulder either currently fashionable or particularly becoming to you. It curves over the top of the shoulder, continues in a slightly curved line to the crease where arm and body meet. (This is the point at which notches are placed in the pattern.) The armhole swings into an underarm curve about 1" to 1½" below the armpit. The curve of the front armhole seam is deeper and somewhat shorter than the back armhole seam which in turn is longer and shallower.

The waistline fits snugly at the natural waistline or where you would like your waistline to be.

The side seams hang straight to the floor in a plumb line. When the arms hang naturally at the side, the middle fingers touch the side seams of the skirt.

The skirt length is set at a *fashionable* length. Don't hold back or you'll look outdated. On the other hand, you don't have to adopt extremes in fashion if these are outrageously unbecoming to you.

Sleeves

A long sleeve ends at the wristbone. A short one is as short as the season, the fashion, and the build of your arm will permit. If there is one elbow dart it is placed *at* the elbow; if two, one either side of the elbow; if three, one at the elbow, one above and one below. Fullness in place of darts is distributed in this small elbow area.

The artist's eye

You could follow all the rules and still not achieve a flattering fit. This is where your artist's eye must play an important role. If a shoulder seam placed as directed makes you look too round-shouldered, move it back. If a side seam following the above directions results in magnifying an already mountainous situation, for heaven's sake move it so that the front of the skirt is larger than the back and create an optical delusion. If you are short-waisted and big-bosomed, a natural waistline will make you look dumpy; drop it. If you are longwaisted, a natural waistline will emphasize your length to a disproportionate degree; raise it.

Fine fit is composed of many things: a great style in the right size, accurate layout and cutting; skillful sewing and pressing. Undoubtedly a good foundation garment helps. But above all, fine fit depends on a wise adjustment of a standard size pattern to conform to your figure and secondly on those refinements in fitting that are made as the construction of the garment progresses.

The sewer has all the lines

The woman who buys her clothes has very little choice. If she is not too sensitive about fit, she accepts what she finds. If she is discerning, she must resort to alterations—frequently expensive.

The woman who sews "has all the lines" literally. She has the advantage of being able to custom-fit her clothes. Many women are drawn to sewing for this very reason.

Anyone can learn to sew. The proof is in the fitting!

THE PATTERN AND YOU

Alter the pattern rather than the garment

It is a bore as well as a chore to alter a garment after it is finished. To cut a garment to the standard size with the expectation of fitting it to your figure in the cloth is a mistake. It may be too laborious and too late. The safest procedure is to adjust the pattern as nearly as your calculations can bring it to your measurements and then perfect the fit as work progresses on the fabric.

In your first few ventures the pattern alterations should be minimum if you choose the right size in an easy-to-make style.

You will need to check length, width at bust, waist, and hips, and the correct location of the darts.

Check the pattern length against one of your dresses of good length. It is easier to compare the two if the styles are similar.

Make whatever simple additions or subtractions are required for bust, waist, and hips in the seam allowances.

Relocate the dart if necessary in the pin fitting.

Since your sewing won't stay at this level, future choices of style will become more intricate. Then changing the pattern to fit the figure becomes a little more complicated. For that you will need a little more information about you, about your pattern, and about how to alter it.

More about you, more about your pattern

The list of measurements that follows by no means exhausts the possible body measurements for a comprehensive knowledge of your figure. There are enough of them, however, to enable you to alter any standard-size pattern so it will come close to your needs.

You'll need the help of an understanding friend. You cannot

possibly take all these measurements yourself. Besides, you may need some comforting when you read the tape measure.

The best measurements are taken in a slip over your foundation garments. Wear shoes of the heel height you plan to wear with the dress since this will affect your posture.

Tie a piece of string around your natural waist or push it into a position that is more becoming to you. Your waistline can be where you wish it. The string provides a fixed point for measuring lengths.

Make a chart like the one opposite. Or, use this one. It's a handy record of the pattern as well as you. You can see at a glance just where the changes need to be made and in what amount.

How to take your body measurements

General measurements

Bust—over the high point of the bust and across the fullest part of the shoulder blades in back.

Waist—in the hollow of the waist or where you would like your waist to be.

Hips—from 5″ to 7″ below the waist or around the fullest part of the hips; note how much below the waist.

The Bodice

Center front—from the hollow of the collarbone to the waistline string.

Center back—from the socket bone to the waistline string.

Bust-point height—from the highest point of the bust to the string.

Bust-point width—from bust point to bust point.

Shoulder width front—from shoulder point to shoulder point straight across the front.

Shoulder width back—from shoulder point to shoulder point straight across the back.

Across the chest—from the crease where arm meets body to the opposite crease.

Across the back—With arms forward, measure from the crease where arm meets body to the opposite crease.

Item	Me	Plus Ease	Total	Pattern Including Ease	Changes + or −
General measurements					
Bust		3″			
Waistline		½″ to 1″			
Hips		2″			
The Bodice					
Center front		½″			
Center back		½″			
Bust-point height		none			
Bust-point width		none			
Shoulder width front					
Shoulder width back					
Across the chest		½″ to 1″			
Across the back		½″ to 1″			
The Skirt					
Center front length		none			
Center back length		none			
The Sleeve					
Total arm length		bent arm provide ease			
Shoulder to elbow		none			
Girth		2″			

The Skirt

Center front length—from the waistline string to the floor; subtract the number of inches from the floor the skirt is to be worn.

Center back length—from the waistline string to the floor; subtract the number of inches from the floor the skirt is to be worn.

The Sleeve

Total arm length—with the arm bent, measure from the shoulder point to the elbow, to the wrist at the little finger.

Shoulder to elbow—while the tape is still in position, note the measurement; the *elbow to wrist* length can be determined by subtracting the shoulder to elbow length from the total arm length.

Girth—around the heaviest part of the upper arm; usually about midway between the shoulder and elbow.

How to measure the pattern

All measurements in the pattern are taken *from seam line to seam line*. They do not include anything which will end up in some seam or some dart. Use your tape measure like an adding machine. Measure to the dart, skip over the dart, continue measurement: 1″ to 4″—dart—4″ to 7″.

Remember that *your width measurements are whole measurements* while *the pattern measurements are only half*. You will need to halve your width measurements to correspond to those of the pattern.

Remember, too, you must add ease to your body measurements (see column 2 of measurement chart), while the pattern already includes all the ease necessary for the size and the style.

Place the front and back patterns together with hips touching and center front and center back parallel to each other.

General measurements

Bust—across the fullest part of both front and back; this measurement is ½″ above the point of the waistline dart and *directly in line* with any underarm dart.

(*All* pattern darts are shortened darts. They provide a softer effect and easier fit than if the darts were to be stitched to the high point.)

Waist—across the front and back waistlines; remember not to include the darts in your measurements.

(It sometimes helps in measuring if the darts are pinned closed as they will be when stitched. What remains is the waist.)

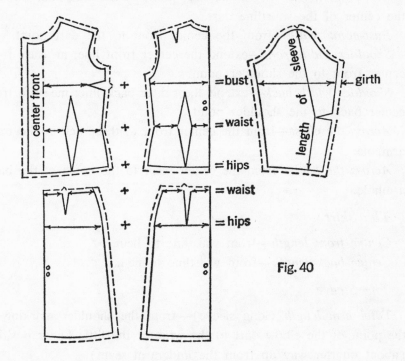

Fig. 40

Waist in blouses and shift-type dresses—located at the widest part of a waistline dart.

(If there are no darts by which to determine the waist, look for the waist pattern symbol or judge the location from the indented shape at the side seam. Where there is little or no shaping, it really doesn't matter where the waistline is.)

Hips—across the fullest part of the hips below the darts; note how far below the waistline the hipline is.

The Bodice

Center front length—from natural neckline to waistline.
Center back length—from natural neckline to waistline.

(If the garment has a natural—jewel—neckline, this is easy to determine. However, if the garment has either a raised or a dropped neckline, it is impossible by these measurements to determine the center front and center back lengths. The simplest thing to do is to use as a guide a similar dress that fits you well.)

Bust-point height—from the dart point to the waistline, through the center of the waistline dart.

Bust-point width—from the center front to the dart point.

Shoulder width front—extend the center front line; measure from center front to the shoulder point.

Shoulder width back—extend the center back line; measure from center back to the shoulder point.

Across the chest—from the center front to the notch at the front armhole.

Across the back—from the center back to the notch at the back armhole.

The Skirt

Center front length—from waistline to hem.
Center back length—from waistline to hem.

The Sleeve

Total arm length (long sleeve)—from the shoulder marking to the point of the elbow dart to the wrist at the little finger position (about quarter way up from the underarm seam).

Shoulder to elbow—from the shoulder marking to the point of the elbow dart.

Elbow to wrist—from the point of the elbow dart to the wrist at the little finger position.

Girth—from the underarm seam to the underarm seam midway from shoulder to elbow dart (about 1" below the armhole at the underarm seam).

You and the pattern: a comparison

Compare all your measurements with those of your pattern. Decide what needs changing and how much. Very small changes—¼" or less—can always be made in the seam allowances. If you have to make too many changes or consistent overall changes of 2" or more, get the next size pattern. There is a 2" difference between pattern sizes. If most of the pattern fits but some 2" changes are indicated, work with the pattern you now have.

A CHANGE FOR THE BETTER

Some sewers are so in awe of their patterns that they're fearful of moving a dart even a fraction of an inch without official sanction. While patterns come to you of necessity in standard sizes, this doesn't mean that they have to stay that way in your hands. Chances are that yours is not the mythical "standard figure."

You need not be a slave to a pattern! Change it to fit you!

All it takes to change a pattern for the better is a little arithmetic, a little courage, a little judgment—and the following information.

General information on pattern changes

You will need a ruler, a yardstick, lead and colored pencils with sharp points, Scotch tape, paper-cutting scissors, any tissue, shelf, or other unlined paper.

Keep in mind that we are not trying to change the style. We are only trying for better fit of an already appealing style.

Don't make general changes; make changes only where needed.

When there is more than one change to be made, make them one at a time. Don't try to do everything at once.

Make all changes right on the pattern. Write notes to yourself, slash the pattern, tuck, insert tissue, patch, do anything that will make the change clear to you. When you have finished making your alterations, the pattern should be ready for use without any further ado. These changes and alterations should be understandable when you pick the patterns up again later, without having to puzzle out its messages or decode any of its cryptic symbols.

When you make a change in one pattern piece, remember to make a corresponding change on all pieces that join it.

When you slash and spread for extra length or width, fill in the spread area with paper. Scotch-tape to position.

The following changes are such as are indicated by the measurement chart and your arithmetic. Further changes may be made in the trial fitting.

How to make the pattern changes

A pattern may be changed on any outside line or within the pattern itself. Changes may be balanced (even) throughout the pattern or they may be in one place only.

The easiest changes to make are *overall, balanced changes in length.* If the pattern has straight lines, make the changes at the bottom (Fig. 41a). If the pattern is shaped (Fig. 41b) or styled (Fig. 41c), make the change within the pattern to preserve the style line. Most patterns designate the place to make the change (Figs. 41b and c).

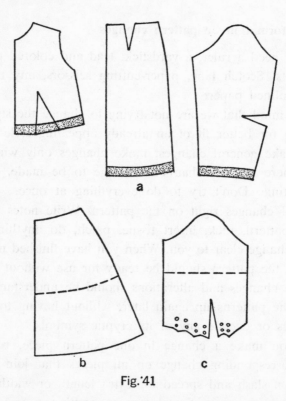

Fig. 41

Overall changes in width may be made at center front (Fig. 42a), center back (Fig. 42b), side seams (Fig. 42c) or through the center (Fig. 42d). Such changes should be no more than a seam allowance (⅝″) at the most. Anything larger than this distorts the shape of the neck, armhole, waistline, sleeve cap, etc. When larger changes must be made, make them in several places in small amounts (Figs. 42e, f, and g). This preserves the style line while changing the pattern proportionately.

Changes may also be made on any inside seam line (Figs. 42h, i, j).

Fig. 42

Changes within the pattern

Changes within the pattern may also be made on the principle of *slash and spread* or its reverse, *slash and overlap* or tuck.

Patterns may be made larger or smaller in one of two ways. When the change is an equal one either in width or length across the entire pattern, it is called a balanced change (Figs. 43a and b). When the change is in one place only it is called a change for circularity (Figs. 43c and d).

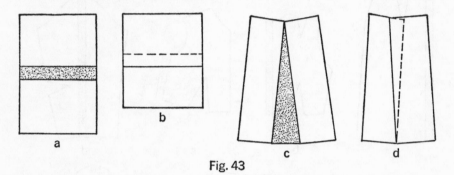

Fig. 43

To make the pattern larger

1. Draw a slash line at right angles to the grain where the change is to be made.

2. Slash and spread to the desired amount; equally for a balanced change (Fig. 43a), in one place only for circularity (opens like a fan) (Fig. 43c). The shaded area shows the change.

3. Insert tissue in the spread area. Fasten with pins or Scotch tape.

To make the pattern smaller

1. Draw a line at right angles to the grain where the change is to be made.

2. Slash and overlap or tuck the pattern to the desired amount, equally for a balanced change (Fig. 43b), in one place only for circularity (Fig. 43d).

3. Pin or Scotch-tape to position. The broken lines indicate the change. Changes may be vertical or horizontal as you can see by the above exercises.

When the pattern is slashed and spread (Figs. 44a and b) or slashed and overlapped (Figs. 44c and d) to produce a change in one place only, it is thrown out of kilter.

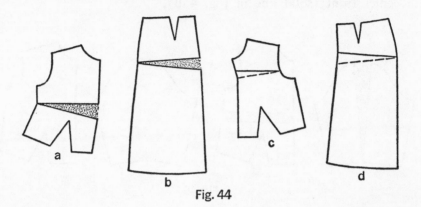

Fig. 44

This calls for a correction.

1. The shaded areas in Fig. 45a are amounts that have been added.

2. Extend the center front lines to establish the new center fronts (shaded area) (Fig. 45a).

3. Subtract from the jutting area the amount just added to the front (broken line in Fig. 45a) to balance the measurement.

OR

1. The jutting lines at the center fronts in Fig. 45b are the result of the slash and overlap.

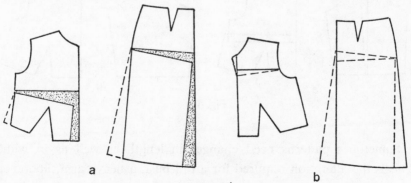

Fig. 45

2. Extend the center front lines to establish the new center fronts (solid line in Fig. 45b).

3. Add to the other side an amount equal to what was subtracted at center front (solid line in Fig. 45b).

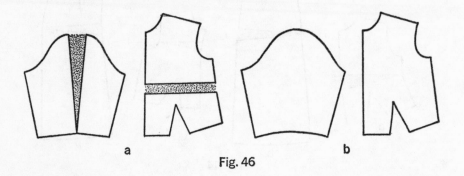

a   b

Fig. 46

Whenever an undefined space results from a slash and spread (Fig. 46a) a new line must be drawn to connect the ends of the broken line (Fig. 46b).

Whenever a jagged line results from overlapping or tucking the pattern (Fig. 47a) a new line must be drawn to correct the projecting pattern (Fig. 47b). Draw a line beginning at the point where it originates to the point at which it ends, cutting off all projecting jogs.

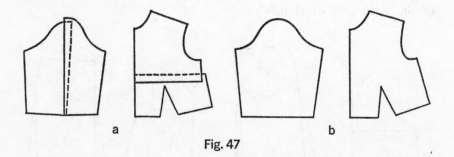

a   b

Fig. 47

Sometimes patterns need changes in length as well as in width. This is the alteration required for a full bust, a heavy arm, abdomen, or seat.

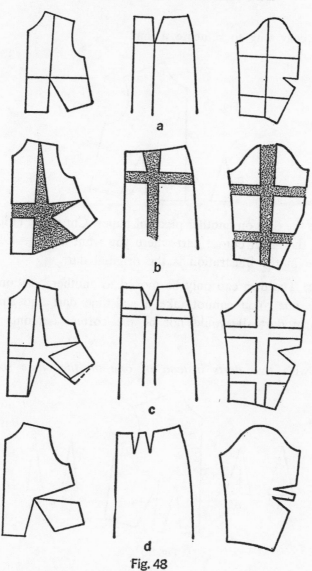

Fig. 48

1. Draw a vertical as well as a horizontal line for slashing (Fig. 48a).

2. Slash and spread, first in one direction, then in the other (Fig. 48b).

3. Relocate the dart (Fig. 48c).

4. If there is too much dart control in the resulting dart, divide it into two darts (Fig. 48d).

Here is an easy way to relocate a dart

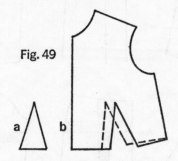

Fig. 49

1. Trace the dart on another piece of paper. Cut it out (Fig. 49a).

2. Place the paper cutout dart where you want it (Fig. 49b). The broken line in the illustration is the original dart.

CAUTION: The dart can only be moved to another position *on the same seam line.* You cannot take a waistline dart and shift it to an underarm dart. It would not be the correct amount, size, or length.

If you wish *two darts instead of one on the same seam line*

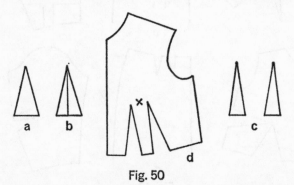

Fig. 50

1. Trace the dart on another piece of paper. Cut it out (Fig. 50a).

2. Divide the dart into two equal parts (Fig. 50b). Cut them apart.

3. Make the dart legs equal in length (Fig. 50c). You will find one shorter than the other as the sections are cut.

4. Place the new dart sections into position on either side of the bust point (X) and about 1″ apart at the seam (Fig. 50d).

5. Trace the darts in their new positions.

Here are the pattern alterations for the two adjustments most frequently required

Where a little more ease is desired across the bust or the back

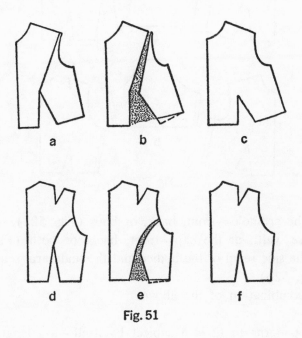

Fig. 51

1. Cut out the entire dart.

2. Draw a slash line from the shoulder point (Fig. 51a) or the armhole (Fig. 51d) to the dart point.

3. Slash and spread to the desired amount of ease (Figs. 51b and e).

4. Relocate the dart in the center of the spread area (Figs. 51c and f).

5. Correct the drawing where necessary (Figs. 51b and e).

To relieve strain across the upper sleeve

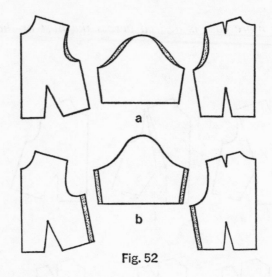

Fig. 52

Add to the armhole—front, back, or both (Fig. 52a).

Add more width at the cap—front, back, or both (Fig. 52a).

Add to the side seam of the bodice and the underarm seam of the sleeve (Fig. 52b).

Or any combination of the above.

Altering patterns to fit is a subject by itself—too lengthy for a book of this kind and perhaps too bewildering for beginners. With the few principles described above, it should be possible for you to make simple changes. Apply the theory of slash and spread or slash and overlap to any part of the pattern that needs change. Add or subtract on any seam allowance. You may even take liberties with the darts, adding and subtracting dart control to improve the fit. Above all, remember the pattern is there for you to use. Make it work for you!

PART III
GET SET!

GET SET!

As automatic as brushing one's teeth and hair at the start of a day is preparing the pattern and the fabric at the start of a new dress. These are the first "musts" of actual construction.

PREPARE THE FABRIC FOR CUTTING

Grain perfection essential

In weaving cloth, one set of lengthwise yarns (warp) is placed side by side in a row on a loom. Another set of crosswise yarns (filler) is threaded over and under the warp yarns. These lengthwise and crosswise yarns, interlaced at right angles to each other, produce a length of cloth that is rectangular in shape.

As cloth comes from the loom, the grain is correctly set. (The grain is either the lengthwise or crosswise yarn.) Sometimes as the miles of fabric pass through the finishing process, some may be pulled "off grain"—that is, out of its rectangular form. Salespeople who cut cloth may not be aware of this. They cut in what appears to be a straight line but may actually be off grain.

To assure correct cutting, stitching, pressing, and fitting—all of which are done with the grain—you must make certain that the horizontal and vertical grains are in their original rectangular form.

You will have no problem with the vertical grain, for that is the selvage of your material. Don't cut it away! We use it as a guide for the correct placement of the pattern. Should it be a little tight, making the material pucker beyond it, clip every inch or so to release the strain. (If it is pretty enough, the selvage can even be used as a finished edge in your garment, which indeed it is in the cloth. It makes a lovely trimming.)

However, you will need to *establish the correct horizontal grain*.

If the fabric tears easily without damaging the material, this is the easiest way to establish the crosswise grain. (You may even ask the salesperson to do this for you instead of cutting the material.) Test a small section of the fabric. Snip through the selvage; make a short clip with the point of the scissors; tear.

If the fabric does not tear easily or if tearing injures it, then straighten the grain by this method: pull a crosswise thread and cut along the space left by the drawn thread (Fig. 53).

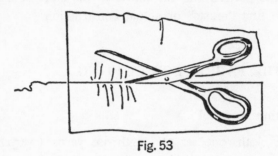

Fig. 53

Don't try to do the whole width at one time. Pull a short distance; hold the fabric up to the light so you can see the space where the thread has been removed; cut along this space; pull a little more, examine, cut. Repeat until you are across the entire width of your fabric.

If the fabric has a prominent yarn, rib, line, stripe, etc., cut along this line.

Both ends of the fabric must be straightened. It is not sufficient to correct only one end.

Fig. 54a—Fabric as it may come to you from the bolt—rectangular but off grain.

Fig. 54b—A pulled thread establishes the correct horizontal grain.

Fig. 54c—The grain is accurate but the fabric no longer looks rectangular.

Fig. 54d—Pull grain in the opposite direction (on the bias) until Fig. 54e—the fabric is restored to its correct position.

If pulling dry fabric on the bias doesn't straighten the grain, dampen the cloth first or press with a steam iron on the wrong side. Fabric is often more manageable in a damp state.

Caution: Do not dampen silk; instead pull and press the dry material into position.

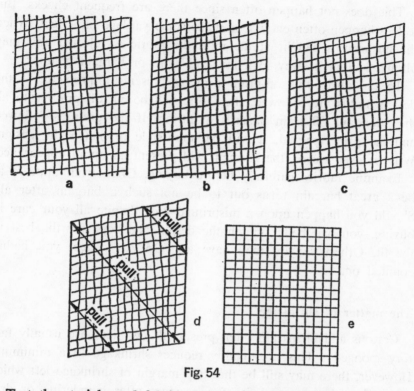

Fig. 54

Test the straightened fabric against any right angle—the corner of the cutting table or cutting board will do. If you wish to use a professional tool, get a tailor's square or a 45° triangle.

The problem presented by off-grain printing

Sometimes in the printing process the design may be printed off grain (Fig. 55).

Fig. 55

This does not happen often since there are frequent checks. But it does happen often enough to make some yardage imperfect. When the misprint is caught at the mill, the fabric is rejected and may ultimately find its way to a mill-end store or bargain counter.

To the sewer this off-grain printing presents a problem. If the design motifs are followed, the fabric will be cut off grain with all the attendant off-grain hazards in fitting. If the grain is followed and the print ignored, it will be impossible to match the design. What is even worse, the garment will present an uphill appearance.

Examine fabrics carefully before buying. Often what appears to be a great bargain turns out to be not such a bargain after all. Should you happen upon a misprinted area despite all your care in buying, you had better match the design and hope for the best in the fit. Otherwise you may have an "Op Art" effect you hadn't counted on.

The matter of shrinkage

Cottons and linens are often preshrunk (woolens are usually factory sponged). This presumably reduces shrinkage to a minimum. However, there may still be that tiny margin of shrinkage left which may affect the size and fit of a garment after laundering or dry-cleaning.

Most cotton and linen fabrics may be safely preshrunk at home. Use lukewarm to cool water for white or light-colored fabrics, cold water for dark ones. A fabric softener in the water helps to preserve the finish and makes ironing easier. Follow this procedure:

1. Establish the grain.

2. Fold the fabric in half lengthwise with the right sides together. Baste both straightened edges and both selvages.

3. If you have an automatic washer: run the fabric through the rinse cycle. If you don't have an automatic washer: allow the fabric to soak thoroughly for several hours in a tub or basin.

4. Spin dry or squeeze out the excess moisture. Twisting or wringing produces wrinkles.

5. If possible, dry flat. Or, hang over a clothesline, a shower rod, or a door that has been well padded with Turkish towels.

6. Smooth out all wrinkles.

7. Make sure the horizontal and vertical grains are in the right position.

8. Allow the fabric to drip dry. Turn once while drying.

9. Ironing is usually not necessary. Should it be, iron when slightly damp on the wrong side. Do *not* iron the fold line.

How to sponge woolen fabric

1. Straighten the grain.

2. Fold the fabric in half lengthwise with right sides together. Baste the straightened edges and both selvages.

3. Make a preshrinking cloth at least 40″ wide and long enough to cover all the fabric. An old sheet or two old sheets sewn together are fine for this purpose.

4. Wet the sheet and wring out the excess moisture. It should be damp but not wet. (If you have an automatic washer, run the sheet through the rinse cycle. It comes out just the right dampness.)

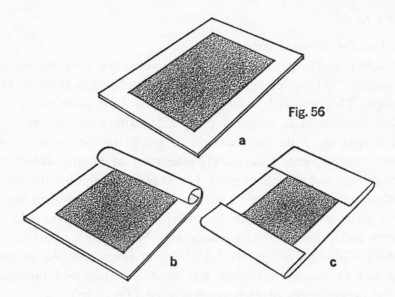

Fig. 56

a

b

c

5. Place the fabric on the sheet, smoothing out any wrinkles. Be sure the horizontal and vertical grains are in the correct position (Fig. 56a).

6. Roll the wool and the preshrinking cloth into a cylinder (Fig. 56b), or fold loosely into sections (Fig. 56c).

7. Cover completely with a Turkish towel, brown paper, or a plastic bag to prevent uneven absorption of the moisture.

8. Let stand for several hours.

9. Unroll. If possible, dry flat. If not, hang over a shower rod or a door that has been well padded with Turkish towels.

10. Smooth out all wrinkles. Check the grain.

11. Turn the wool once while drying as if you were drying a sweater.

12. Allow to dry naturally. Do *not* press dry.

Do remember that sponging or preshrinking is only a *partial* elimination of shrinkage. Don't overdo it to the point of destroying the beauty and luster of the fabric finish.

PREPARE THE PATTERN FOR CUTTING

Things to do

1. Use the adjusted pattern.

2. Select all the pattern pieces which will make your version of the design. Fold up all unnecessary pieces and return them to the envelope. They will only confuse you if you keep them about.

3. If the pattern is wrinkled, press it flat with a warm iron.

4. Extend the grain line (straight of goods) to the *entire length* of each pattern piece. Theoretically measuring an equal distance between selvage and straight of goods in two places establishes the grain parallel to the selvage. Acting on this principle, most pattern companies provide a short grain line (Fig. 57a). But fabric, like a squirmy child, doesn't always remain still. What may be parallel in the middle may be completely out of line at either end. For proper hang and fit, the correct grain line must be established throughout the entire length of each pattern piece (Fig. 57b).

5. If you haven't already done so, cut off all the unnecessary margins beyond the cutting line.

6. If a pattern needs to be used more than once or reversed, it is very helpful to trace and cut out an extra one. This can be used to complete the entire layout without lifting the original pattern from the

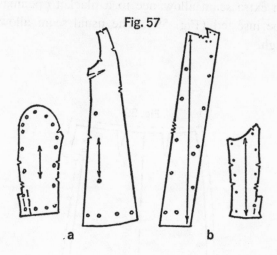

Fig. 57

.a   b

cloth for replacement. If a whole pattern rather than the usual half makes the layout easier, trace another half and Scotch-tape it to the original pattern.

7. Whenever there are two thicknesses of fabric, an upper and a lower, the seam that joins them is rolled to the underside so that it will not show. This means that the upper layer must be a little larger than the under layer. (Nothing gives away amateur sewing so much as the visible seam that joins an upper and lower layer of cloth in facings, collars, cuffs, lapels, welts, flaps, etc.)

Here are two ways in which to do this:

a. Add a little to the outside edges of the upper surface pattern (Fig. 58). Do not add anything to the edge that joins the garment.

b. Use a little less of the upper layer seam allowance of the fabric. The amount added or used depends on the thickness of the material—more for heavy fabrics, less for lightweight ones.

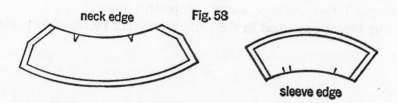

neck edge   Fig. 58

sleeve edge

8. Add an extra seam allowance to a placket opening in which a zipper will be inserted (Fig. 59). The usual seam allowance is not always enough.

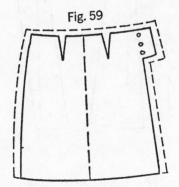

Fig. 59

These few additions to your adjusted pattern should make cutting easier, stitching more accurate, and finish more professional.

PLACING THE PATTERN ON THE FABRIC

The guide for placing the pattern on the fabric is the layout chart.

The layout chart is like one giant jigsaw puzzle that has been solved for you. Without it you would have to spend long hours of dove-tailing all those strange shapes of pattern tissue.

The layout contained in the pattern may not be the only possible

one. Women have been known to invent their own, either because they don't have enough fabric (in which case compromises
must be made) or because the pattern has been altered in some
way.

Beginners would do well to work with the layout chart provided
in the pattern. This is a photostatic copy (in scale) of all the actual
pieces necessary to complete the garment. This particular placement
of pattern makes an economical use of the fabric while strictly re-
specting the grain which provides the hang intended by the designer.
Innovations can come later.

Which of the many layouts?

You will notice that a number of layouts are offered for each design. This is to accommodate the variety of shapes of pattern pieces,
the varying widths of cloth as well as the varying widths of sewers as
represented by the size of the pattern.

Select the layout planned for your size, the view of the design
you are making, and the width of your fabric. Circle the chart with
colored pencil so that the eye will light on it easily (Fig. 60). Constant interruptions (a seeming plot directed against any woman
bent on sewing) may cause you to look up from or even leave your
work. If you don't mark the layout you are using, you may find
yourself working on another style in another size.

Fig. 60

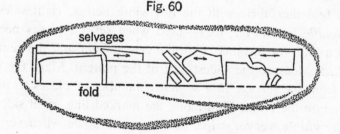

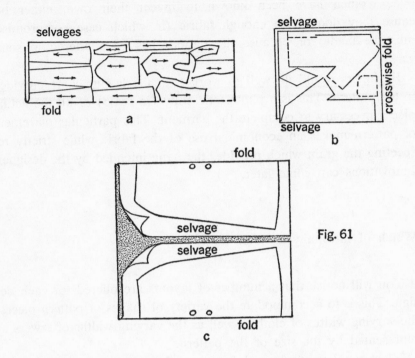

Fig. 61

Folding the material

As previously stated, most patterns are placed on a double thickness of fabric whenever possible. This is accomplished by folding in any of the following ways:

A lengthwise fold (Fig. 61a)—that most frequently used; fold the material lengthwise with the right sides inside.

A crosswise fold (Fig. 61b)—for fabrics *without* nap or directional design and for pattern pieces too wide to fit half the width of the fabric; fold the fabric with the full width across, right sides inside.

A double fold (Fig. 61c)—used when several pieces need to be cut on a fold, for instance, both the center front *and* the center back of a skirt. Measure the widest part of the pattern. Mark the required depth from the selvage in a sufficient number of places to provide a fold line on the grain. Fold along the marked line, right sides inside. Use any visible weave, stripe, or check as a guide whenever possible instead of measuring.

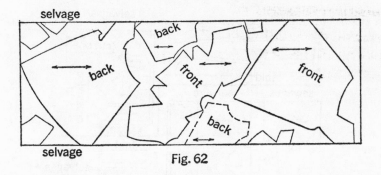

selvage

back

back

front

front

back

selvage

Fig. 62

Full width (Fig. 62)—the patterns for asymmetric and bias designs are usually complete and cut individually: place on the right side of a single thickness of fabric opened to full width.

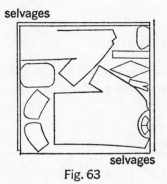

selvages

selvages

Fig. 63

Open double—(two thicknesses of full-width fabric) (Fig. 63)—for fabric with nap, pile, or directional design and for patterns too wide to fit half the width of the fabric; measure the length of fabric that will be needed for the pattern: cut along the crosswise straight of goods; swing the fabric around so that the nap or design is going in the same direction on both thicknesses; place both thicknesses together, right sides inside.

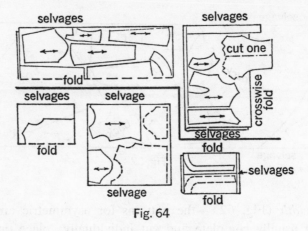

Fig. 64

Combinations (Fig. 64)—there are all sorts of combination lay-outs. Part of the garment may be placed on one type of fold, a second part on another. For layouts of this kind, pin and cut out the fabric on the lengthwise fold first; then fold the fabric again for the new layouts.

Hints for pattern placement

Whenever possible, fold with the right sides inside. This both pro-tects the fabric and makes marking simpler. Most marking is done on the wrong side.

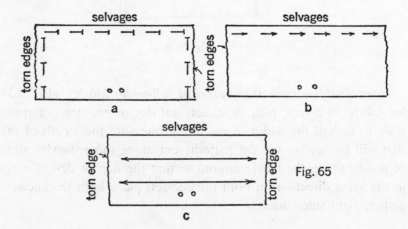

Fig. 65

The selvage edges and the torn or straightened edges are placed together and either pinned or basted to position (Fig. 65a).

Mark the direction of nap or directional designs with arrows along the selvage so you won't have to wonder or make repeated decisions as to which way the nap or design is going (Fig. 65b).

Mark the grain in several places with tailor's chalk on the wrong side of the fabric for use in areas which will fall away in cutting but which must be used again for other pattern pieces (Fig. 65c).

When a pattern is cut by twos or on a fold, it doesn't matter whether the printed side of the pattern is up or face down. Some pattern companies use a shaded area on the chart to indicate that the pattern is placed face down.

When a pattern is placed on the right side of the fabric opened to its full width, it is placed with the printed side up exactly as it will appear in the finished garment. One piece only is cut at a time. Should this pattern piece need to be used a second time in a reversed position, the printed side must then be faced down on the right side of the fabric. What is even more helpful is a traced identical pattern placed as directed along with the original pattern so the layout can be complete before cutting.

Match the identifying letter or number of the pattern with that on the chart. Note by its shape the position of each piece on the fabric.

Notches are also a good clue. The number and direction show how the pattern piece is placed and when it is reversed.

Be sure you know which pieces are to be cut on a fold and which just by twos.

Note particularly when cutting by twos which twos are in pairs— a right and a left (like sleeves) (Fig. 66a) and which are duplicates like pockets (Fig. 66b).

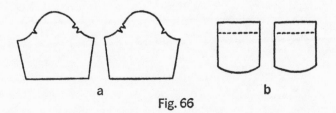

a   b

Fig. 66

When the layout chart shows a complete pattern piece, half of which is drawn in a solid line and the other half in a dotted line, it means the pattern is cut on a fold in that space. A complete pattern indicated by dotted lines means it is to be used a second time (Fig. 67).

Fig. 67

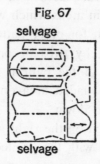

If a pattern piece is shown extending beyond a folded edge (Fig. 68), it means this piece must be cut in that space after all the other pieces have been cut and the remainder of the cloth is opened out. Just make sure that you mark the grain line on the material before the surrounding pieces are cut away. Otherwise you will have all the trouble of re-establishing the grain with perhaps not enough fabric to do it.

Fig. 68

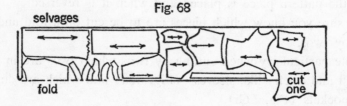

THE PRELIMINARIES ARE VITAL

Too often women speak of sewing solely in terms of machine stitching. They consider anything that may postpone this operation a disagreeable and frustrating preface with which they are only too willing to dispense. In reality, the actual sewing is like the eighth of an iceberg that is visible as against the seven-eighths that is submerged. That seven-eighths is all the vital preliminary deliberation necessary for a beautiful finished garment. In ready-to-wear clothes all of this is done for you by a staff who give considerable time and thought until every tiny detail of design and production is worked out. Now you must do all of this for yourself.

A good habit to get into from the very start of your sewing career is this: think much, plan much, decide much, prepare much before you ever put scissors to cloth.

NO TRIAL, MUCH TRAVAIL

What a nuisance to get the pattern securely pinned to the fabric only to discover as you near the end that you can't quite make it. Usually this is more a matter of faulty pattern placement than of lack of yardage. It's easy enough to unpin the pattern and replace the pieces, but what a lot of work and what a mass of pins!

A trial layout can avoid all this. While it may seem to be extra work at a point when you are very anxious to get on with the cutting, it is in reality a great time saver. Don't skip it.

The fabric on the cutting table

Place the fabric on a flat surface in the proper fold. The folded edge and the selvages are in the same relative position on the cutting table as they appear on the layout chart. Line up the straight edges of the fabric with the straight edges of the cutting surface. Weight the fabric in this position. If both surface and fabric are the kind that can take it, pin or tape the material to the cutting board. Support the weight of the material beyond the edge of the cutting table on an ironing board, a chair, or any other handy piece of furniture. This will prevent its being soiled by trailing on the floor or tugging at the end you are pinning.

The pattern on the fabric

Starting at one end of the fabric, place each pattern piece on it following its position on the layout chart. Pin the grain line first, starting at the widest part of the pattern. Measure an equal distance from the selvage to the straight of goods in a number of places along the entire length of the pattern. This places the grain parallel to the selvage—its true position. Don't rely on your eye! Measure!

Place the pattern pieces close together. Half inches have a way of adding up to inches. If you are Lady Bountiful in placing large margins around each piece, you may end up short of fabric.

Since this is only a trial layout, use as few pins as are absolutely necessary to hold the pattern in place. Should you need to change the layout, you won't have to undo a pound of pins.

As the pattern is pinned, fold the completed end and pull up more cloth.

When you are satisfied that all pattern pieces are rightly placed with the grain in perfect position, go back and pin for the cutting.

Pin for cutting

1. Pin the straight of goods every 2" or 3" along the entire length of the pattern.

2. When the straight of goods is set, smooth the pattern toward the outer edges and pin.

3. Keep the pattern and the fabric flat. Try not to raise them from the table any more than you can help.

4. Use one hand as an anchor, the other to pin.

5. The pins must go through the pattern and both layers of the material.

6. Place the pins at right angles to the cutting edge 2" to 3" apart.

Pin the corners diagonally (Fig. 69a). Curves take more pins than straight edges (Fig. 69b).

Fig. 69

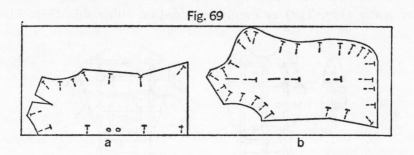

a   b

7. Pin in enough places to give a true cutting edge but not so much as to make the material pucker.

8. Compare your layout with the layout chart. Check off each part of the pattern you have pinned to the cloth. This is the best time to locate any missing pieces.

Now at last! You are ready to cut that gorgeous fabric.

PARENTHESIS—PATTERN PLACEMENT ON FIGURED FABRICS

If you limit yourself to solid-color fabrics (but who does?) laying out the pattern on the material is comparatively simple. When you get into the layout of figured fabrics, a little more time and thought are required.

Consider the most *effective placement of the motifs, checks, plaids, stripes.* A motif may be placed at center for a balanced effect (Fig. 70a), to one side for an asymmetric effect (Fig. 70b), or unexpectedly (Fig. 70c).

Fig. 70

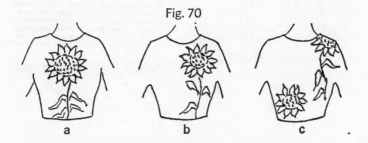

a   b   c

A dominant vertical stripe, bar, check, or color may be placed at center (Fig. 71a) or evenly balanced on either side (Fig. 71b).

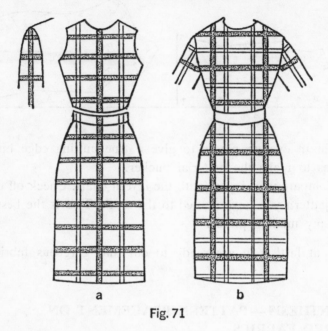

Fig. 71

How to "read" a plaid or a group of stripes

Stripes and plaids are designed with an even or uneven placement of lines, bars, or colors. Study the fabric to determine whether it has an up-and-down or a right-and-left movement. Find the

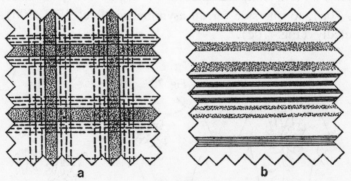

Fig. 72

center or dominant line of each plaid or group of stripes. "Read" the
the lines above and below, to the right and to the left.

If these are the same on all sides, the stripe or plaid is said to be
"balanced" (Fig. 72a). The layout for such fabrics is comparatively
simple. The pattern may be placed in any direction.

If, in reading the lines, you find they are different on each side,
the stripe or plaid is said to be "unbalanced" (Fig. 72b). Fabrics
like this must be treated as one-way designs (which, indeed, they
are). All pattern pieces must be placed going in the same direction.

Meticulous matching

Stripes, plaids, and checks need meticulous matching (Fig. 73a).

All crosswise lines must match at side seams, shaping seams, and
center front (or back) closing.

The vertical lines of the bodice must match the vertical lines of
the skirt.

The crosswise lines of the sleeves must match the crosswise lines
of the bodice.

The dart legs should be centered on straight lines and must match.

If there is a collar, the center back of the collar must match the
center back of the bodice.

Pockets, belts, and buttonholes must match the area in which
they are located.

a   b

Fig. 73

Design: the way out

Sometimes for design reasons and often simply to avoid this meticulous matching, the designer (or the sewer who is, in this respect, a designer) may plan to use one part of the pattern on one grain and another part on a different grain (Fig. 73b).

As you can see, there are many considerations in using figured fabric. If you are wise you will postpone working with these materials until a little more experience makes you more confident of your ability to handle them. That is—if in the meantime you don't find a checked, striped, plaid, or figured fabric you just can't resist!

CUT IT OUT!

That beginners are apprehensive about cutting into beautiful fabric for the first time is very understandable. More experienced sewers feel just that way, too. One is always haunted by visions of ir-remediable mistakes. A cut is so final! Fortunately, ingenious sewers can devise rescue operations. But it really is best to save the cutting for a time when one feels fresh and alert. Anyone who cuts when tired invites avoidable mistakes.

1. Keep the cloth as flat and as still as possible on the cutting table.

2. Move around the table as you cut rather than turning the fabric toward you. The latter may displace the pattern, pull the pins out, and shift the material.

3. Use long, firm strokes for the straight edges, short strokes for the curves.

4. Beginning sewers are safer cutting the notches outward beyond the edge of the pattern (Fig. 74a). Two or three notches may be cut as one (Fig. 74b). They can be matched to the same size "bumps" on the adjoining section.

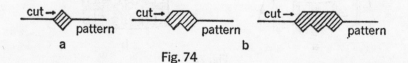

Fig. 74

5. Do not use pinking or scalloping shears for cutting. They do not give an accurate cutting line; they make it too difficult to judge seam allowances in sewing; they make cutting through paper and two thicknesses of cloth much too hard; and they may have to be trimmed away anyhow. Pinking and scalloping shears are best used as an edge finish.

6. Support the weight of the uncut end of the fabric on any handy piece of furniture so that it does not trail on the floor or tug at the rest of the cloth.

7. As each section is cut out, lay it flat or hang it on a hanger. If your storage space is such that you must fold the garment after cutting, make as few loose folds as possible. Keep the pattern side out so that you can easily identify each piece as well as protect the fabric.

8. Pull the new section to be cut, carefully into place, without disturbing the pattern or the pins of the trial layout.

There is no doubt about it. Layout and cutting are hard work. But they are also a sure sign that you are well on your way.

MARK EVERYTHING!

The pattern is clear. All those enigmatic little symbols on it are now understandable to you. Obviously you can't stitch the pattern into the garment. What happens when you remove the pattern from the cloth? How will you ever know what to do with that uncharted expanse of material? The answer is simple: transfer all the pattern markings to the fabric.

Mark everything! The more time you take to mark, the less puzzlement, the quicker the work will progress.

What marks to transfer: all darts, seams, placket openings, notches, button placement, pocket placement, pleats, dart tucks, areas of controlled fullness, special joinings, or any other meaningful markings which facilitate the joining of the garment sections.

What marks not to transfer: the grain line, the cutting line, printed identifying letters or numbers or any printed directions.

Markings on the wrong side of the fabric: construction seams and darts.

Use tailor's chalk

The safest marking is done with tailor's chalk, which is both easy to apply and easy to brush off. Since this comes in assorted colors, use a color that contrasts with your cloth so that it can easily be seen.

Chalking can best be done through a perforation. If the pattern doesn't have perforations, you can easily make them with a stiletto or the pointed end of an orange stick through the medium-sized "O's" of the darts and seams.

Place a pin through the newly created perforation, catching both thicknesses of fabric. Chalk the area caught by the pin on both upper and under side. (Fig. 75).

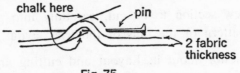

Fig. 75

Since tailor's chalk brushes off easily, it is best to chalk just prior to sewing. If you mark this week and sew next, you may not find any chalk marks left.

Use dressmaker's carbon paper

The longest-lasting marks (indeed, permanent in some cases) can be made with dressmaker's carbon paper and a blunt tracing wheel.

This marking makes for precision stitching. It's a great method IF your fabric can take it.

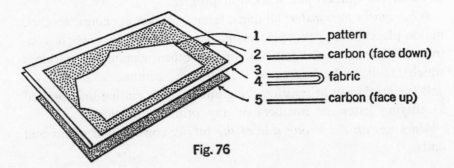

1 —————— pattern
2 ========= carbon (face down)
3 ═══════⟩ fabric
4
5 ========= carbon (face up)

Fig. 76

1. Unpin a small section of your pattern.

2. Slip a sheet of dressmaker's carbon paper of contrasting color between the pattern and the fabric. Slip a second sheet of carbon under the lower thickness of cloth. In each case the carbon side is against the fabric. The cloth is enclosed by the carbon so both sides can be marked simultaneously.

3. Replace the pattern and pin in just enough places to hold all in position (Fig. 76).

4. For straight-line marking, run the tracing wheel along the edge of a ruler. For curved-line marking, trace freehand, following accurately the line of the pattern.

5. Unpin the pattern, remove the carbon, and slide it along to a new section. Make sure the new marking will join the old.

6. Repeat Steps 2 to 5.

Caution

While chalk does brush off easily, it may leave a tonality on white, light-colored, or sheer material.

Carbon markings show brightly, clearly, and forever as they come through to the right side of white, light-colored, or sheer materials.

In vari-colored or textured fabric neither of the above methods may produce visible markings.

For many fabrics, the safest and most effective method of marking is with basting thread of contrasting color.

Right-side markings

Some markings are absolutely necessary on the right side of the garment, while the work is in progress. They must be such that they can be easily removed, without leaving any trace that they have been there. The safest (and incidentally the oldest) method of right-side marking is with basting thread of contrasting color.

Guide basting marks the center front and back, the fold line of a facing, the fold of a pleat, *any line* of marking necessary for either construction, finishing, or trimming.

1. Using a double thread, make a line of basting through the pattern and both layers of the fabric.

2. Leave 1″ loops of thread between each stitch (Fig. 77a).

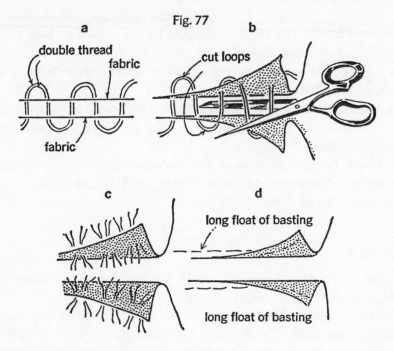

Fig. 77

3. Open the layers of the fabric carefully and cut the threads between them (Fig. 77b).

4. Clip the stitch on the upper surface to release the pattern (Fig. 77c).

5. Immediately run a line of basting along the tufts before you lose their marking. Make a long float of basting on the right side and a short stitch on the wrong side (Fig. 77d) so the guide basting shows as an almost continuous line.

Tailor's tacks—for "spot" markings

1. Use a double thread of contrasting color.

2. Take a stitch through both thicknesses, leaving a 1″ end.

3. Take another stitch in the same place making a 1″ loop.

4. Repeat Steps 2 and 3, making a double loop. Cut the thread, leaving a 1″ end (Fig. 78a).

5. Carefully separate the two layers of fabric until a stitch appears on each outer side.

6. Clip the thread between the layers, making small tufts on the right side of each layer (Fig. 78b).

7. Clip the stitches on the upper and lower surfaces to release the pattern.

8. Remove the pattern carefully.

9. The remaining tufts are the tailor's tacks (Fig. 78c).

Fig. 78

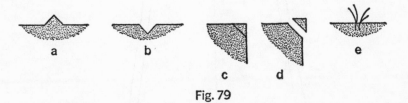

a   b   c

The trick in successful tailor's tacks is *not* to cut the loops until the layers of fabric have been separated. If you cut them before, the tufts are apt to pull out as you separate the two thicknesses.

Notches—to facilitate joining of garment sections

Notches may be marked in several ways: they may be cut out beyond the cutting line (Fig. 79a) while cutting the fabric, see page 112; a tiny V-shape may be cut out of the seam allowance (Fig. 79b); the fabric may be folded and snipped diagonally across the corner (Figs. 79c and d); several loops of basting thread of contrasting color may mark the notch in fabrics that ravel easily (Fig. 79e).

a   b   c   d   e

Fig. 79

Whatever method of marking is used, the marking should above all be accurate. If it isn't, the stitching can't be accurate. The marking should be clearly visible so you won't have to hunt for it. Choose that marking which, while effective, will also be safest for the fabric.

Careful marking is a time-saving device, not a delaying action. Mark everything! A well-marked fabric takes the guesswork out of joining the sections of the garment.

STAY STITCHING SAVES THE SHAPE

In the ensuing hours of construction, all those carefully cut and accurately marked sections of your garment will be subjected to

Fig. 80

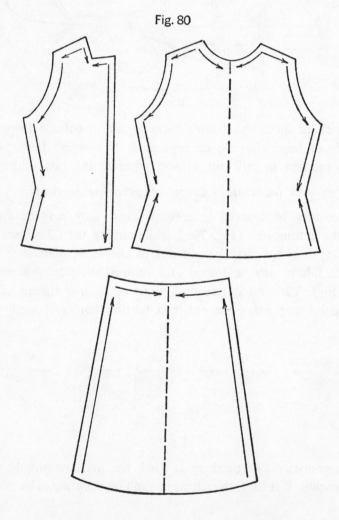

much handling. If unprotected, these precious pieces may be pulled or stretched out of shape. To prevent such a mishap, each single layer of fabric is stay stitched.

Stay Stitching is a line of machine stitching ½″ in from the cut edge that fixes the size and shape of each section of the garment as cut. It may be removed when the garment is completed or it may remain permanently in the seam allowance where it will be invisible from the right side.

Use any thread and 8 stitches to 1″—small enough to stay the edge, large enough to be removed should you wish. *Stay Stitching is directional* to preserve the grain of the fabric. There are two rules: stitch from high to low and from wide to narrow. The rule wide-to-narrow takes precedence over high to low. Some patterns indicate the direction of the stay stitching by arrows (Fig. 80).

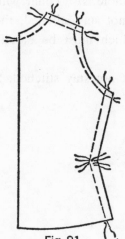

Fig. 81

Never make a continuous line of stitching around a corner. Break the thread at the end of each row and begin again in the new direction (Fig. 81).

On a curve, stitch from the high to the low point of the curve, break the thread, stitch the rest of the curve from high to low until it meets the previous line of stitching.

When the stay stitching is completed, test each piece of fabric against the pattern. Just keep in mind that stay stitching is intended to preserve the original shape and size, not to distort it. Make any necessary adjustments—pulling up the thread on any stretched edge or clipping and releasing a few stitches on a tight edge—until the cut edge of the fabric matches the pattern.

The following edges require stay stitching: neck, shoulders, armholes, side seams, waistline, all edges on curves or sharp angles, all straight edges of ravelly material.

The following edges should not be stay stitched: those cut on a true lengthwise or crosswise grain in non-ravelly material; hidden edges which don't join anything, like the outer edge of a facing; any edge which needs to be eased into another, for example: the sleeve cap needs to be eased into the armhole so *it* is not stay stitched though the armhole is: a collar which must be eased around neck and shoulders is not stay stitched, though the neckline is; the top edge of a hem which must be eased against the skirt is not stay stitched.

True bias is best left not stay stitched. Stay stitching restricts its drape and hang.

PROGRESS REPORT

Your dress is now cut out, marked, and stay stitched.

Fold your pattern up neatly and save it for another time. You're a rare one if you can fold it back into that small, neat, compact package it was at the start. Often one can't even jam it into the envelope in which it came. Try a manila mailing envelope, large enough to take it comfortably. Paste the front and back of the original envelope on the face of your new container for easy identification and needed information.

Do save your patterns for a reasonable length of time. You may find to your dismay that the very pattern you discarded last Tuesday has a wonderful collar or neckline you would just love to have this Friday. A reference collection of used (and unused) patterns can be very useful.

BUILT-IN BEAUTY

The French have well-known words for it—*trompe l'oeil*—fool the eye. It's interesting to reflect that the French, who gave us this phrase, also gave us Fashion. A connection between the two?

Certainly in fashion, things are not always what they seem. What meets the eye may be anything a designer's flight of fancy may conceive. What remains hidden from view is the fashion engineer's sub-structure which makes it possible. Subtle or exaggerated, the shape of fashion depends on undercover support. Fabric alone can seldom sustain the lines.

The inside story
Part One—concerning wear

All outside edges of a garment need a finish. If the edge is a straight one, the finish is a hem. If the edge is a curved one, the finish is a facing.

All outside edges of a garment, straight or curved, are subject to stress and wear. To reinforce these areas and strengthen them, the garment needs an interfacing in addition to the facing.

An *interfacing* is just what the word implies: a layer of reinforcing material between (inter) the facing and the garment. The interfacing is generally cut from the facing pattern.

It has the same shape and the same grain. An interfacing material should be compatible with the fabric it interfaces, that is: lightweight fabric takes a lightweight interfacing, mediumweight fabric takes mediumweight interfacing, heavy fabric takes heavy interfacing.

Part Two—concerning style

In times gone by, chiffon was always reserved for fluttery, flimsy, feminine styles. Everyone knew that chiffon had no mind and no body for a slim, seductive sheath. Yet, it is being shown today that very way. What accounts for the transformation? Point of view and an underlining of crepe. Now that lovely muted look of chiffon merely camouflages the shaping quality of the crepe. Many present-day fashions call for just such treatment.

Any fabric can be used for any style regardless of its texture IF it is propped up by a *backing or underlining*. (These words are used interchangeably.)

Underlining does *not* have to be compatible in weight or texture with the outer fabric. It may be anything that will support the shape. Use the same pattern pieces for the backing as for the outer fabric (Fig. 82).

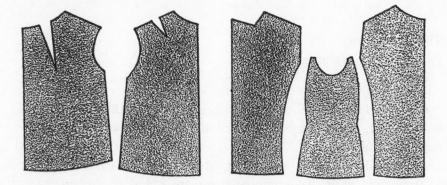

Fig. 82

Underlining a sleeve is optional. If the fabric needs bolstering because it is too limp, by all means underline the sleeve. If the shape of the sleeve requires support, back it entirely (Fig. 83a) or in part (Fig. 83b). Bear in mind that an underlined sleeve is heavier, warmer, tighter, stiffer than one that isn't. Should an underlining be essential to the design, consider a backing that is softer and lighter in weight than that used for the rest of the garment.

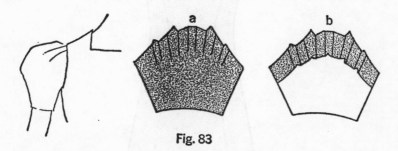

Fig. 83

Apply the same principle to a kimono sleeve: back it with the same material as the rest of the garment (Fig. 84a), omit it (Fig. 84b), or substitute a softer backing for the sleeve (Fig. 84c). In the latter two instances, the bodice backing is carried to a point ½" beyond the shoulder and curves slightly to the underarm seam.

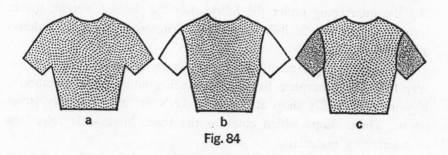

Fig. 84

Know the combination

A garment may have a combination of both interfacing and underlining if the style calls for it. Each functions in a particular way in a specific part of the garment. In fact, many a garment has an entire undershell composed of several different types of interfacing and backing fabric (Fig. 85).

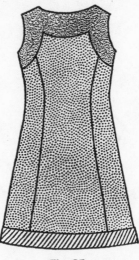

Fig. 85

What to use

There are so many interfacing materials and so many companies making extravagant claims of merit for their products that it is hard to decide which to use. Your *choice depends on the fabric and the style*. The safest thing to do is to take a sample of your fabric and a picture of the design with you when you shop for interfacing. Slip the interfacing under the fabric. Let the desired weight, finish, texture, degree of flexibility, softness, firmness, or crispness determine the choice.

While many department stores carry large stocks of dress fabrics, very few carry complete lines of interfacing and backing materials. If you can possibly shop at a dressmaker's or tailor's supply store, do so. These shops which cater to the trade have wide selections of interfacing materials.

Don't assume that the salesperson is better informed on the use of these materials than you are. After all, salespeople sell what they have for sale. This may not be at all what is best for your style. Furthermore they have no way of knowing just what is the end effect that you have in mind. While you may accept advice, you alone must make the final judgment. Let the fabric and the style guide you.

Often dress fabrics can be used for both backing or interfacing: organza, organdy, net, lawn, crepe, muslin, taffeta, linen, batiste, etc. If the dress or blouse is of wash fabric, self-fabric makes a fine interfacing. It has the same color and the same shrinkage. (Self-fabric also makes a very satisfactory interfacing for fabrics of other fibers.)

In addition, there are many interfacing and underlining fabrics designed especially for the purpose.* You will no doubt recognize some of the names in the following list.

The wovens	The non-wovens	The iron-ons
Formite	Evershape	Adheron
Siri	Keybak	Interlon
Veriform	Interlon	Keybak—Hot Iron
Capri	Kyrel	Pellomite Detail
Sta-shape	Pellon	Pellomite—Shape
Si-bonne		Retaining
Everflex		Pressto
Silesia		Sta-Flex
Wigan		Weldex
Hair canvas		

They vary in character—limp to stiff. They vary in weight—light to heavy. They vary in width—18″ to 72″. They vary in price—but none are as cheap as cotton. Some are washable, some dry-cleanable. Some come in colors—others may be dyed to match the fabric when color is an important factor.

Woven interfacings are best used in areas that need shaping or suppleness. Non-woven interfacings are fine for belled and bouffant effects. Because they stiffen the area in which they are used, they are not desirable for more general use.

---

* A detailed list of interfacing, underlinings, and other shaping materials can be found in *The Complete Book of Tailoring* by this author, published by Doubleday.

Part Three—concerning luxury

One looks back with nostalgia on a day when a summer dress was just one thin layer of cool fabric. Today's dresses are so much heavier, weighted as they are with backings, interfacings, and linings.

The use of lining as a finish is and always was a distinguishing mark of professional custom work as against home sewing, high-priced couture clothes as against inexpensive ready-to-wear. Add to

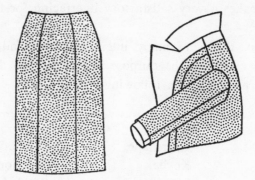

Fig. 86

this the naturally sumptuous feel of silk or very fine cotton and it is easy to understand why luxury by lining has become a status symbol and why practically all dresses come to us lined these days.

A lining is used primarily as a finish, hiding the inner workings of the garment (Fig. 86).

Or, it may be used as a stay to preserve the planned shape (Fig. 87) of the garment.

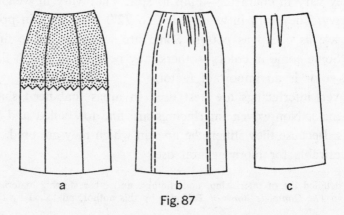

a   b   c
Fig. 87

Fig. 87a—A half lining for the back of a skirt to prevent a "seat."

Figs. 87b and c—The front fullness of this skirt is held where it belongs—in front! Were it not for the stay (Fig. 87c), the skirt would just look big and baggy.

A drape of any kind looks better when its fullness is held in place by a lining stay (Fig. 88).

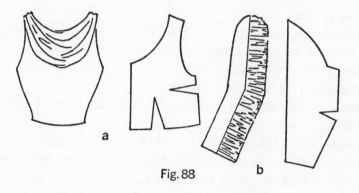

a

Fig. 88

b

Fig. 88a—The cowl neckline is held in place by a fitted bodice lining which acts as a stay.

Fig. 88b—The shirred fullness of the sleeve is held in place by a fitted sleeve lining.

While there are technical differences in function between a lining, a backing, and an interfacing, in effect there is a good deal of duplication. A lining provides more body for the outer fabric; in doing so it serves as a backing. A dress backed with China silk has the feel of a lining. A lining or a backing joined at the outside edges reinforces and finishes those edges performing the role of an interfacing.

We always come back to the same thought: whether you choose to interface, to underline, or to line depends on the fabric and the design.

Special effects

There are times when even interfacings, linings, and backings are not quite enough to produce a particular effect. For that purpose stiffer materials are used. (Because millinery production deals with this problem continually, you will find millinery supply stores an endless and wonderful source of foundation and shaping fabrics.)

Here are a few stiffening aids:

Hair braid (horse hair)—used to stiffen laces, sheer fabrics, and hems of gowns

Featherboning—attached to vertical shaping seams of fitted bodices, strapless or off-the-shoulder dresses; it may also be used for standing collars, wide belts, etc.

Belting—for waistbands and belts

Crinoline and buckram—wherever a very stiff area is called for; both of these grow limp when washed or dry-cleaned

Flexible wire (silk covered)—used for shaped edges

Cotton wadding, cotton flannel, lamb's wool, felting—provide a soft, padded look to satins, brocades, and heavy silks; may be used as a backing for the entire garment or in unpressed hems

SHOULDER PADS—SHOULD I?

The memory of those football shoulders fashionable in the thirties and forties lingers and colors many a present attitude. One of the questions most frequently and most fervently asked in dressmaking and tailoring classes is, "Do I have to use shoulder pads?"

A little padding goes a long way

While present styles bypass the exaggerated padding of yore, there is no doubt that some padding does help. A little bit can go a long way to provide just that smidgen of support that will keep the shoulder area and sleeve cap from collapsing.

If the pattern calls for shoulder pads, you should use them. Not only is this necessary for the style but for the fit. The pattern has been cut to include them. If you omit the pads, the pattern must be recut to exclude them or the shoulder area will require very special fitting. You really do not need to use the pad exactly as you buy it. Should there be too much "stuffing" for your taste, remove some of it.

Ready-made pads come in a number of types and shapes. In selecting one, keep in mind the design of your garment. Some pads are meant for set-in sleeves, others for kimono or dropped-shoulder styles. Avoid those that sit like little bumps on your shoulder.

"Lifts" or supports to make yourself

A cap lift (Fig. 89)—for a set-in sleeve

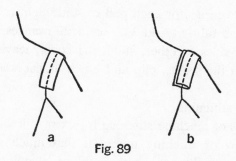

a   b

Fig. 89

1. Cut a bias strip of self-fabric (if it is firm enough) 6″ long by 1½″ wide. Should it be too limp, too stiff, too heavy, or too bumpy, use Siri-soft, flannelette, or any similar fabric.

2. Push the armhole seam allowance (graded) into the sleeve. You may as well take advantage of this extra bit of padding, also.

3. On the underside and holding the sleeve and shoulder in the position in which it will be worn, place the strip over the shoulder— half to the front and half to the back. Extend the strip ⅝″ into the sleeve cap. Pin to position.

4. With tiny hand stitches, fasten the strip to the seam allowance close to the armhole seam (Fig. 89a).

If you think a double strip of fabric will work better, cut one 6″ long by 3″ wide. Fold it in half lengthwise. Extend the folded edge ⅝″ into the sleeve cap. Stitch to position. Grade the raw edges (Fig. 89b).

Crescent pad (Fig. 90)—for set-in sleeve

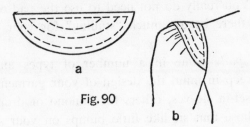

Fig. 90

1. Cut two crescent shapes (Fig. 90a) of some stiff material in a suitable size.

2. Cut two coverings for each pad of some lightweight material—perhaps the dress fabric. Add ¼″ seam allowances.

3. With right sides together, stitch the cover, leaving the straight edge open. Trim the seams, clip and notch as necessary, turn to the right side.

4. Insert the stiffening.

5. Make rows of machine stitching for extra stiffening (Fig. 90a). Each added row of stitching makes it that much stiffer.

6. Close the straight edge with hand or machine stitching.

7. On the underside, attach the pad to the armhole seam by hand stitching (Fig. 90b).

Strip pad (Fig. 91)—for set-in sleeve

Fig. 91

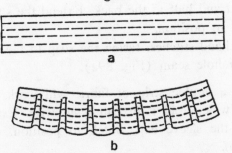

1. Cut a strip of taffeta to three times the desired length and twice the width.

2. Fold in half lengthwise. Insert any stiffening material—crinoline, Pellon, etc.

3. Make several rows of machine stitching to add to the stiffness (Fig. 91a).

4. Pleat the stiffened strip. Stitch across one lengthwise end to stay the desired length (Fig. 91b). (This could be bound instead, if you like.)

5. Attach the bound or stitched edge in place in the armhole.

Any stiff fabric or ribbon can be used as well as the taffeta suggested.

TRIAL FITTING

This is the first of many times you will try the garment on—sometimes for work, sometimes just to admire your handiwork.

If you were making a standard-size garment and you neither knew nor cared who was to wear it, fitting would be no consideration and no problem at all. Since you are sewing for yourself (or someone in whom you are interested) you are very much concerned about flattering fit.

Fabrics fall differently

Pattern changes alone do not insure perfect fit. Fabrics have characters of their own: they fall differently; they may or may not "give"; the color and texture affect the "look." This is the time—before stitching—to make whatever other changes may be necessary. A trial fitting is a must.

Baste or pin?

Many dressmakers like to baste a garment for the trial fitting. They feel this gives a truer picture of how the garment looks on.

Perhaps it does, but pin-fitting is faster and more practical for a first trial. It is so much easier to remove a pin, make the adjustment, and repin than it is to rip a line of basting, fit, pin, and rebaste. Endless basting has discouraged many a would-be sewer.

Aides and aids

It's easier and more fun to work with a friend or neighbor who loves to sew as much as you do. You can train each other to see the fine points of fitting. However, you may be surprised to find how much you can actually do for yourself.

A dress form that duplicates your body (and only that kind) can be an invaluable help. A standard-size form is no more help than a standard-size pattern. If an individual dress form is not commercially available, make your own. Carefully fit a muslin to your figure. Stitch it and pack it tight with shredded foam rubber (the kind used to stuff toy animals), with tissue paper, or with cotton wadding.

In time you may want to make a basic pattern. This is a flat tag pattern traced from a carefully fitted muslin. It is a portrait of your figure that depicts all the many little ways in which it differs from the standard. The basic pattern is used as a guide in changing standard-size patterns to fit you. It takes the guesswork out of pattern alteration.

If you know that you have a real figure problem, make a trial muslin first. All necessary corrections can be made on the muslin and transferred to the pattern *before* you cut your material. A trial muslin is also a good idea if you are uncertain of the becomingness of a style. It is better to change your mind about a muslin than about expensive material.

Seeing is deceiving

Most figures are not symmetrical. Yet we want our garments to look balanced. This takes a little doing. Fortunately, we have myriad body movements and optical illusions to assist us in disguising the body's asymmetry.

We are not generally given to standing at rigid attention or sitting like Egyptian statues. Our heads may be tilted or turned, the shoulders inclined, the waist bent, one arm raised while the other hangs at the side, one foot forward, another back. All these many body movements, however slight, make for an informal body balance which happily disguises its asymmetry.

Because of this illusion of balance, some parts of the garment may be fitted individually to shape and size while others must be faked to look balanced. For instance: the right shoulder may have a different slope than the left one. If each is fitted separately, somehow the garment will look symmetrical; if both are made the same, the unfilled-out excess material of one will emphasize the difference. On the other hand, even if the shoulders are not alike in width, they must be made the same or the garment will look lopsided.

MORAL: fit where you can, fake where you must. Seeing can be very deceiving.

Fit the shell of the garment

Use only those sections that make the outer shell of the garment —no double thicknesses, no facings, no collars, no cuffs, no sleeves unless any of the above are cut all-in-one with the pattern. Our concern is chiefly with the seams and darts.

First sewing projects are simple ones, so fitting problems are held to a minimum. If our mathematical calculations are correct, the garment as cut from the adjusted pattern should be close to your figure needs. Such minor changes as are necessary may be made in existing seams and darts.

1. Pin all the darts and seams that complete the dress front.
2. Pin all the darts and seams that complete the dress back.
3. Pin the front and back together at the shoulders and the side seams, leaving the placket open.

Place the pins fairly close together to provide a continuous line. Take *the full seam allowance.* If, in your fear of making the garment too small, you pin close to the cut edge, you may make the dress a full size larger.

4. Try on the garment. Pin it closed at the placket or the opening extension (if any).

5. If you are planning to use shoulder pads, set them in place.

6. Now examine the fit.

Fit from the right side

Though the garment is pinned (or basted, if you insist) on the wrong side where the markings are clear, *all fitting is done from the right side.* Were this not done, you would be fitting the garment in reverse.

Examine the fit critically in your mirror. Make any changes you deem necessary. Use safety pins rather than straight pins: they won't fall out when you remove the dress. Pin one side only for symmetrical changes and duplicate the other side. Pin each side individually where it is essential.

Make it fit

Fitting with grain

Your first clue to good fit is the grain. The vertical grain marked by guide basting hangs at right angles to the floor. The horizontal grain across the chest, across the bust, across the hips is parallel to the floor (see Fig. 40, page 79).

If the grain is not in the correct position, release the nearest seam involved, lift or lower the fabric as necessary, and repin. For instance, if the grain does this (Fig. 92a), make it do this (Fig. 92b) on the bodice. If the grain does this (Fig. 92c), make it do this (Fig. 92d) on the skirt.

Fig. 92

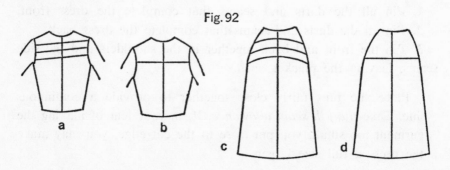

a   b   c   d

If the lengthwise grain of a sleeve tilts forward as in Fig. 93a or backward as in Fig. 93c, "dial" it to the correct position as in Fig. 93b.

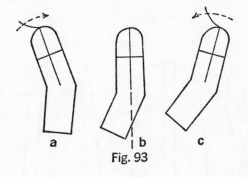

Fig. 93

Fitting for shape

Check the position of all darts. Remember that they must head toward the high point of the curve under consideration no matter

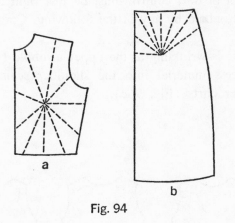

Fig. 94

what seam they come from. For instance: all bodice darts head for the high point of the bust (Fig. 94a); all back skirt darts head for the high point of the buttocks (Fig. 94b).

If the darts on your garment produce fullness or bulges above, below, or beside the high point, unpin and reposition the darts.

All shaping seams must pass over the high point of the curve being fitted or within 1″ either side of it unless there is auxiliary shaping by means of other seams, darts, or fullness (Fig. 95).

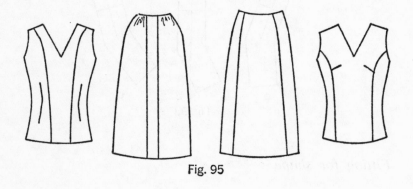

Fig. 95

The amount of dart control must be just right for your figure or you may be troubled by any of the following. Correct them in these ways.

Where there is wrinkling at the upper armhole (Fig. 96a), unpin, push the excess material into the shoulder seam (Fig. 96b), or make shoulder darts (Fig. 96c).

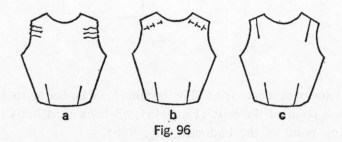

a   b   c

Fig. 96

Where there is wrinkling at the lower armhole (Fig. 97a), push the excess material into an underarm dart (Fig. 97b), or a shoulder dart (Fig. 97c).

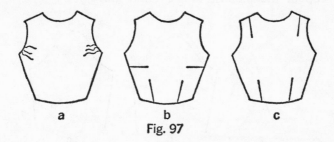

a   b   c

Fig. 97

If the center front bodice "hikes" up (Fig. 98a), you need a larger dart at the waistline, or the underarm (Fig. 98b).

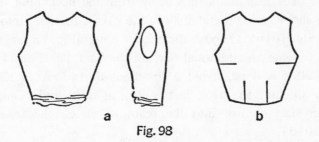

a   b

Fig. 98

A skirt that pokes out at center front or back needs more dart control (Fig. 99a). Unpin the side seams above the hips, make a larger dart or two darts (Fig. 99b), repin the side seams, shaping as necessary.

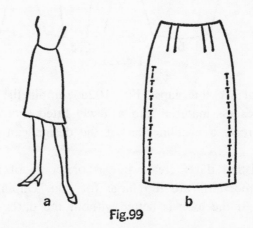

a   b

Fig.99

Where a short sleeve pokes out (Fig. 100a), the sleeve cap needs more length. If the fabric is already cut, use what you can of the seam allowance. If you can anticipate this correction, add to the sleeve cap of the pattern (Figs. 100b and c).

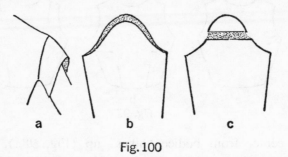

a   b   c

Fig. 100

If the back neckline stands away from the neck (Fig. 101a), unpin the shoulder seam and smooth the excess material into the seam, repin (Fig. 101b). Or push the excess material into a larger shoulder dart; or, create an additional dart on the back neckline (Fig. 101c). If the latter is done, avoid a too-many-darts look in the shoulder area by stitching the neck dart control as darts and easing the back shoulder dart control into the seam to match the front shoulder (Fig. 101d).

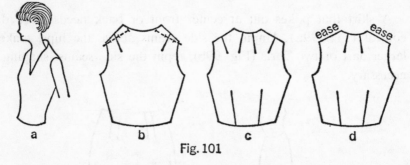

a   b   c   d

Fig. 101

If the front neckline gaps (Fig. 102a), unpin the shoulder seam, smooth the excess material into a newly fitted shoulder seam (Fig. 102b), or create a neckline dart if the design can absorb it (Fig. 101c).

If the existing darts create bulges or poufs of material at the dart point, the darts are too large for you. Unpin, make smaller darts, repin. If the look is better without the darts, eliminate them

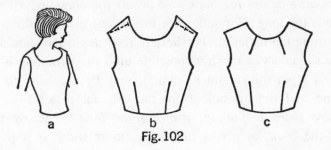

a   b   c
Fig. 102

entirely and shape the garment on the nearest seam. This is often
a good correction for skirts that puff out at the hips.

Whenever you make a change in a dart—either to make it smaller
or larger—the seam from which it originates is altered in length,
perhaps even in shape. Match it to the seam that joins it. If it is
too long, cut some off. If it is too short, add what is needed (or
possible) in the seam allowance. *All corresponding seams must
match in length and shape. Each pair of dart legs must match in
length.*

Wrinkles that appear in a skirt or bodice indicate one of several
things: the grain is not right, more dart control is needed, added
length or width is required, or a nearby seam is not in the right
place. Check out each of these.

Corrections for wrinkling at the waistline (Fig. 103a): Unpin the
side seams as far as is necessary to release the strain and wrinkling.
Check the grain and the darts. Refit and repin the side seams (Fig.
103b). Tie a string around the waist and mark the new waistline
(Fig. 103c). Add seam allowance and trim off any excess fabric.

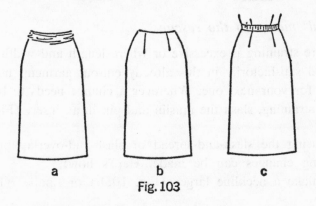

a   b   c
Fig. 103

Wrinkling across the back and across the chest indicates that the bodice is too long. Correction for this is best made in the pattern before cutting the material. To shorten now, unpin the shoulder seams, lift the shoulders as much as possible until the wrinkling is removed, refit and repin the shoulder seam. It may be necessary to recut the neckline and the armhole from the original pattern.

Where there is pulling, drawing, or binding across the chest, across the back, or across the sleeve, more width is required. It is difficult to add width at this stage. Use what you can of the seam allowances. To correct the pattern before cutting the material, see page 83.

If the garment keeps sliding to the back, the back neckline is too short. Use the back shoulder seam allowance to add length. Better yet, if this is a correction always called for in your garments, add ⅝" to ¾" to the entire back shoulder seam before cutting.

If the neckline is too tight, lower it (Fig. 104a). If it is too low, build it up (Fig. 104b). The solid lines indicate the new necklines. Use the seam allowance in this fitting. Fill in the pattern for future garments.

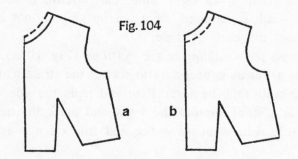

Fig. 104

Trial muslin to the rescue

Where straining is excessive or where length and width cannot be adjusted satisfactorily in this already cut-out garment, make a trial muslin for your next one. Wherever a change needs to be made to relieve straining, slash the muslin and pin in an insert (Fig. 105).

By using the slash-and-spread or slash-and-overlap method, the following changes can be made. Here's how:

To make a neckline larger (Fig. 106b) or smaller (Fig. 106c)

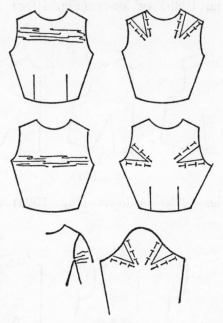

Fig. 105

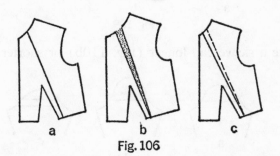

Fig. 106

To make the shoulders broader (Fig. 107b) or narrower (Fig. 107c)

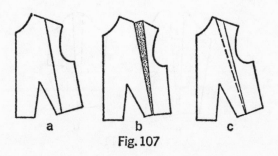

Fig. 107

To raise (Fig. 108b) or lower (Fig. 108c) a shoulder at the armhole

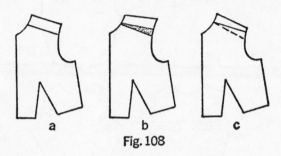

Fig. 108

To raise (Fig. 109b) or lower (Fig. 109c) a shoulder at the neckline

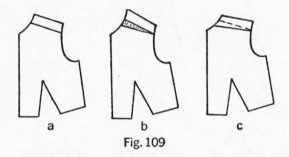

Fig. 109

To make a sleeve cap longer (Fig. 110b) or shorter (Fig. 110c)

Fig. 110

To make a sleeve cap wider (Fig. 111a) or narrower (Fig. 111b)

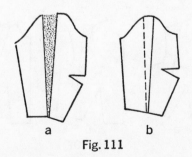

Fig. 111

Remember that you have the entire perimeter of the pattern to which you can add or from which you can subtract a needed amount.

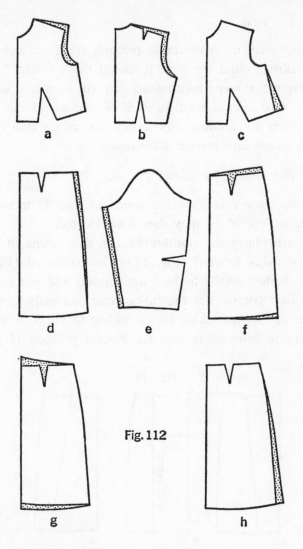

Fig. 112

Shaded areas show where to add on for

a. square shoulders   d. larger waistline skirt
b. broad shoulders   e. muscular arm
c. larger waistline bodice   f. sway back
   g. large abdomen
   h. side seam that swings forward (or backward)

Obviously, these few suggestions can't solve every possible fitting problem, but they may give you a method for dealing with them.

Fitting for ease

Make the garment comfortable through the bust and waistline. Swish the skirt around the hips; it should move easily. Try sitting.

Don't forget that some adjustments can still be made on the seam allowances. One quarter inch on each of four seams may give you that extra inch for comfort. Conversely, too much ease can be removed by taking larger seam allowances.

Fitting the silhouette seams

Reread the section on silhouette seams on page 73 to refresh your memory as to just where they should be located.

Check particularly the position of the side seams of the skirt. Should they swing forward (Fig. 113a) or backward (Fig. 113c), release the seams; establish the correct grain and pin at the hips; check the dart control; let the fabric hang naturally from hips to hem; repin the seams, taking off or adding to either front or back as necessary to bring them into the correct position (Fig. 113b).

Fig. 113

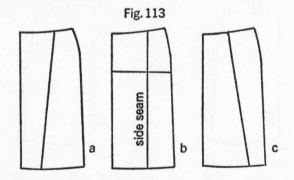

Check the position of the shoulder seam. It may be moved forward or backward in its entire length or in one place only at neckline or shoulder.

When you are satisfied that you have made all the changes that you can at this time, remove the garment. Transfer all corrections to the wrong side of the fabric with tailor's chalk or with basting thread—whichever is safest for your fabric. Repin or baste the corrections. Try the garment on again. Refine the fit. Unfortunately, there is no substitute for repeated fittings.

Fit to flatter

You must train your eye to see the fine details that make for good fit. As your perception grows, you'll probably grow more demanding. Feel free to make any changes that will make the dress more becoming. Would it be more becoming *if*

the shoulders were wider? or narrower?

the shoulder seams were moved backward? or forward?

you had more ease across the chest? across the back? across the bust? across the upper sleeve?

the waistline was looser? or tighter? raised? or lowered?

the hips had more ease? or less ease?

the sleeves were wider? or narrower? or shorter? or longer?

there was more shaping? or less shaping?

the side seams were moved forward? or backward?

Ask yourself honestly if the style is becoming. Does it bring out your good features and hide your bad ones?

One dress that fits well is worth a ton of misfits. You'll find yourself reaching for it constantly, for you know you always look your best in it.

PART IV

KNOW!

THE HEADWORK IN HANDWORK

Any sewing technique that contributes to the realization of a particular style is legitimate and right; any that doesn't is needless and wrong. Fortunately, there is a great body of information on which to draw. Then, too, most successful sewers, like other artists, are innovators: they make a creative and original use of classic techniques. They have even been known to invent their own.

There are many possible methods for achieving a result. Anything goes in construction if it attains the effect that you or the designer have in mind. Any amount of hand or machine sewing may be right. Any use of fabric may be right. Any interfacing or underlining may be right. Any lining material may be right. Any changes for style or fit may be right.

It all depends on you

While this knowledge may free you from fear of erring, it also puts the burden of choice on you. Did you think there was no headwork in handwork?

Making a choice presupposes a background of basic information. Do get all the help you can on the mechanics of sewing. It's wonderful to know what you are doing and how to do it. This part of the book deals with fundamental sewing techniques that every sewer needs to know.

Test-stitch first

Before you begin your machine stitching, it is wise to do some test-stitching on scraps of the fabric that have fallen away in cutting. In this way you can:

1. check the correctness of the machine stitching.
2. perfect your stitching techniques.
3. get the feel of the fabric as it passes through the machine.
4. have a sample seam and dart for test-pressing.

The machine is properly set for your fabric if

1. the fabric "rides" smoothly—there is no puckering or creeping.

2. the tension is neither too tight nor too loose.

3. the stitches are balanced and lock perfectly on both sides.

4. the length of the stitch makes for a strong seam.

It "seams" to me

A seam is a line of stitching which holds two (sometimes more) pieces of fabric together permanently. The material is placed with right sides together while the stitching is done on the wrong side. When completed, the right side shows only the line of the seam but no stitching. The stitching appears only on the wrong side. Even this is concealed when the seam allowance is pressed open.

To hold the layers of the fabric together and in place until the seam is stitched, it is necessary to pin or baste them.

Basting is long, tedious, and not necessarily effective. However, there are times when it should be used—usually on silks or other slithery fabrics. Machine stitching is done beside the basting, never directly over it which would make it difficult (if not impossible) to remove the basting when the stitching is completed.

Pinning is fast, easy, and sure. Pin at the beginning and end of a seam line, at all notches, and in a sufficient number of places between. Pins may be placed at right angles to the seam line (Fig. 114a) or lengthwise—points face the top of the seam, heads are toward you (Fig. 114b). Fabrics that bruise easily are pinned in the seam allowance rather than on the stitching line (Fig. 114c), so the pin marks won't show.

They say that with a flexible presser foot you can stitch right over pins placed at right angles to the seamline. Unfortunately, you always stand a chance that the needle may hit a pin, bending it and breaking the needle. (This usually happens at a time when you have no other needle!)

Pins placed lengthwise are easy to pull out as you go along. Remove them just before the presser foot reaches them. This may slow up the sewing somewhat but it is far the safer of the two methods.

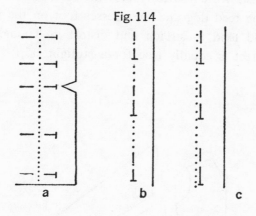

Fig. 114

a   b   c

How to stitch a seam

1. Compare the pattern seam lengths of the sections to be joined. If they are equal you must stitch so they remain so. If one length is really meant to be longer than the other, the extra amount must be eased in (see page 156).

2. Lock the stitches at the beginning and end of each seam with back-and-forth stitching.

3. Stitch the seam slowly. Speed stitching is of no particular value to home sewers. There are not so many yards of machine stitching in any garment that the time saved is worth the risk of faulty stitching.

4. Keep your eyes on the stitching. Guide the cloth with your right hand, anchor it with your left (or vice versa, if that is more comfortable for you).

5. If you need to go back over a line of stitching to correct it, be sure to remove the first stitching. Every added row of machine stitching makes the area that much stiffer.

6. Seam stitching, like stay stitching, is directional to preserve the grain, the length, and the shape of the fabric (Fig. 115).

FOR EXAMPLE: In stitching a flared skirt, start at the hem and stitch to the waist. Were you to reverse the direction (waist to hem) the action of the feed dog and the presser foot on the angle of the seam line would tend to stretch and distort it. Though less exaggerated, this effect is equally true for a straight skirt.

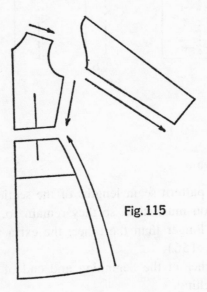

Fig. 115

7. Be sure to stitch the full seam allowance—either that planned for in the pattern or that determined by your fitting. An eighth of an inch may not seem much to you at the time but a little arithmetic will quickly disclose that ⅛″ on each of two thicknesses equals ¼″. Two ¼″ equal ½″. Four ¼″ equal 1″. Without much ado you could be adding anywhere from 1″ to 2″ on your garment and grading it up to the next size.

Assorted darts

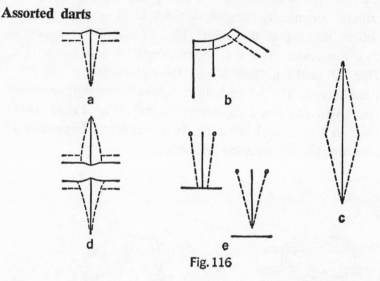

a   b   c

d   e

Fig. 116

How to stitch a straight dart—the familiar triangle type (Fig. 116a) or the neckline dart indicated on the pattern by a straight line (Fig. 116b).

1. With right sides inside, fold the dart on the center **(a)** or straight line **(b)**. Match the dart legs. Pin.

2. Place the fabric in the machine with the wide end of the dart at the top and the point of the dart toward you. Set the fabric so that the stitching line rather than the fold line is directed toward your body at right angles (Fig. 117a). Were you to reverse this position, making the *fold* at right angles to you, the stitching would need to be done on an angle (Fig. 117b). This makes it too difficult to stitch an accurate dart.

Fig. 117

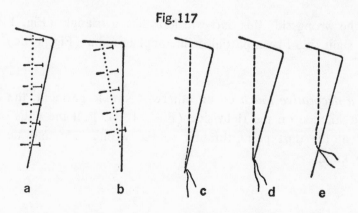

a   b   c   d   e

3. Stitch from the wide end to the dart point. Keep the last two or three stitches practically parallel to the fold (Fig. 117c) before tapering off to nothing at the point (Fig. 117d). Don't swoop in suddenly as you realize you are approaching the dart point (Fig. 117e). This will make a "bubble" on the right side.

4. Cut the thread. Tie the ends in a square knot: right over left and left over right (all you former Girl Scouts) (Fig. 118a). Don't attempt back and forth lock stitching. It is practically impossible to get back on the line of stitching accurately.

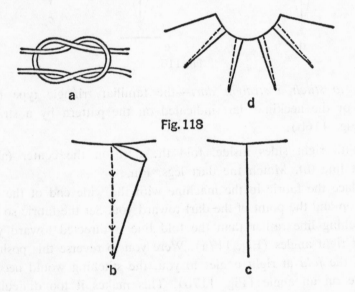

Fig. 118

On the wrong side this dart will look like a triangle (Fig. 118b); on the right side like a partial or incomplete seam (Fig. 118c).

For a decorative touch on an otherwise simple garment, the darts may be stitched on the right side (Fig. 118d). Pull the ends of the thread at the dart point through to the wrong side and tie in a square knot.

How to stitch a double-pointed dart (Fig. 116c)—commonly used for waistline fitting in a one-piece dress or overblouse.

1. Fold the dart on the center line and pin.
2. An exception to the rule: bring the needle down at either dart point. Leave long enough ends of thread to tie a square knot.
3. Make a continuous line of stitching from one dart point to the other. Arrange your work so the line of stitching is at right angles to your body. This calls for a resetting of the fabric at the widest part of the dart.
4. Observe all the stitching rules for tapering off the points of the dart.

How to stitch a curved dart—either an outward curve or an inward curve (Fig. 116d).

Follow the same procedure as for a straight dart. Stitch on the curved lines.

How to stitch a dart tuck or released dart (Fig. 116e)

Some darts never do get stitched all the way to the point. The stitching stops part of the way up. This releases fullness as an unpressed pleat does. It is the kind of control frequently used in blouses.

1. Fold through the center of the dart tuck.
2. Match the stitching lines and pin.
3. Stitch from the narrow end to the wide end and across the wide end to the fold. This holds the fullness in place.

How to ease-in fullness

Off-grain stitching (Fig. 119a)—useful for easing fullness in a sleeve cap or a shaping seam over the bust; also a good method to prevent the top layer of fabric from slipping forward.

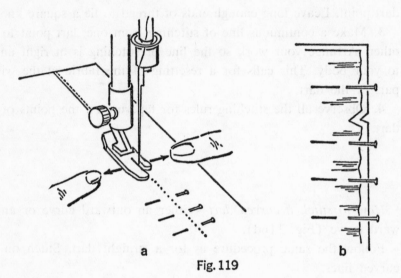

Fig. 119

1. Place the forefingers either side of the presser foot.
2. Pull the fabric horizontally as it feeds into the machine.
3. Stitch a little bit at a time slowly, easing in the fullness to the desired amount.

Ease by stretching (Fig. 119b)—an easy method when the amount to be eased is slight and the fabric obliging.

1. Pin the ends of the seam with the shorter side up.
2. Stretch the shorter length to match the longer length and pin to position.
3. Stitch with the shorter side up, taking advantage of the tendency for the upper layer to stretch somewhat in stitching anyway.

Fullness controlled by gathering, shirring, gauging (Fig. 120)

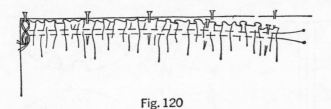

Fig. 120

1. Section off the length to be gathered—halves, quarters, eighths, etc. Mark with pins, notches, or basting thread.

2. Section off the length to which the fullness is to be joined in a similar manner.

3. Make at least two rows of hand or machine gathering, one slightly above the seam line, the second ¼" above the first.

For machine gathering, use a basting stitch; wind the bobbin with buttonhole twist or coarse thread which is easier to pull up.

For hand stitching, make *tiny* gathering stitches, using a double thread, buttonhole twist, or coarse thread.

4. With a pin, anchor one end of the shirring at the edge to which it is to be joined. Wind the ends of the thread around the pin in a figure 8.

5. Draw up the fullness until it equals the exact fixed length. Pin, wind the ends of the thread around the pin as before.

6. Match the markings for each section. Pin.

7. With the point of a needle, distribute the fullness evenly in each section.

8. With the fullness on top, stitch on the seam line, correcting and redistributing the fullness where necessary.

How to reinforce a slash line (Fig. 121a)—gussets, sleeve openings, neck openings, etc.

Stitch either side of the slash line close to and an even distance from it. Take one stitch across the end to provide the space for the slash.

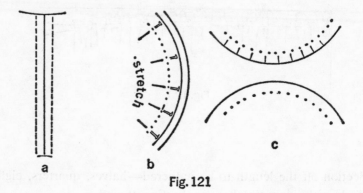

Fig. 121

How to stitch a curve when one side is concave and the other convex

1. Stay stitch each curve.

2. Clip the concave curve (inside curve) to within an inch of either end (Fig. 121c).

3. Stretch it to match the convex curve (Fig. 121b). Pin.

4. Stitch.

How to stitch a scallop (Fig. 122)

The scallop is a recurring and charming edge which calls for precision marking and stitching.

1. Use some guide for the scallops. Either trace the scallop seam line very carefully on the fabric, use the pattern itself as a guide, or trace the scallops to tissue paper. Pin the pattern or tissue to the fabric, stitch through both, tear away the tissue.

2. Stitch on the scallop seam line, taking one stitch across each point (Fig. 122a).

3. Clip the seam allowance into each point. Take care not to clip the stitching (Fig. 122a).

4. Trim the seam allowance close to the stitching. Notch to prevent bulk when the scallop is turned to the right side (Fig. 122a).

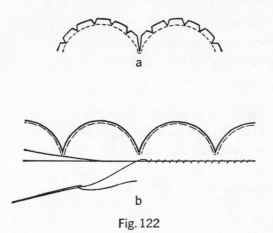

Fig. 122

5. Turn the scallops to the right side, working out the edges with a blunt needle until they are smooth (Fig. 122b).

6. Baste close to the edge with silk thread (this is less likely to leave press marks) and press (Fig. 122b).

How to stitch a bias seam

Loosen the top tension slightly and use a small stitch. This provides elasticity and more thread to accommodate the stretch of bias fabric.

OR

Pin a strip of tissue paper along the seam line. With the tissue on top, stitch through both paper and fabric. Tear away the tissue when the seam is completed.

How to stitch a corner

In very sheer fabrics:

1. Stitch the seam, ending with the needle in the fabric at the corner.

2. Raise the presser foot and pivot a 90° angle.

3. Lower the presser foot and continue stitching in the new direction.

In lightweight fabrics:

1. Stitch the seam almost to the point of turning.
2. Take one stitch across the corner.
3. Continue stitching the other side.

In heavy fabrics:

1. Stitch the seam almost to the corner.
2. Take three stitches to turn the corner.
3. Continue stitching the other side.

How to miter a corner (Fig. 123)

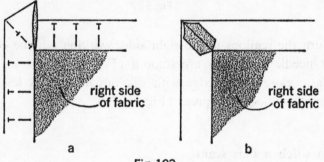

right side of fabric

right side of fabric

a   b

Fig. 123

1. Turn the fabric to the right side (Fig. 123a).
2. Pinch the corner into a dart (Fig. 123a).
3. Pin the dart diagonally across the corner (Fig. 123a). It must be tight against the under layer.
4. Stitch the seam line of the dart. Trim and press open (Fig. 123b).
5. Turn to the inside. Gently work out the corner with an orange stick or a blunt needle.

How to join matching cross seams

1. Press seams open.
2. Trim to reduce bulk at the seam line. (See page 167.)
3. Place both thicknesses of fabric together so that the seams match.
4. Put the point of a pin through the matching seams of both

thicknesses. Slide it along the seam line of the under surface and bring it up on the seam line of the upper surface. The pin spans the area of the cross seam.

5. Stitch across the pin very slowly and very carefully to run less risk of striking it.

If you insist on using thread to hold the cross seams in place, use a back stitch rather than a basting stitch.

How to stitch an enclosed or encased seam (Fig. 124)

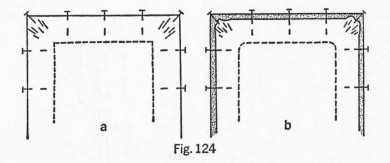

Fig. 124

Whenever a section of a garment consists of two layers, the seam that joins them should never be visible from the surface. The seam is rolled to the underside. This calls for a little extra material on the upper layer to negotiate the turn. There are two methods by which this may be accomplished.

METHOD I (Fig. 124a)

1. Cut the upper layer slightly larger than the under layer.
2. Pin the corners together diagonally, edges matching.
3. Push a little bubble of fullness into each corner on both sides of the pin. Pin to position.
4. With the shorter layer on top, stretch to match the longer one. Pin with edges matching.
5. Stitch a seam allowance in from the edge of the under layer.

METHOD II (Fig. 124b)

1. Cut both layers the same size.
2. Set the raw edge of the upper layer down from the raw edge

of the under layer. How much depends on the thickness of the fabric.

3. Stitch the two a seam allowance in from the edge of the under layer.

Using less of the seam allowance of the upper layer has the effect of adding to its size.

Sometimes, despite all these efforts, the seam which joins garment and facing does slip into view. To make certain that this never happens, the two thicknesses are held in place with either topstitching or understitching, depending on which is appropriate to the design.

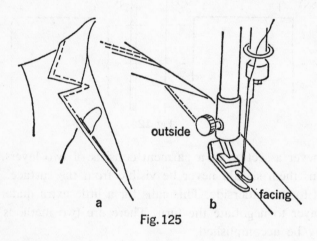

Fig. 125

Topstitching (Fig. 125a)

Topstitching is a line of decorative stitching done an even distance in from the edge either by machine or by hand through both thicknesses of fabric.

Machine Topstitching—may be done with a stitch of regulation length and the thread used for the rest of the garment; particularly interesting when the stitch is lengthened and buttonhole twist is used in place of the regular thread. Several rows spaced evenly apart in a contrasting color are very attractive.

Hand stitching—use matching mercerized thread, buttonhole twist, or several strands of embroidery floss; any of these stitches may be used: *glove stitch* (small basting ¼" to ½", even on both sides), *saddle stitch* (uneven basting with longer stitches on the outside and shorter stitches on the underside), *seed stitch* (tiny back stitch made of two or three strands of embroidery floss, pulled up unevenly making a tiny irregular stitch on the surface).

Understitching (Fig. 125b)

Understitching is a line of machine—or hand stitching made through the facing and the seam allowances of both garment and facing.

Open the garment and the facing out with right sides up. Place the seam allowances directly under the facing. If necessary, clip to make them lie flat. Stitch through the facing and the seam allowances close to the seam line.

When understitching a collar or lapel, stitch to within 1″ of the corner.

How to stitch a style line that comes to a point or a corner (Fig. 126)

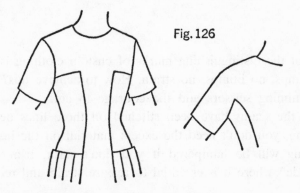

Fig. 126

1. Mark the matching points very carefully.
2. Reinforce each with stay stitching.
3. With right sides together match the markings. Pin.
4. Bring the needle down directly on the matched marking. Stitch away from the marking to the end of the seam.
5. Pull the threads at the corner through to the one side and tie.
6. Clip the seam allowance at the corner to the stay stitching in order to facilitate the matching and stitching of the second side.

7. Once more, bring the needle down into the marking at the clip where the previous stitching started. Stitch away from the marking in the opposite direction to the end of the seam.

8. Again, pull the ends of the thread at the marking through to one side and tie. Make sure that the two lines of stitching just meet at the corner.

Stitch one side at a time. Stitching the entire corner in one continuous line is not only too difficult, it is hazardous. The action of the presser foot and the feed dog may displace the fabric at a point that calls for precision stitching.

THE COURAGE TO CUT

One of the distinguishing marks of custom clothing is its trimness —no lumps, no bumps, no strain. How to achieve this? Your trusty little trimming scissors and the courage to cut.

Once the seams have been stitched on those lines determined by the fitting, you don't need the excess material on the inside. Indeed, the fitting will be hampered if you don't slash, trim, clip, notch, and grade* where it is essential to release strain and reduce bulk.

*slash—to cut open with a sweeping stroke
   trim—to cut away excess fabric
   clip—to make a short snip in the seam allowance using the point of the scissors at right angles to the stitching line
   notch—to cut a small V-shape in the seam allowance
   grade—to trim away one seam allowance so that it is narrower than another, giving a staggered or layered appearance

Most *seam allowances* may be trimmed back to ½"—that is, unless you contemplate gaining weight. (Trimming them may be an incentive to staying the way you are.)

When seam allowances are to be pressed to one side, they must be *graded* to prevent bulk. Trim each seam to a slightly different width (Fig. 127a). This applies to as many layers of fabric as are stitched into any one seam. Width is determined by the thickness of the fabric—sheer fabric requires less width than heavy fabric.

Wide darts and darts in heavy fabrics—slash open to within ¼" of the dart point (Fig. 127b); snip across the unslashed end of the dart almost to the seam line; press the dart open where slashed, press to one side where unslashed (Fig. 127c). (Narrow darts and darts in very sheer fabrics remain uncut.)

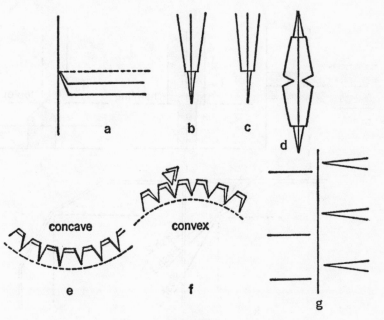

Fig. 127

Waistline darts—trim to ½"; clip at the waistline so the dart is released to do the shaping for which it was intended; slash the dart open above and below the clip in the same way as for a wide dart (Fig. 127d).

When an *outside edge is shorter* than the seam line, *clip* to release the strain (Fig. 127e).

When an *outside edge is longer* than the seam line, *notch* to prevent rippling (Fig. 127f).

When a curved seam is pressed open, note which seam allowance strains and clip it, which ripples, and notch it. When both are necessary, *notch between the clips* to reduce the strain on the stitching (Fig. 127g).

If notches and clips are directly opposite each other, the fate of the seam literally hangs by a few threads.

All *cross seams* should be *trimmed* before being stitched (Fig. 127h).

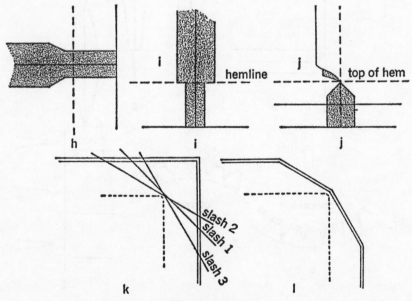

Fig. 127 (cont.)

To reduce bulk in a hem: grade the seam allowance of the hem area to the fold line (Fig. 127i).

To reduce bulk where a pleat seam enters a hem: clip at the top of the hem and press the graded seam allowance to one side; trim and press open the seam allowance of the hem (Fig. 127j).

To free a corner of excess bulk: make three slashes—one diagonally across the corner, a second diagonally further into the seam allowance on one side, a third diagonally further into the seam allowance on the other side. Cut close to the stitching line (Figs. 127k and l).

Correct clipping, trimming, notching, grading, and slashing may make all the difference in the world between a sleeve that fits comfortably and one that does not, a waistline dart that shapes and one that does not, a corner that turns easily and one that does not. Your trimming scissors are as important a tool as your sewing machine and your iron. Have them handy. Have the courage to use them.

INSIDE INFORMATION

Pride in craftsmanship dictates that the inside of the garment be just as beautiful as the outside. Often beauty and function go hand in hand. An attractive finish for a raw edge may enhance its appearance; it also prevents it from raveling.

All raw edges of seam allowances and darts are finished off in some way. There are as many types of finishes as there are functions, fabrics, and fancies of creative sewers.

Seam finishes

Plain

When a lining covers the "works," a plain seam needs no special finish. Without a lining and exposed to view, it does. Here are several from which to choose (Fig. 128).

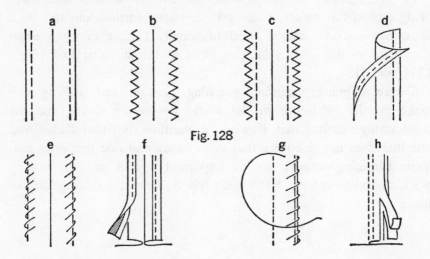

Fig. 128

Fig. 128a—a row of machine stitching along each raw edge of the seam allowance

Fig. 128b—a chance to use your pinking or scalloping shears

Fig. 128c—a row of machine stitching *and* a pinked edge

Fig. 128d—a hand- or machine-stitched turned-under edge

Fig. 128e—a raw edge overcast by "easy" hand stitches—or by machine, if you are lucky enough to have one that performs this operation

Fig. 128f—a raw edge bound with commercial seam binding or bias strips of the lining of the garment

Fig. 128g—both seam allowances closed, overcast, and pressed to one side

Fig. 128h—for very sheer fabrics: make two rows of stitching ⅛" apart for the seam; trim both seam allowances close to the second row of stitching

And fancy

Anything your imagination can devise. (Fig. 129—a few that others have invented and enjoyed.)

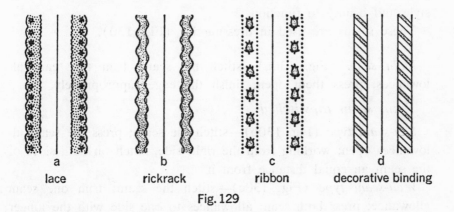

a	b	c	d
lace	rickrack	ribbon	decorative binding

Fig. 129

Fig. 129a—baby lace edging: lap the lace over a turned edge
Fig. 129b—rickrack edging applied in same way as baby lace
Fig. 129c—interesting narrow ribbon lapped over raw edge
Fig. 129d—raw edge bound in plaid, striped, or figured seam binding

How to apply a binding

seam binding: fold the binding in half lengthwise; slip the raw edge of the garment into the fold; stitch by hand or machine close to the edge of the binding.

bias binding: open out one edge of the bias binding (it comes in folds); place the right side of the binding on the right side of the edge to be bound, raw edges matching (stretch or ease as necessary); machine stitch along the fold of the bias; trim the edges close to the stitching if necessary; roll the rest of the binding over the raw edges, enclosing them and bringing the fold to the seam line. Hem.

Seam and variations

A structural detail is often turned into a decorative one—making a virtue of necessity. Take the simple seam, for instance. It is *the* basic structure of a garment. Yet, in its many variations, it lends style and beauty to function.

These seams are used in dressmaking (Fig. 130).

Plain seam (Fig. 130a)—stitch the seam; trim the seam allowances; press them open; finish the edges appropriately.

Plain seam topstitched

Slot-seam type (Fig. 130b)—stitch the seam; press the seam allowances open; working from the right side, stitch on both sides of the seam an equal distance from it.

Welt-seam type (Fig. 130c)—stitch the seam; trim one seam allowance; press both seam allowances to one side with the longer enclosing the shorter; working from the right side; topstitch an even distance from the seam on one side through all thicknesses.

French seam

(Fig. 130d)—with wrong sides together (an exception) stitch the seam on the right side $\frac{1}{4}''$ in from the raw edge; trim the seam allowance to $\frac{1}{8}''$; turn to the wrong side; crease along the seam line; stitch a second seam, enclosing the seam allowances.

Felled French seam or standing fell

(Fig. 130e)—stitch the seam; trim one edge to be enclosed; turn under the edge of the upper seam allowance, bringing the fold to the seam line; hem.

Lapped seam or overlap seam (worked from the right side)

Straight lapped seam (Fig. 130f)—turn under the seam allowance of one raw edge and press; lap the turned edge over the raw edge of the undersection, raw edges matching; pin; topstitch an even distance from the fold.

Curved lapped seam (Fig. 130g)—clip the seam allowance of the curved edge to be lapped frequently enough so it will curve; turn under the seam allowance of the clipped edge; press in a

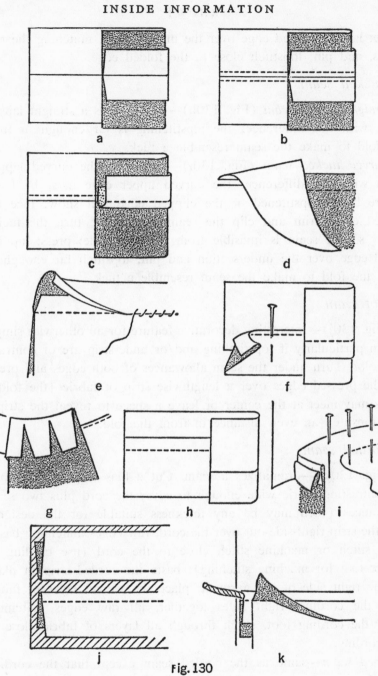

Fig. 130

curve; lap the turned edge over the undersection, matching the raw edges, and pin; topstitch close to the folded edge.

Tucked seam

Straight tucked seam (Fig. 130h)—the same as a straight lapped seam with this difference: the topstitching is far enough in from the fold to make the seam resemble a tuck.

Curved tucked seam (Fig. 130i)—similar to the curved lapped seam with this difference: the curved upper edge must be faced before being topstitched or the clipped edge will show; face the curved edge; trim and clip the seam allowances; turn the facing under so the seam is invisible from the right side; press; lap the faced edge over the undersection and pin; topstitch far enough in from the fold to make the seam resemble a tuck.

Slot seam

(Fig. 130j)—interesting decorative feature for an otherwise simple design particularly if topstitching and/or understrip are of contrasting color. Turn under the seam allowances of both edges and press; lap the pressed edges over a lengthwise strip of fabric (the folded edges may meet at the center or leave a space to reveal the strip); pin; topstitch an even distance in from the fold.

Corded seam

(Fig. 130k)—dramatizes a seam. Cut a bias strip of self-fabric or contrasting fabric wide enough to cover the cord plus two seam allowances (cord may be any thickness suitable for the design); fold the strip right-side-out over the cord, raw edges matching; baste, back stitch or machine stitch close to the cord (use cording or zipper foot for machine stitching); baste the corded strip in place on the right side of the garment; place the second layer of fabric over the cording, right sides together, all raw edges matching; using the cording foot, stitch through all layers of fabric close to the cording.

Piped seam—same as the corded seam except that the cording is omitted.

This great variety of seams should give you a choice for every style and fabric.

THE NEEDLE POINTS THE WAY

Despite the practically push-button sewing machine, hand sewing is still an important part of clothing construction. Everyone expects it of the haute couture. Its presence in ready-to-wear denotes a prestige product. Here is where the home sewer can shine! She can take the time and acquire the ability to add all those hand touches that make for better fit and finish.

There is also a very special satisfaction in hand sewing. Part of it is the sheer pleasure of working with one's hands. Another element is the feeling of control over materials—particularly true for beginning sewers.

Hand sewing will go much easier if you know that:

The thread is cut with sharp scissors to a length about 15" to 16". Breaking the thread produces a ragged end, difficult to thread. Long threads tend to snarl and knot, as do double threads, which in addition do not pull up evenly.

The needle is threaded with the thread end that has been cut from the spool at an angle.

Stitching starts with the thread knotted at one end

and ends with several over-and-over stitches. The knot is always hidden on an underside.

The left hand holds the fabric while the right hand does the stitching (Fig. 131). (Vice-versa if you are left-handed.)

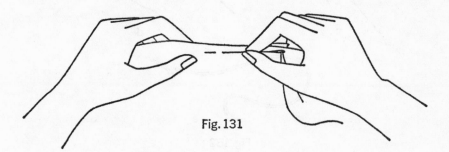

Fig. 131

The thumb and forefinger hold and guide the needle through the fabric and draw up the thread. The middle finger, protected by the thimble, pushes the needle forward; the ring finger and the little finger hold the material down. The thumb on top and the forefinger under the fabric hold it in place while the rest of the other hand supports it. As you can see, in hand sewing all the fingers are busy little members, indeed.

How to make a knot in the thread (Fig. 132)

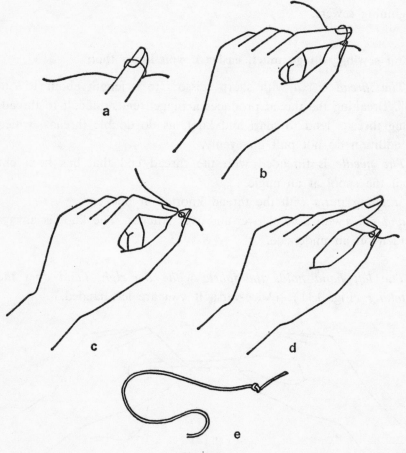

Fig. 132

1. Wind the thread around the top of the forefinger of the left hand (Fig. 132a).

2. Twirl or roll the end of the thread forward with the thumb (Fig. 132b).

3. Slip the forefinger out of the loop (Fig. 132c).

4. Pull down on the loop with the middle finger (Fig. 132d).

5. Draw it up to form a knot (Fig. 132e).

Legacy from the past: a stitch for every need

Left over from the day when all sewing was done by hand are a considerable number of hand stitches for every conceivable sewing need.

Hand stitches may be temporary or permanent. Temporary hand stitches are used while the garment is in process of construction and removed when the permanent stitching is completed. Permanent hand stitches are *the* construction. They must remain for the life of the garment.

Temporary hand stitches

Temporary hand stitches are all variations of the basting stitch. They may be done with single (or double, if necessary) thread of a contrasting color so they can be readily seen. Use cotton thread for most fabrics though it is advisable to use silk thread for basting velvets, fine silks, woolens, or any other fabrics which may be marred by heavier thread.

The stitches should be "easy," "lazy" so they can be easily removed. To remove the basting, clip the thread at frequent intervals before pulling it out. Pulling a long thread through a length of fabric may injure it or crease it.

Baste beside the seam line so that the machine stitching will not be directly over it. Otherwise it is impossible to remove the basting without breaking the machine stitching.

Always remove basting *before* pressing. You wouldn't want to permanently press an imprint of the basting into your beautiful fabric.

Temporary hand stitches

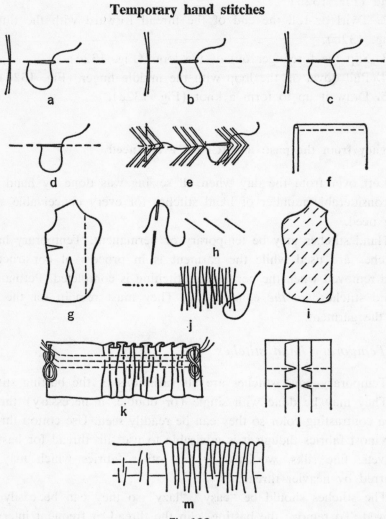

Fig. 133

Even basting (Fig. 133a)—both stitches and spaces are of equal length on both sides of the fabric.

Uneven basting (Fig. 133b)—stitches and spaces are unequal in length, being longer on the surface and shorter on the underside.

Dressmaker's basting (Fig. 133c)—one long stitch and two short ones.

Running stitch (Fig. 133d)—tiny, even basting stitches woven through the material with an up-and-down motion of the wrist while the fabric is held still; when the needle is full of stitches the thread is drawn through.

Slip basting (Fig. 133e)—sometimes called alteration basting. Work from the right side; slip the needle along a fold of fabric, bringing it out about ¼" from the point of entry; push the point of the needle into the lower layer of cloth directly under the point from which it emerged on the upper fold; make a ¼" stitch on the wrong side of the fabric; stitches alternate between the fold and the single layer of cloth, producing a line of basting on the wrong side which can be used as a guide for machine stitching; the stitches are invisible from the right side.

Edge basting (Fig. 133f)—roll the joining seam of two thicknesses of fabric to the underside; baste on the right side close to the rolled edge to hold it in place.

Guide basting (Fig. 133g)—uneven basting with long floats (threads) on the side that needs the marking.

Diagonal basting (Fig. 133h)—diagonal stitch on the upper side, short horizontal stitch on the underside; used to hold several layers of cloth together without slipping.

Tailor basting (Fig. 133i)—diagonal basting with *long* diagonal stitches on the upper side; used to join two layers of fabric, for example: the outer layer and the interfacing or backing.

Gathering (Fig. 133j)—running stitches drawn up to a predetermined length with the fullness evenly distributed.

Shirring (Fig. 133k)—several rows of gathering evenly spaced apart; to eliminate bulk in a seam to be gathered, notch as illustrated (Fig. 133l).

Gauging (Fig. 133m)—several rows of uneven basting with long and short stitches of each row placed directly under each other; when drawn up, the material falls in deep folds; useful for gathering great lengths of material into a small space.

Permanent hand stitches

Permanent hand stitches held garments together long before the sewing machine was even thought of. Though they take longer to do, when correctly done they are as strong as machine stitching. This does not mean to imply that one should revert to hand sewing. In a machine age, it would be somewhat anachronistic to put a dress together by hand. Often, however, hand sewing does accomplish the construction of details more easily, more quickly, and more effectively.

Permanent hand stitches

Fig. 134

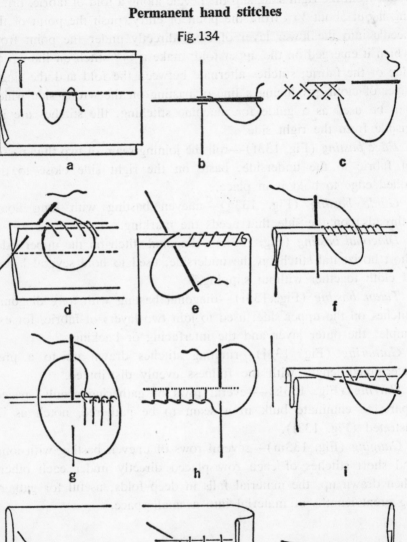

a

b

c

d

e

f

g

h

i

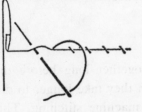

j

k

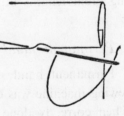

l

Back stitch (Fig. 134a)—the strongest of the hand stitches. Start with a running stitch at the right end; bring the needle up on the right side one stitch ahead; working back to the right, insert the needle at the point where the preceding stitch ended, slide it along the underside and once more bring the needle out one stitch ahead; you are really encircling the cloth with the stitches; this produces a line of hand stitching which resembles machine stitching.

A *half back stitch* is sometimes used when less strength is required. The stitch is made in the same way as the back stitch with this exception: instead of bringing the needle back to the end of the preceding stitch, bring it over only half the distance.

Over-and-over stitches (Fig. 134b)—reinforcing stitches—two or more back stitches worked over each other in place rather than advancing to the left.

Catch stitch (Fig. 134c)—work from lower left to upper right, taking a small back stitch on an imaginary line of the undersurface and picking up only one or two threads; complete the stitch by taking a tiny back stitch to the lower right on an imaginary lower line; the movement is to the right, the needle points to the left shoulder each time.

Overcasting (Fig. 134d)—a series of loose, slanting stitches worked over either a single or double raw edge deep enough to prevent the material from raveling; stitches are even in depth and evenly spaced, "easy"—not drawn up tight; the thread encircles the raw edge.

Whipping stitch (Fig. 134e)—like an overcasting stitch but used on a rolled edge instead of a raw one; the needle passes over and under the roll in a winding motion but never through it.

Overhanding (Fig. 134f)—produces a strong, flat seam. Hold the needle perpendicular to the edge; take small stitches close together over and over the edge; make stitches just deep enough to catch the edges; they should not be drawn up tight so that the seam can open flat when finished; use a short needle.

Buttonhole stitch (Fig. 134g)—work from right to left; stitches are very close together and even in depth; the loop is formed by placing the thread behind the eye of the needle and under its point; the needle is held vertically and goes through the loop of thread.

Blanket stitch (Fig. 134h)—similar to the buttonhole stitch except that it is worked from left to right and does not form a purl; the needle is vertical and the thread which forms the loop is under its point.

Running-hemming stitch (Fig. 134i)—a series of small, very loose running stitches weaving back and forth between the garment and the edge of a hem, picking up only a thread or two of the right side of the fabric.

Slant hemming (Fig. 134j)—the strongest but most conspicuous of the hemming stitches. Work a small, diagonal basting stitch through both fabric and hem; both the needle and the stitch are slanted.

Vertical or straight hemming (Fig. 134k)—the stitch used on most hems—can be made practically invisible. Use a single thread; take a tiny stitch, catching only one thread of the fabric on the right side parallel to the hem; bring the needle up on a slant to the edge of the hem, catching it with a tiny stitch; the beginning of the next stitch is directly under the ending of the upper stitch; stitches on the wrong side are vertical, stitches on the right side are horizontal.

Blind hemming (Fig. 134l)—the slip basting worked on the hem; the needle picks up only a thread or two of the fabric on the right side and is concealed in the fold on the wrong side.

Slip stitch (blind stitch)—an invisible permanent joining worked through an upper and lower fold of fabric; done exactly like the slip basting except that the stitches weave from one fold to the other.

This lengthy list of hand stitches doesn't begin to include all the wonderful and decorative stitches used in tailoring and embroidering, but should provide a working knowledge of those most useful for dressmaking.

PRESS AS YOU SEW!

The iron is just as important to sewing as the sewing machine. The greatest sewing in the world looks unfinished and amateurish if unpressed.

It is not enough to wait until the project is complete for one mighty pressing binge. You must press as you sew!

Press every dart and seam before stitching it to a cross seam.

Press each section of the garment before joining it to another.

For a crisper edge, press open all enclosed seams before turning.

Press all edges before topstitching.

Turn and press the seam allowance before inserting the zipper. This not only makes it easier to sew the zipper but eliminates the necessity for pressing it when garment is completed.

Press the hem before you bind and attach it; the result is smoother and flatter.

The rhythm of work is always: sew and press, sew and press, sew and press—until the garment is completed and the final hand pressing administered.

Set up your pressing equipment along with your sewing equipment. Place a chair or table close to the ironing board to support any fabric that may otherwise trail on the floor. Hang up each pressed section as soon as pressing is complete. If you must store the fabric between sewing sessions, keep it as flat as possible; avoid unnecessary folding.

A great part of all sewing equipment is pressing equipment. There is a tool or gadget for every style, every shape, and every fabric. Some of the following pieces of equipment are familiar parts of your household equipment. Some, designed especially for professional pressing, may be new to you. All will make the job of ironing and pressing very much easier and more effective.

Fig. 135a—press board: a small ironing board that can be placed on a table; since most pressing is done in small units this could replace your ironing board in your sewing room.

Fig. 135b—sleeve board: absolutely essential for normal laundry ironing as well as for your sewing; women's sleeves are never ironed with a lengthwise crease (Fig. 136a).

Fig. 135c—clapper or pounding block: used to "spank" flat the seams of firmly woven and hard-surfaced woolens.

Fig. 135d—hardwood non-resinous press block: used in combination with the clapper (a cheese block or bread board will do nicely).

Pressing Equipment

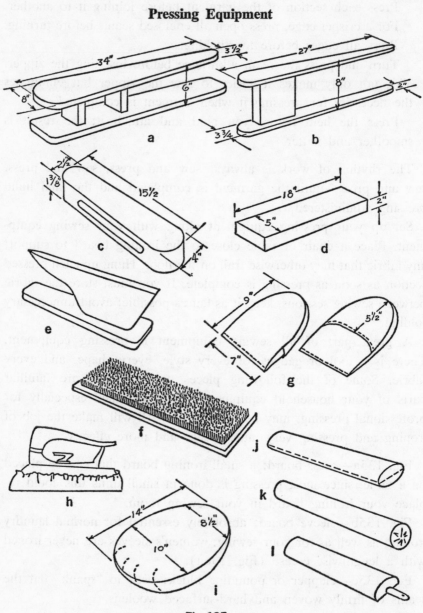

Fig. 135

How to use the board and clapper:

Place the right side of the fabric against the press block. Place a dampened press cloth over a small area to be pressed. Lower the iron on the cloth until steam is produced. Lift the iron, whisk off the press cloth, slap the clapper on the seam with some force. Let it rest there a minute and then remove the clapper. Move on to another section and repeat.

NOTE: all wood equipment is used uncovered.

Fig. 135e—edge and point presser: very useful for getting into those hard-to-reach corners of collars, cuffs, lapels, welts, etc.

Fig. 135f—needle board: used for pressing naps and piles (Fig. 138).

Fig. 135g—cloth press mitt: handy all-around useful piece of equipment for curved seams, sleeve caps, and hard-to-reach places (Fig. 136b).

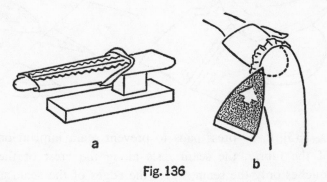

a   b

Fig. 136

Fig. 135h—steam-iron slipcover or hood: slip over the iron and use in place of a press cloth; when this is in place on the iron it is very easy to see what you are doing.

Press cloths: rectangular strips 4″ to 6″ wide by 12″ to 18″ long, of unsized muslin, lawn, drill, linen, cheesecloth, or terry cloth; make certain that all sizing and lint have been removed.

Shape well before using

Since practically all garments have some shaping, it is easier to press them over a curved surface rather than a flat one. There is an assortment of pads for pressing and shaping purposes. Of the many, the following are most useful for dressmaking.

Fig. 135i—tailor's ham: purchase or make your own; cut and stitch together two egg-shaped pieces of heavy, firmly-woven cloth to the given dimensions; leave one end open; pack *very tightly* with hardwood sawdust; stitch closed.

How to press a curved seam or dart over the ham

Place the curved seam over the tailor's ham, face down. Press with the lengthwise grain in the direction of the stitching (Fig. 137a).

Place the opened dart over the tailor's ham. Press from the wide end to the dart point (Fig. 137b). Use a slight rotary motion at the dart point to smooth out the "bump" of the dart.

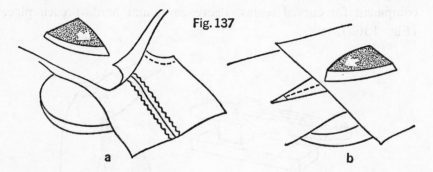

Fig. 137

a   b

Figs. 135j, k, l—press pads to prevent seam imprint on the right side of the fabric; the seam rests along the crest of the pad; the iron touches only the seam, never the edges of the seam allowances, thus preventing a ridge on the right side.

Fig. 135j—an oblong pad made in the same way as the tailor's ham; use a bias strip of firmly woven cloth, 9″ by 12″, fold in half lengthwise, stitch leaving one end open, pack tightly with sawdust, close the end.

Fig. 135k—a tightly rolled magazine covered with unbleached muslin to hold its shape.

Fig. 135l—a rolling pin that has been split in half lengthwise, the varnish removed, and the pin sanded.

You certainly wouldn't want or need all three of the above. Choose the one most readily obtainable.

An even simpler way to prevent seam imprint is to use folded strips of wrapping paper or tissue paper as a cushion between the fabric and the seam allowance of darts and seams (see page 187).

Pressing and ironing

Pressing and ironing (there is a difference!) are accomplished by three elements—heat, moisture, and pressure. To be safe, always test your fabric to determine just how much of each is necessary for a good pressing job.

Ironing—a gliding motion used to smooth washable fabrics like cotton, linen, some synthetics.

Pressing—an up-and-down, lower-and-lift motion used for silks, woolens, and some synthetics which require more pressure to smooth them and which can easily be pushed out of shape by the gliding motion of ironing.

Heat

On the iron, use the heat setting suitable for the fabric. Cottons and linens take high heat; silks and woolens take a moderate heat (animal fibers are burned by high heat as your skin would be); acetate, Dacron, and other synthetics take a cool iron (heat melts them). In combinations of fibers, use the heat setting for the most delicate fiber present; for instance, handle cotton and acetate as if it were all acetate.

Holding a moderate iron on one spot for any length of time intensifies the heat. For slow work, reduce the heat of the iron.

Moisture

Most fabrics press better with some degree of moisture. There are many ways of applying moisture: sprinkling, spraying, rolling in a damp cloth, sponging, applying a damp press cloth or a steam iron, or simply by partially drying the fabric.

The steam iron, wonderful as it is, is not always enough. Sometimes it is necessary to create moist heat with a damp cloth and a dry iron.

Iron *cotton* while damp until it is dry. Limp cotton wrinkles.

Iron *linen* while damp with a hot, dry iron until the linen is dry. Damp linen musses.

Press *wool* with moist heat and a moderate iron. Handle it very carefully while damp. Allow it to dry naturally.

Press *silk* with a dry, moderate iron. Moisture or steam may waterspot silk. If dampness is necessary (and sometimes it is) protect the fabric with a dry press cloth so the moisture doesn't come in direct contact with the silk.

Synthetics are generally pressed dry. Better check the label that comes with the fabric.

Pressure

All fabrics require some pressure to smooth them. The very word "press" implies this. But pressure may be anything from the merest touch of the iron to the 1600 pounds of pressure per square inch applied to one edge of a man's coat in clothing factories.

In home sewing, an ordinary iron supplies enough pressure for most fabrics. The exception to this is wool, which requires more— anything from patting with a press mitt for lightweight woolens to "beating or spanking" with a pounding block for firm and heavy woolens.

Pressure must be used judiciously, however. You certainly wouldn't want to flatten out a raised surface that is *the* attraction of the material. Many fabrics need protection more than pressure.

Protection for

Raised, nubbed, slubbed, looped, ribbed fabrics: Place the right side of the material against a strip of self-fabric or terry cloth. Steam from the wrong side. Apply the lightest touch of the iron: pressure will flatten the raised surface.

Crinkled, blistered, puckered, embossed, or other novelty sur- faces: Finger-press seams and darts. If the iron is used, press very lightly. For many such fabrics it is sufficient to hold the steam iron ½" above the surface and allow the steam to play over it. The iron should never come in direct contact with the cloth.

Deep fleece, fake furs, furry fabrics, naps and piles (Fig. 138): Place the right side of the material against a needle board. Steam from the wrong side. Avoid pressure.

When the right side of any of the above fabrics is turned to the wrong side as seam allowance, hem, or facing, it, too, needs protection. Use a strip of self-fabric. Place the raised surface of the strip against the raised surface of the turned-back cloth. Or, if you can afford it (they're expensive!) use two flexible needle boards (Fig. 138).

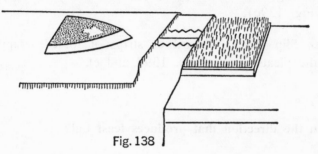

Fig. 138

A protective cushion prevents imprints of

Seam allowances: Slip folded strips of wrapping paper between the seam allowance and the wrong side of the fabric; press (Fig. 139a).

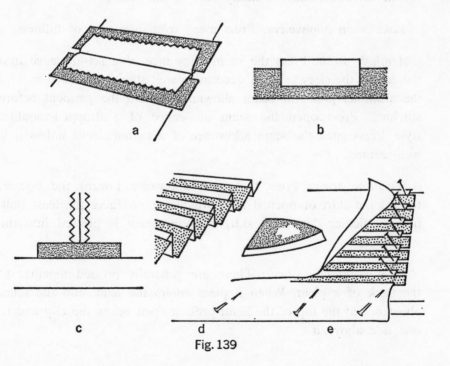

a   b

c   d   e

Fig. 139

Pockets, welts, and flaps: Slip folded strips of wrapping paper between pockets, welts, or flaps and the right side of the garment; press (Fig. 139b).

Hems: Slip strips of wrapping paper between hem and garment; press (Fig. 139c).

Pleats: Slip thin cardboard or strips of folded wrapping paper under the pleats; press (Figs. 139d and e).

Press in the direction that produces least bulk

Uncut darts: Unless otherwise noted in the pattern (for a specific reason), all horizontal darts are pressed down (gravity will pull them down anyway). Elbow darts are pressed down. Vertical darts are pressed toward the center. When an uncut dart in a lining falls directly over an uncut dart of the outer fabric, press the garment dart in one direction and the lining dart in the other.

Yoke seam allowances: Press away from any type of fullness.

Armhole seam: Press the seam allowance of a set-in sleeve into the cap of the sleeve. When decorative welt stitching is used around the armhole, press the seam allowance toward the garment before stitching. Press open the seam allowance of a dropped-shoulder style. Press open the seam allowance of a raglan sleeve unless it is welt-seamed.

Waistline seam: Press the seam allowance toward the bodice, toward the skirt or opened flat—whichever produces the least bulk in a particular design. A skirt waistline seam is pressed into the waistband.

Pleat seam allowances: These are generally pressed together at the back of a pleat. When a pleat enters the hem, clip the seam allowance at the top of the hem; press it open below the clip and to one side above it.

How to press fullness

Gathering: Use lengthwise strokes, working the toe of the iron into the gathers (Fig. 140a). Don't press over the gathers.

Shirring and smocking: Hold the steam iron ¼" to ½" above the right side of the fabric and apply the steam slowly over the area (Fig. 140b).

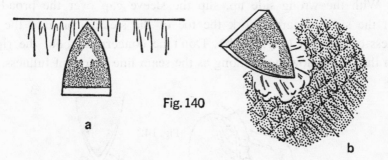

Fig. 140

a

b

Do not touch the surface with the iron or you will flatten the decorative raised surface.

Curved hems: Put a line of gathering along the top of the hem. Pull up the thread until the hem fits the skirt (Fig. 141a). Distribute the fullness evenly. (Cushion the hem with paper.) Shrink out the fullness by steaming. Work the toe of the iron from the fold of the hem to the top of it (Fig. 141b).

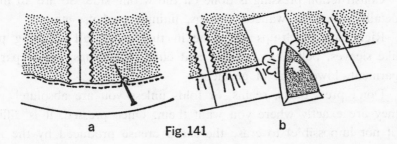

a   Fig. 141   b

How to shrink and shape the sleeve cap

It is much easier to set and stitch a set-in sleeve if the ease has been removed by shrinking and the cap has been shaped in the process. It has the added advantage of eliminating that final right side pressing of the armhole seam.

Stitch the sleeve seam, press it open. Gather across the cap and draw up the gathering to a cap shape (Fig. 142a). Distribute the fullness evenly.

With the wrong side up, slip the sleeve cap over the broad end of the sleeve board. Work the toe of the steam iron into the fullness of the cap (Fig. 142b). Don't be concerned about the ripples in the seam allowance so long as the seam line is free of fullness.

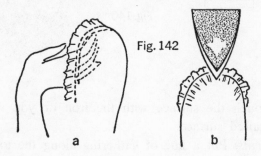

Fig. 142

a   b

Hints and helps

If pressing is done while the garment is in construction, it will only need a right-side touch-up when it is completed.

Construction pressing is done on the wrong side. So are all inside details—seam allowances, facings, linings, pockets, etc.

Right-side touch-ups are done in this order: all dangling parts like sleeves, belts, etc., collars and cuffs, trimmings, upper part of garment, lower part of garment.

Don't press darts, seams, or folds unless you are absolutely sure they are exactly where you want them. Once pressed, it is difficult (if not impossible) to erase the sharp crease produced by the iron.

Don't press over pins and basting: they leave press marks.

Don't press until you are sure how your fabric responds to heat, moisture, and pressure.

Always press with the grain. Pressing, like stitching, is directional. Off-grain pressing pushes the material out of shape.

Press all napped material with the nap.

Press all darts and shaping seams over suitable press pads to preserve the curves.

Always protect the right side of the fabric with a press cloth or tissue paper. Direct contact with the iron produces a shine.

It is easier to glide the tip of the iron along a seam if it has first been pressed open with the thumb or forefinger. This is known as finger pressing.

It is easier to press a neckline on a sleeve board (a little bit at a time) or on a curve of the tailor's ham than on a straight ironing board.

In double thicknesses of fabric (collars, cuffs, facings, etc.) press the underside first, then the upper side.

Avoid over dampening and over pressing.

Pressing problems

The sad truth is that the fabrics we lose our hearts to invariably present some pressing problems which take a bit more handling.

Cotton and linen in *white* and *light* colors may be ironed on the right side if the shine is not objectionable. *Dark* and *dull* colors should be ironed on the wrong side to avoid right-side shine.

Synthetics should be ironed on the wrong side. If sizing sticks to the iron, producing brown streaks, protect the fabric with tissue paper.

Embroidered fabrics are treated like raised-surface fabrics. Press face-down on a soft pad—terry cloth is fine.

Press *lace* face-down on a soft pad, too. Work the tip of the iron crosswise from the inside to the outside to open the design. Protect fragile laces with tissue paper or thin lawn (a fine handkerchief makes a great press cloth).

Press *chiffon* very lightly; protect with tissue paper.

Avoid overpressing or too much pressure on *crepe*. This smooths out and stretches its crinkled surface. Press very lightly over terry cloth. The same caution must be used in pressing *matelassés* or fabric created by using plain yarns and crepe yarns shrunken in such a way as to produce a puckered effect.

Embossed designs need little ironing. Some are labeled "never iron." It is so easy to flatten out their raised surfaces.

Heat yellows *white silk*. Press as little as possible with low heat.

Press *satin* lightly with very little or no moisture. The surface is always protected by a dry press cloth. Steam or moisture leaves an imprint and destroys the luster. Don't try for sharp edges or completely flattened seams; softness looks better in satin, anyway.

Brocades are treated like satin.

Lamés and metallics are pressed very lightly with a warm, dry iron. Moisture tarnishes them. Protect with tissue paper.

Shantung, pesante, and Thai silk are pressed with a moderately warm, dry iron and a dry press cloth.

Test *moire* to see if it is water-resistant; moisture makes the moire pattern disappear in some fibers. Use the steam iron if the fabric is water-resistant; press dry if it is not.

Knit fabric is pressed very lightly with a lengthwise rib. Too much pressure or too much moisture will stretch the fabric. It is next to impossible to press out the fold of knitted fabric as it comes to you by the yard. Plan to lay out your pattern on the fabric to avoid it.

Soft woolens, gauzy woolens, mohairs are lightly pressed with a steam iron over self-fabric. Pat seams and darts flat with the press mitt.

Hard-surfaced woolens and worsteds are pressed with a damp press cloth and a dry iron. The right side is placed against the wood surface of the press block. All seams and darts are flattened with the clapper or pounding block.

Laminates require little pressing. Use a damp press cloth and a warm dry iron or the steam iron and a dry press cloth.

Please note how often the direction is to *press rather than iron*. The gliding motion of ironing can stretch or destroy the surface interest of the above fabrics. The lower-and-lift motion of pressing preserves the surface.

PART V

SEW!

SEW RIGHT — RIGHT FROM THE START!

You have undoubtedly discovered by now that there is a long interval between dream and dress. When someone tells you boastingly that she whipped up a dress one fine morning and wore it to dinner that night, you are entitled to raise your eyebrows. Even with your present limited knowledge of sewing, you know better!

With all the time-consuming preliminaries out of the way, the work of assembling and sewing will proceed more quickly. It will, that is, *if* you organize your work, have everything you need handy, and save the most difficult procedures for a time when you feel your freshest.

First things first

In the beginning you will have plenty to think about if you concentrate on the layout, cutting, marking, assembling, stitching, and pressing! For these very first projects it is wise to omit all interfacings, underlinings, and linings. However, as soon as you feel confident enough, move right on to include them. Don't delay this too long for these are the hallmarks of all fine custom clothing (which is the only kind you are interested in sewing).

Start with a plan

The simplest plan is that of *unit construction*. By this method all work is completed as far as it is possible to do so on one section of the garment before going on to the next. Most pattern directions, particularly for easy-to-make dresses, follow a unit work plan.

The units in a shift dress, jumper, or overblouse (Fig. 143)

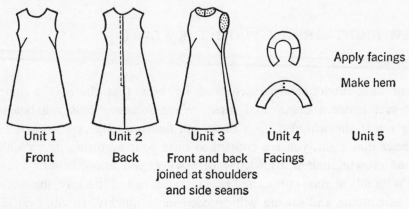

Apply facings

Make hem

Unit 1	Unit 2	Unit 3	Unit 4	Unit 5
Front	Back	Front and back joined at shoulders and side seams	Facings	

Fig. 143

Units in a basic skirt (Fig. 144)

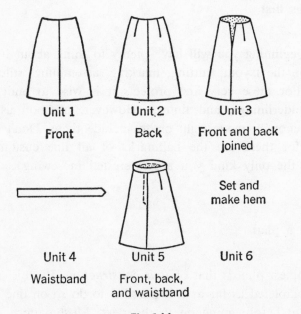

Set and make hem

Unit 1	Unit 2	Unit 3
Front	Back	Front and back joined

Unit 4	Unit 5	Unit 6
Waistband	Front, back, and waistband	

Fig. 144

To complete each unit

1. Stitch all darts and seams.

2. Apply interfacings and backings. (Optional for first few projects; essential for subsequent work.)

3. If there are any style details (pockets, tabs, etc.), apply them.

4. If there are any bound buttonholes, make them. Machine- or hand-worked buttonholes can be made after the garment is finished.

5. If a zipper is called for, insert it.

Join the completed units as outlined in Figs. 143, 144, and 145.

Use this suggested procedure in conjunction with the pattern instructions.

Fitting is done at any time and as many times as necessary.

Alternate work plan

When precise fitting isn't necessary, as in children's clothes, house-dresses, etc., the sequence for completing the units may be different.

1. Complete the bodice front and back; complete the skirt front and back.

2. Join the bodice front and the skirt front.

3. Join the bodice back and the skirt back.

4. Join the shoulders.

5. Make the sleeve.

6. Stitch the sleeve into the armhole.

7. In one continuous line of stitching, join the underarm sleeve seam and the side seam of the garment.

8. Make the hem.

This is the method followed in manufacturing inexpensive and utility clothing, also men's shirts. Keeping the work flat as long as possible increases the speed of construction. Unfortunately, it also decreases the chance for accuracy in matching the seams and the surface pattern of the material.

Units in a basic shirtwaist dress or tailored blouse (Fig. 145)

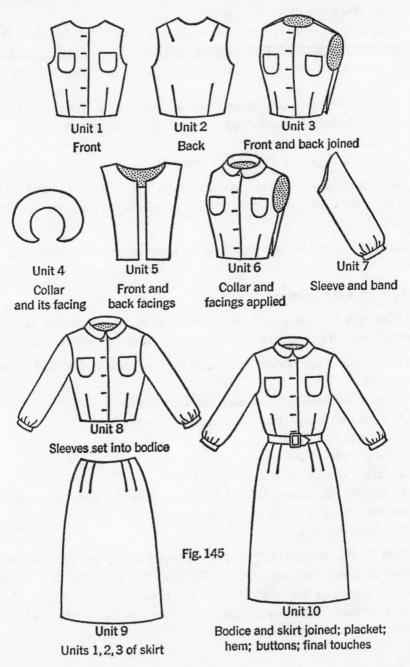

Unit 1
Front

Unit 2
Back

Unit 3
Front and back joined

Unit 4
Collar
and its facing

Unit 5
Front and
back facings

Unit 6
Collar and
facings applied

Unit 7
Sleeve and band

Unit 8
Sleeves set into bodice

Fig. 145

Unit 9
Units 1, 2, 3 of skirt

Unit 10
Bodice and skirt joined; placket;
hem; buttons; final touches

Plan for the sleeveless, collarless shift dress, jumper, or overblouse of cotton. Use in conjunction with the pattern instructions. Techniques of planning, layout, cutting, stitching, pressing are contained in Parts II, III, IV.

New information for this garment: how to handle the facing, interfacing, underlining, and lining; how to set and stitch the zipper, how to mark and make the hem.

1. Get the pattern in the right size. Make any necessary adjustments. Prepare it for layout.

2. Get the material. Establish the grain. Prepare it for cutting.

3. Get all the necessary findings—see the pattern envelope.

4. Study the diagram of the pattern sections on the instruction sheet.

5. Identify each pattern piece. Make sure you understand every construction symbol.

6. Study the layout chart. Select the layout that suits the view you are making, the pattern size, and the width of the fabric.

7. Following the chart, place the pattern on the material for a trial layout.

8. When you are satisfied with the trial layout, pin the pattern to the cloth and cut.

9. Mark everything that will facilitate the joining of the sections of the garment.

10. Remove the pattern. Stay stitch each section of material.

11. Pin the dress, jumper, or overblouse for the first fitting. Make any necessary modifications.

12. Decide what interfacing, underlining, or lining may be necessary to support the design. (Optional for first few projects; essential for subsequent garments.)

13. Cut and mark any of the above.

14. Stitch all darts and seams which complete the front and back units.

15. (Optional) Stitch all darts and seams which complete each unit of the interfacing, underlining, or lining as decided upon.

16. Press the outer fabric and the underpinnings when used.

17. (Optional) Apply the interfacing, underlining, or lining as decided upon from alternate methods.

18. Pin or baste the front and back together at the shoulders and side seams for the second fitting. Make any necessary refinements in fit.

19. Stitch the shoulders and side seams.

20. Apply the facing to the garment at the neck and armholes.

21. Set and stitch the zipper.

22. Finish all inside seams.

23. Set and make the hem.

24. Sew on the hooks and eyes, snaps, or other fastening.

25. Attend to any necessary hand finishing.

FACING — A SAVING DEVICE

Without a facing, the garment is rimmed with raw edges. This not only offends aesthetically but invites disaster. Unfinished edges fray. Who wants a dress with an unwelcome fringe?

If the edge is a straight one, the facing may be turned back to form a hem. The hem of a skirt is in reality a facing.

If the edge is a curved one, obviously it cannot be turned back. So, a facing is provided in the same shape and the same grain as the outer fabric.

A facing is not only a finish, it is a support. It adds body, sustains the shape, and reinforces every outside edge subject to stress and wear. For this latter reason you will always find an interfacing wherever you find a facing.

If, in fitting, you changed the shoulder and/or side seam, you must make similar changes on the facing (and interfacing). Facing seams must match garment seams to provide identical shape and fit.

To make the facing seams match the garment seams (Fig. 146)

1. Place the facing over the garment, right sides together.

2. Match the center front and the center back. Pin both edges, top and bottom, of the facing to the garment.

3. Working out from the center, smooth the facing toward the seams. Pin to position on both edges.

4. When you reach the seams, fold the facing back against itself. The fold follows the seam line of the garment.

5. You will have a pair of folds just touching at every seam (Figs. 146a and b).

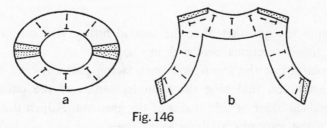

Fig. 146

When the neck facing and the armhole facing are cut separately (Fig. 146a):

6. Slip stitch the folds.

When the neck and armhole facing are cut all in one (Fig. 146b):

7. Baste along each fold. Do not join them.

In both cases:

8. Unpin and remove the corrected facing.
9. Make the interfacing match the facing.

If the adjustments in fitting make the neckline too high and/or the armholes too small, a new neckline and a new armhole must be cut from the original pattern to provide the necessary comfort in wearing (Fig. 147).

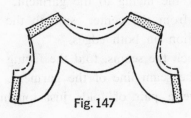

Fig. 147

1. Unpin the garment after the second fitting. (Be sure you have marked the corrections before doing so.)

2. Superimpose the front- and back-facing patterns over the neck and/or armholes, matching the shoulder seams of the pattern with the altered shoulder or side seams of the garment. Adjust the patterns to match the garment at these seam lines.

3. Let the rest of each pattern drop on the garment to the center front and/or center back and to the side seams. The pattern must lie flat regardless of the amount of the drop. Pin to position.

The broken lines in Fig. 147 show the smaller neckline and armholes of the garment after fitting the shoulders and side seams. The solid lines show the neck and armholes of the original pattern in position to be recut.

4. Cut the new neckline and/or the new armholes from the original facing patterns.

To apply separate neck and armhole facings

1. Stitch the seams of the facing beside the guide basting formed by the slip stitching (page 201, step 6). Make the facing slightly smaller than the edge to be faced. This somewhat shortened length fits the inside of the garment rather than the outside. It also helps the garment to lie flat against the body.

2. Press the seam allowances open.

3. Trim the seam allowances of both garment and facing, freeing the neckline cross-seam area of bulk (Fig. 148a).

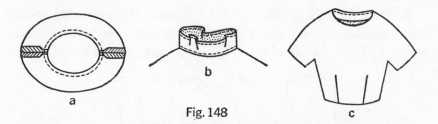

a   Fig. 148   c

4. With right sides of fabric together, stretch the slightly smaller facing to fit the garment and pin to position. Match all seams.

5. Stitch the facing to the garment with the facing side up. Keep the seam an even distance in from the raw edge.

6. Press the seam open. Since this is a curved edge, press a small section at a time, clipping as necessary to release the strain.

7. Turn the facing to the wrong side, rolling the seam to the inside. Press in this position.

8. Working from the right side, understitch the facing to the seam allowances close to the seam line (Fig. 148b). (See page 163.)

9. Trim the seam allowances close to the understitching line. There is not much chance the edge will rip through the two rows of stitching. If you leave any seam allowance, grade it.

10. Turn the facing to the wrong side in position (Fig. 148c).

11. Finish the outer edge of the facing in any of the ways suggested for seam finishes. (See page 168.)

A facing correctly sewn in never shows from the right side, is smooth (no bumps), and is flat (no drawing up).

To apply an all-in-one neck and armhole facing

1. Stitch the side seams of the garment. Do not stitch the shoulder seams. Stitch the side seams of the facing; do not stitch the shoulder seams. Make the facing slightly smaller than the garment.

2. Press all the seam allowances open. Trim them to ½". Free all cross seam areas of bulk.

3. Place the right side of the facing against the right side of the garment, matching the side seams, center front, and center back. Stretching the facing slightly to match the garment, pin or baste to position.

4. With the facing side up, stitch around the neck and around the armholes but do not stitch the shoulders. Stop the stitching about 1" from the shoulder (Fig. 149) each time you come to it.

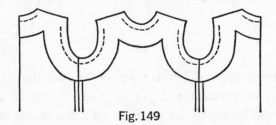

Fig. 149

5. Trim and clip all seam allowances to the end of the stitching.

6. Turn the facing to the wrong side through the opening at the shoulder.

7. Press all edges, rolling the seam to the underside.

8. With right sides together, stitch the shoulder seams of the *outer fabric only.*

9. Press the seam allowances open. Trim them. Trim the bulk from the cross seam area.

10. Turn under the seam allowances of the remaining neck and armhole edges. Press. Catch stitch (see page 179) to the shoulder seam allowance.

11. Turn under the facing seam allowances at the shoulder. Bring the folds to the shoulder seam. Slip stitch (see page 180). Trim seam allowances.

12. Turn under the facing of the remaining small openings at the neck and armhole edges. Pin. Slip stitch.

To apply all-in-one neck and armhole facing when the length and bulk of the garment are not too great and when there is a center front or center back opening (Fig. 150)

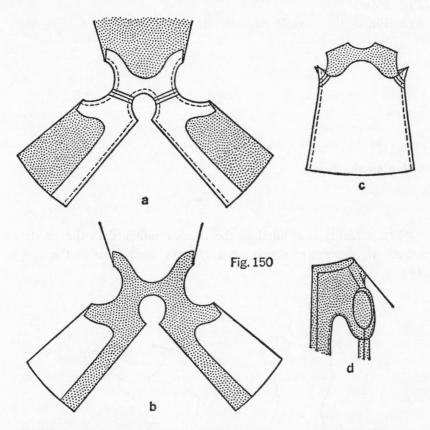

Fig. 150

1. Stitch the garment at the shoulders but *not at the side seams.*

2. Stitch the facing at the shoulders but *not at the side seams.*

3. Press all seam allowances open. Trim.

4. With right sides together, stitch the facing to the front opening and neck edges. Stitch the facing to the armhole edges (Fig. 150a).

5. Trim all seam allowances. Clip all curves.

6. Turn the facing to the wrong side, bringing the front through the shoulders toward the back (Fig. 150b).

7. Press all edges, rolling the seams to the underside.

8. Open out the facing so it extends the side seam (Fig. 150c).

9. With right sides together, make one continuous line of stitching along the facing and the side seams (Fig. 150c).

10. Press the seam allowances open. Trim and clip where necessary.

11. Turn the armhole facing to the wrong side. Press the edges (Fig. 150d).

12. Finish the outside edge of the facing.

Facing to the fore

When a facing is applied to the outside rather than the inside of a dress, its decorative shape (it may have one) adds to the design (Fig. 151a).

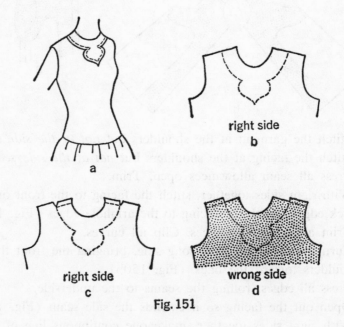

right side
b

a

right side
c

wrong side
d

Fig. 151

1. Mark the depth and the shape of the facing on the right side of the fabric with basting (Fig. 151b).

2. With wrong sides together, stitch the shoulder seam of the garment on the right side from the neck edge to within a few stitches of the marking line.

3. Clip the seam allowance at the end of the stitching. Trim to ¼" (Fig. 151c). Press open.

4. With right sides together, join the remaining shoulder seam on the wrong side (Fig. 151d). Trim and press open.

5. With right sides together, join the front facing to the back facing at the shoulder seams. Make the facing *slightly longer* than the garment; it must fit the outside of the garment. Trim the seam allowances and press them open.

6. Place the *right side of the facing against the wrong side of the garment,* stretching the shorter neck edge of the garment to match the facing. Match the shoulder seams and the center front and back. Pin to position.

7. With the garment side up, stitch an even distance in from the neck edge.

8. Trim the seam allowance to ¼". Clip around the curve.

9. Turn the facing to the right side of the garment. Now both facing and garment are right side up.

10. Roll the neck seam to the underside. Press to position.

11. Lifting the facing carefully so as not to disturb the roll, understitch the seam allowances to the garment close to the seam line.

12. Pin the facing to position on the right side matching center front and back and shoulder seams. Baste if necessary to keep it flat. Make sure the seam is rolled to the underside.

13. Clip the seam allowance of all curves and corners on the outside edge of the facing.

14. Turn under the clipped seam allowance of the facing and bring the folded edge to the marking line. Baste to position.

15. Topstitch.

Bias facing

A strip of bias may also be used for a facing but this must be limited in size to 1″ to 1¼″ plus ¼″ seam allowances. This amount can be swirled into shape to match the garment edge to be faced. Anything wider cannot.

1. Cut a strip of fabric on the true bias to a length which fits the *outer* edge, not the neck edge. Add ¼″ seam allowance to each end. The cut is made on the straight of goods.

2. For rounded shapes, join the ends of the bias strip (Fig. 152a). For square or V-shapes, miter (Figs. 152b and c) (see page 160). Press the seam allowances open. Trim.

a   b   c
Fig. 152

3. Trim the garment seam allowances to ¼″.

4. With right sides together, pin and stitch the bias facing to the garment, easing where necessary (Figs. 152a, b, and c). Clip the seam allowances at curves and corners.

5. Turn the bias to the inside, rolling the seam under. Press to shape.

6. Understitch the bias strip to the ¼″ seam allowances very close to the seam line.

7. Turn under the outside edges of the bias strip and stitch. Hand stitching is easier than machine stitching, which tends to ripple the bias.

8. Tack the outer edge of the facing to all seams and darts to hold it in place.

How to make a bias strip (Fig. 153)

1. Bring the lengthwise grain to meet the crosswise grain (Fig. 153a).

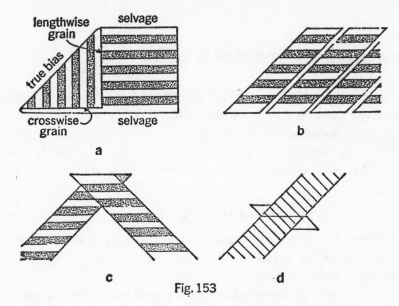

Fig. 153

2. Cut along the fold which is the true bias.
3. Rule off strips parallel to the bias edge and cut (Fig. 153b).
4. Join the strips on the straight grain (Fig. 153c).
5. Press the seam allowances open (Fig. 153d). Trim.

Swirl into shape

Bias of the 1″ to 1½″ width suggested for a facing may be swirled into a curve before it is pinned to the garment (Fig. 154).

Use a steam iron. Keep the side of the iron parallel to the edge. Work the iron inward (follow the arrows in the illustration) from the outer or longer edge to the inner or shorter edge, easing in the fullness while at the same time shaping the strip.

Grosgrain ribbon of this width can be shaped in the same way.

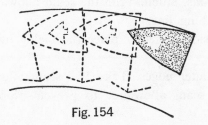

Fig. 154

HOW TO APPLY THE INTERFACING

The general rule is to interface the garment rather than the facing. However, there are many times when it is easier and more advantageous to interface the facing.

Apply the interfacing at an appropriate place in the suggested plan. This will depend in large measure on how you elect to apply the facing.

METHOD I (Fig. 155a)

1. Place the interfacing along the edge to be interfaced on the wrong side of the garment.

2. Baste it to position.

3. Treat both garment and interfacing as if they were one material.

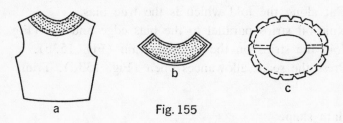

a   Fig. 155

METHOD II (Fig. 155b)

1. Place the facing over the interfacing and stay stitch.

2. Handle as if they were one fabric.

METHOD III (Fig. 155c)

1. Stitch the shoulder and/or side seams of the facing. Press the seam allowances open. Trim.

2. Join the sections of the interfacing by lapping (see page 214, Fig. 158) the seams. Stitch. Trim the seam allowances on both sides close to the stitching line.

3. With right sides together place the facing over the interfacing. Pin.

4. Stitch the outer edges. Take ¼" seam allowance.

5. Notch the seam allowance to prevent rippling when turned (Fig. 155c).

6. Turn to the right side. Press. You now have a finished outer edge.

7. Attach the facing-interfacing to the garment as if they were one fabric.

Always trim an interfacing close to any stitching line to avoid seam bulk when it is turned to the right side.

METHOD IV (Fig. 156)
When a facing is cut all-in-one with the garment

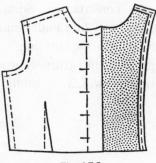

Fig. 156

1. Cut the interfacing only to the fold line. It is not necessary to interface both the garment and the facing. Trim off the seam allowances at the shoulder and outer edge.

2. Turn under the seam allowance of the facing at the shoulder and at the outer edge. Press.

3. Slip the interfacing under the pressed edges, bringing it to the fold line.

4. Stitch the facing to the interfacing close to the turned edges. Be sure to include the interfacing in the seam (Fig. 156).

5. Either machine or hand stitch the inner edge of the interfacing to the facing along the fold line. If the style includes a lapel, the facing will reverse itself to form the lapel. You would not want the stitching to show; end it at the break. Hand stitching is done with a single strand of matching thread, along the fold line, catching only one thread of the outer fabric so the stitching is invisible.

This method may be used as an outside finish for any facing-interfacing outer edge.

HOLD THAT LINE!

There's no doubt about it! Contemporary fashions need under-lining to hold that line!

Most patterns, particularly designer patterns, call for backing as an essential part of the construction. Sometimes in the table of yardage requirements, you will find underlining referred to as "stiff-ening." A better word would be "firming." Fortunately, compara-tively few underlinings are stiff. Stiffness would defeat the present purpose of an underlining, which is subtle shaping.

Back to backing

Cut the fabric and the backing from the same pattern. If a sheer or lightweight backing is used on a sheer or lightweight fabric, cut the underlining the entire length of the pattern. Plan to turn up the hem with the double thickness of backing. This adds just that extra touch of weighting and padding for a softly turned hem that hangs well. In heavier fabrics, cut the underlining just to the fold of the hem. If you are uncertain of the length of the skirt, cut the backing the length of the pattern; then, trim away the backing when the skirt length is set.

The same rule applies when a facing is cut all-in-one with the garment. Lightweight fabrics and underlinings: cut underlining the same as the outer fabric; turn back at the fold line with the facing. Medium and heavy fabrics: cut backing to the fold line only.

The weight of the outer fabric and the underlining also deter-mines the way in which the darts are stitched.

METHOD I
For sheer and very lightweight fabrics

1. Transfer the pattern markings to the underlining only.
2. Stay stitch or tailor baste the outer fabric and the underlining.

To tailor baste two flat unshaped sections: match the centers of both sections, pin and tailor baste, working toward the outer edges, or, match any straight edge, pin and baste, working back from edge.

3. Machine stitch directly down the center of the dart, ending at the dart point through both thicknesses of material.
4. Fold the dart on this line of stitching.
5. Pin and stitch the dart through all layers of material. Start the stitching at the wide end of the dart. Be particularly careful to taper the stitching off the fabric at the dart point.
6. If the finished dart is not too bulky, leave it uncut; if bulky, slash the dart and press it open.

It is very difficult to get a perfectly stitched dart by this method in any but sheer or very lightweight material. The following method produces a much more accurate dart in heavier materials.

METHOD II
For lightweight outer fabric and underlining

1. Transfer the pattern markings to fabric *and* underlining.
2. Pin and stitch the dart in the outer fabric. Pin and stitch the dart in the backing.
3. Press the garment dart in one direction, the underlining dart in the opposite direction to avoid bulk.
4. Join the outer layer and the underlining.

Since this section of the garment has been shaped by the darts, it cannot be worked flat as a straight or unshaped section might be. To preserve the shaping, the two are joined over a curve of the tailor's ham in the following way (Fig. 157).

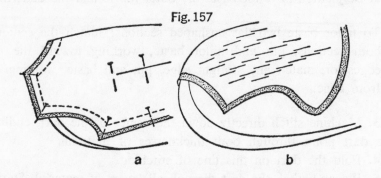

Fig. 157

a

b

a. Place the backing over the tailor's ham wrong side up.

b. Place the outer fabric over the backing right side up; this places the material and backing in the same relative position and shaping in which the garment will be worn.

c. Match the darts and pin (Fig. 157a).

d. Using the dart point as a hub, smooth the fabric toward the outer edges in strokes like the spokes of a wheel; pin.

e. Tailor baste the two thicknesses in rows about 2″ to 3″ apart; start with the dart and work to the outer edges; the long stitches must be on the right side of the fabric or you are working incorrectly (Fig. 157b).

METHOD III

*For medium to heavy outer fabric and crisp or springy
interfacing or underlining (like hair canvas)*

1. Transfer the pattern markings to each.

2. Pin and stitch the dart in the outer fabric. Slash the dart and press it open.

3. *Lap and stitch* the dart in the underlining or interfacing (Fig. 158).

a. Slash on one dart leg to the dart point (Fig. 158a).

b. Lap the slashed edge over the other dart leg (Fig. 158b).

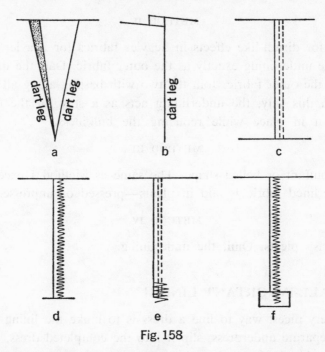

Fig. 158

c. Stitch close to the cut edge, starting at the dart point (an exception) and stitching toward the wide end; this assures a smooth dart point.

d. Make a second line of plain stitching close to the first (Fig. 158c) or use zigzagging to join the dart (Fig. 158d).

e. Reinforce the dart point with either zigzag stitching (Fig. 158e), a patch of seam binding, or tape (Fig. 158f).

f. Trim away the excess material on the underside close to the stitching line.

4. Tailor baste the underlining to the outer fabric by the method described above (page 214).

To underline a garment with fullness

METHOD I

Good for dirndl designs in sheer or lightweight fabric on slim figures.

Cut the underlining exactly as the outer fabric. Join both with stay stitching. Gather both. This produces a very full effect.

METHOD II

Good for dirndl-like effects in heavier fabrics for heavier figures. Cut the underlining exactly as the outer fabric. Dart the underlining; shir the outer fabric. Join the two with basting along all outside edges. In this way, the underlining acts as a stay for the fullness, keeping it in place while reducing the bulkiness.

METHOD III

For bouffant or belled shape. The same as Method I except that the underlined fabric is laid in pleats—pressed or unpressed.

METHOD IV

For crisp pleats. Omit the underlining.

THAT ALL-IMPORTANT LINING

The very nicest way to line a dress is to make the lining as if it were a separate underdress, slip it into the completed dress, and attach it by hand. Handled in this way, it acts as a coverup for the "inner works."

Lining used as a coverup in a fully lined dress (Fig. 159a)

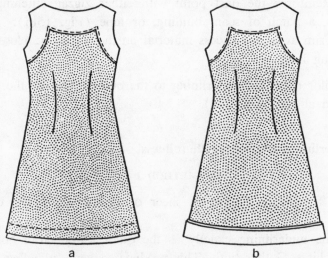

a   b

Fig. 159

1. Complete the dress. Complete the lining, leaving the placket open.

2. Slip the lining into the dress. The finished side of the lining is placed against the body. The wrong sides of the dress and lining face each other.

3. Match the side seams (or any seams which come near the side of the dress). Pin the seam allowances of the dress and lining together and join with permanent basting stitches which are loose, easy. Stop about 8″ from the hem.

4. Match the shoulder seams and pin.

5. Clip and turn under the seam allowances at the neckline and the armhole edges of the lining. Or,

6. Match the clipped raw edges of the lining to the raw edges of the facings. Slip stitch the lining to the facing.

7. Fold under the seam allowance of the lining against the zipper tape and hem.

8. Turn up the hem in the dress and lining separately. Make the lining 1″ shorter than the dress. Use an appropriate finish for each hem.

The staying power of lining

Lining may also be used as a stay to prevent stretching or "bagging" of the outer fabric. It can be greatly aided in this purpose by the character and grain of the lining material. When possible, use fabric with little "give." Or, cut the lining on a crosswise rather than a lengthwise grain—particularly in a skirt (Fig. 160).

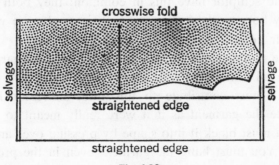

Fig. 160

Cutting the lining so utilizes the non-stretchability of the length-wise straight of goods across the hips where it is needed most. It also makes it possible to use the selvage as the finished lower edge instead of making a hem.

Lining used as a stay in a dress

1. Cut the dress lining from the dress pattern.

2. Mark and stitch the darts and/or shaping seams in both outer fabric and lining.

3. Press all darts and seams.

4. Place the lining over the tailor's ham wrong side up. Place the outer fabric over the lining right side up. This means that the wrong sides are together and the right sides are away from each other (see Fig. 157) and that the finished side of the lining will be against the body. Match the centers and/or darts; tailor baste, working outward toward all edges.

5. When the units of the outer fabric and the lining are "welded together" by the tailor basting, treat them as if they were one fabric. Complete the dress—facings, zippers, and all.

6. Turn up the hem of lining-dress as one (Fig. 159b).

THINKING IN THE ROUND

Sewer and sculptor have this in common: they both think in the round, they both work in the round, their results are viewed in the round, their artistry is judged in the round.

From the moment you stitch your first dart, the garment begins, literally, to take shape in your hands. Everything you do from this moment on must contribute to this three-dimensional form. You must handle the garment as if it were really meant to go *around* a figure. You must block it into shape by pressing over an appropriate press pad. You must hang the garment even in the process of construction; never store it flat. Use a hanger if you must—a dress form if you have one. You are particularly lucky if your dress form is a duplicate of your figure. Then your garment can be trained from the very start to conform to the curves of your body.

Always think "in the round," work "in the round," preserve "the round." Then you, like a sculptor, will truly create a work of art.

NO EXIT?

If you limit your choice of dresses to unfitted styles or stretch fabrics, you will have no problems. You can always crawl into them through enlarged necklines. (Never mind what it does to your new hairdo!) Happily there are easier ways of getting in and out of a dress.

Zip—and you're in—or out!

The simplest of all closings is by zipper. It may be long, short, or in-between. It may be front, side, or back. It may be hidden in a dart or under a pleat. It may be brazenly exposed in a startling color. Inconspicuous or decorative, it is *the* modern, fast, easy way to get into dress or skirt. And, because it is so ubiquitous you must learn to sew it well.

Just because you have the latest-model sewing machine, don't make the mistake of thinking that every operation must be done on it. Some are best accomplished by hand. Take the zipper, for instance. The easiest, fastest, most beautiful way to set and stitch a zipper is *by hand*. While others are busy changing the presser foot to a zipper foot, pinning, basting, stitching, ripping, and starting all over again, you can put in several zippers. Besides, the tiny hand stitches look so much better than that rigid, wavering line of machine stitching.

There are two types of zippered closings—the regulation (Figs. 161a and b) and the slot seam (Fig. 161c).

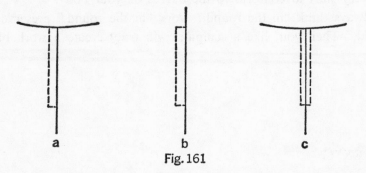

Fig. 161

In the regulation closings (Figs. 161a and b) the zipper is hidden by a lapped fold. Only one line of stitching is visible. The lap may be to the right or to the left depending on which is easier for you to use. Generally a lap to the right is easier for right-handed people, a lap to the left for the left-handed.

In the slot seam closing (Fig. 161c) the zipper is concealed by two folds of material which are centered over the zipper. There are two lines of stitching, one on each side of the seam line. The repetition of vertical lines makes this closing appear slimmer.

Both types are acceptable whatever the location of the zipper. Which to use depends (you've guessed it) on the design and the fabric. Use a slot seam when a symmetrical look is consistent with the design. It makes a trimmer opening for heavy or pile fabrics, faced openings, slashed openings, wrist openings, openings concealed in box or inverted pleats. Use a lapped closing in delicate and lightweight fabrics. There is less danger of catching the cloth in the zipper.

How to make the regulation-zippered closing
for skirt and neck-type openings (Fig. 161a)

1. Buy a neck-type zipper of the proper length.

2. Carefully pin-fit the garment on the placket opening. Mark the seam line with chalk.

3. Transfer the markings to the right side with guide basting. The garment must close on this marked line but this is *not* the line on which the zipper is stitched.

4. Clip the under (back) seam allowance at the end of the opening practically to the seam line (Fig. 162a).

5. Fold the under-seam allowance ⅛" from the line of guide basting so that it forms an extension into the garment (Fig. 162b). Press along the fold.

6. Place the metal slider and top-stop of the zipper ¼" below the top cross seam line. Place the fold of the extension close to the zipper, allowing just enough room to work the metal slider. Pin to position (Fig. 162c).

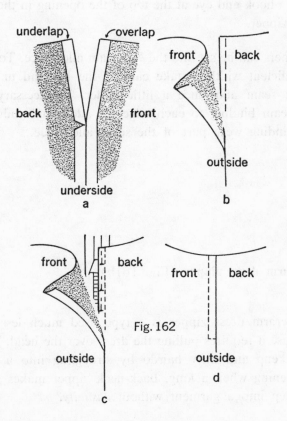

Fig. 162

7. Using a single thread and working from the right side, stitch the zipper with tiny *back stitches*. These may be continuous (full back stitches) like machine stitching, making a strong seam for a garment that will see much wear. Or, they may be half back stitches providing adequate strength while, at the same time, being less conspicuous. The latter method is more appropriate for sheer, fragile fabrics and less frequently worn dresses.

8. Place the folded edge of the overlap so that it meets the guide basting of the underlap (Fig. 162c). This encloses and conceals both the zipper and the stitching. Pin to position.

9. Back stitch the overlap in place (Fig. 162d). Start at the bottom of the zipper; stitch across the end below the bottom-stop; work to the top. Keep the welt uniform. As you approach the top-stop, pull the tab down. This makes it easier to preserve the narrow welt in the slider area.

10. Sew a hook and eye at the top of the opening in the ¼" space above the zipper.

Most zippers can be set into the ⅝" seam allowance. To make sure there is sufficient width to take care of the lap and underlap, cut the placket seam allowance a little wider. If necessary, attach a length of seam binding to each edge for additional width. Proceed as if the binding were part of the seam allowance.

The underarm dress zipper (Fig. 161b)

The underarm dress zipper is a type used much less frequently today because it requires pulling the dress over the head. Who wants to ruin makeup and nifty hairdo by struggling into a dress with such an opening when a long, back-neck zipper makes it so much easier to step into a garment without *casualty?*

If the dress is sleeveless, you may use a neck-type zipper even on an underarm seam. This provides a little more room for manipulation. If the dress has sleeves and a collar that make a center back opening impossible, then use the regulation underarm dress zipper.

This zipper has tiny metal bridges that hold the tapes together at the top of the zipper as well as at the bottom. When set, there is a seam above the zipper and below it making for a partial opening in a dress instead of the complete opening achieved by the neck type. Insert it in exactly the same way as the other types with this slight change: substitute the following for Step 4, page 221.

4. Clip the under-seam allowance at both ends of the placket opening.

How to make the slot-zippered closing (Fig. 161c)

1. Buy a neck-type zipper of the proper length.

2. Fit the garment and mark as for the regulation zipper.

3. Fold under both seam allowances of the placket opening along the lines of guide basting. Press.

4. Place the zipper in the opening so that the top-stop and the metal slider are ¼″ below the top cross seam line.

5. Place one folded edge *slightly beyond the center* of the closed zipper. This slight correction compensates for the pull away from center as the zipper is being stitched. If the opening fold is placed on dead center, this natural pull exposes the teeth of the zipper. Who wants a zipper with bared teeth?

6. Pin the zipper to position.

7. Back stitch, using either full or half back stitches.

8. Place and pin the second side of the zipper in the same way as the first—that is, the opening fold slightly beyond the center of the zipper.

9. Back stitch across the bottom below the bottom-stop and continue up the second side. Keep the welts even on both sides. Lower the pull-tab as you approach the top-stop for easy stitching.

10. Sew a hook and eye at the top of the opening in the ¼" space.

If you've ever struggled with a machine-stitched zipper, you'll find soon that you can do it better by hand.

If you've never stitched a zipper before, following these directions should give you easy mastery.

HAPPY ENDING — THE HEM

By the time you get to the hem, you can start planning your next dress. The end of this one is not far off.

Adopt or adapt a fashionable length

Choose a fashionable length or one that is becoming to you and reasonably within the current fashion. Don't be the last holdout against a new fashion. You'll only have to keep "inching" up or down. Think of all that extra work you can spare yourself if you bow to the inevitable in the first place. However objectionable we may think a new look at the start, so quickly do our eyes become accustomed to it that before long we look queer if we don't adopt it (even if we have to adapt it) as our own.

Settle the fabric and set the hem

Let the garment hang out so the fabric settles—at least overnight for a straight skirt, longer for a gored skirt, as much as a week for a circle skirt. A week, too, for bias cuts, knits, and heavy materials. Settling the fabric prevents a "dippy" hemline.

Wear the foundation garments and the shoes you plan to wear (or ones of similar heel height) with the dress.

Use a skirt marker or a T-square for accurate marking. A yardstick won't do; it can be tilted too easily. A chalk self-marker is uncertain and unsafe for many fabrics. There is this, too, about self-marking: a shift in position on your part may make for an uneven hem. This is another spot where you can use a little assistance from a sewing "buddy." Stand still and let the "buddy" move around you.

Place the pins about 2″ apart on a straight skirt, closer on more circular ones. Fold the hem under along the pin markings, correcting any "jumpiness." Using a gauge, measure and mark the hem an even depth around the skirt. Straight skirts generally take hems of 2″ to 2½″. The more curved the sweep of the skirt, the narrower the hem. Use only that width whose upper edge can be readily eased to fit the skirt without ripples, bumps, or darts. Trim away any material beyond that point. Press the hem, easing the upper edge so it lies flat.

Hem finishes

As with all other raw edges, this one also needs a finish. Here are a variety to choose from. Suit the hem finish to the type of fabric.

Stitches that fasten the hem to the garment are loose, "lazy." They pick up only one thread of the garment so they are practically invisible from the right side. Where there is an underlining, attach the hem to it rather than to the outer fabric.

Bound Hem

The most usual type of hem finish is a binding (Fig. 163a). If the skirt is a straight one, use straight seam binding; if curved, use bias binding. Stitch the edge of the binding to the raw edge of the hem as you would join any other two thicknesses of cloth. Fold the binding over the seam to conceal it. Press the binding flat. Hem it to the garment.

This makes a much neater and stronger finish than the overlap-and-stitch method. The latter often results in an inaccurate, wavering line of machine stitching or one where the binding pulls away as the stitching goes completely off the cloth (a common casualty even with experienced sewers).

A finer touch is to enclose the raw edge of the hem completely with the seam binding and then attach it to the garment in the same way as a French dressmaker's hem (Fig. 163b).

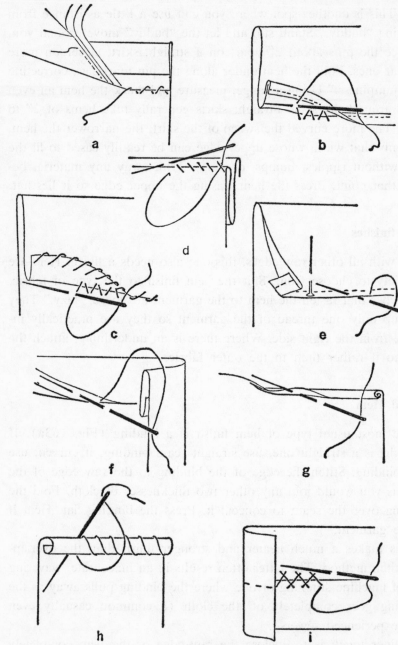

Fig. 163

French dressmaker's hem

Special touch for special dresses (Figs. 163b and c)

1. Overcast the raw edges. (If you can ever get a look at the inside of a haute couture dress, you'll discover that a French dressmaker can't bear to see a raw edge and considers every one she finds a challenge to overcast. There are literally thousands of tiny overcasting stitches on all inside edges.)

2. Fold back the edge of the hem toward the fold of the hem (Fig. 163d). Pin.

3. Fold back the garment toward the outside. This places the folds of both hem and garment opposite each other (Fig. 163d).

4. Using a single strand of matching thread, pick up one thread of the hem, then one of the garment about ¼" to ½" away. Continue across the entire length of the hem, alternating between hem and garment. Use either a running-hemming stitch or a catch stitch.

Edge-stitched hem

(Fig. 163e) for cotton, silk, and very lightweight woolens

Turn under the raw edge. Stitch close to the fold either by hand or by machine. Hem or slip stitch in place.

Slip-stitched hem

(Fig. 163f) used when no matching seam binding is available

Turn under the raw edge of the hem and press. Slip stitch to the garment through the fold.

Double-fold hem

A double-fold hem can be used on sheer or lightweight fabrics. The extra layer of material (the depth of the hem) acts as an interfacing, weighting the hem slightly for a better hang. Fold the raw edge to the fold line of the hem. Fold a second time to position. Slip stitch through the fold.

Rolled hem (Fig. 163g)

A rolled hem is used on very sheer fabrics like chiffon (or on a single layer of a bow). This is the hem of your handkerchief. Stay stitch close to the edge. Trim close to the stitching. Roll the edge toward you with the thumb and forefinger. Hem or slip stitch in place.

Whipped hem (Fig. 163h)

Stay stitch close to the edge. Trim close to the stitching. Roll toward you as for a rolled hem. Stitch in place with whipping stitches.

Catch-stitched hem (Fig. 163i)

To keep the hem of bulky or heavy material flat or to provide stretchability to a knit or bias fabric, catch stitch the raw edge of the hem to the garment.

"Give-'em-the-works" treatment

The opposite to this bare-edge treatment is the "give-'em-the-works" treatment: finish the raw edges with baby lace, rickrack or ribbon, striped, floral, or plaid binding, or any other original (though suitable) finish you can devise.

Whatever the finish, the hem must lie flat. However pretty or ingenious, it must be invisible from the outside. Only you must know what goes on underneath—unless you choose to reveal your handiwork. To the viewer, your dress must come to a graceful, unobtrusive conclusion. To you it is the happy ending of a proud venture.

MAKE A SKIRT

What's easy to make, speedily done, and made with little material? A skirt, of course! A pretty skirt that fits well is worth its weight in—fabric. Several good skirts to wear with your favorite blouses or sweaters can well see you through most of your daytime (and even some evening) needs.

Here is the plan for making a skirt

Straight or gored. Use this in conjunction with the pattern instructions.

New information: How to make and attach the waistband—how to line a skirt—how to handle pleats.

Follow Steps 1 to 10 for making the shift dress, page 199.

Continue as follows:

11. Pin the skirt for the first fitting. Adjust as necessary. Mark the alterations.

12. Decide whether the skirt is to be lined or backed and how much of either. Remember, this is optional for the first few skirts.

13. Stitch all darts and seams that complete each unit of the outer fabric.

14. (Optional) Stitch all darts and seams that complete each unit of the lining or backing. Decide what method to use for inserting either. (See page 212.)

15. Stitch the side seams.

16. Insert the zipper. (See page 219.)

17. Decide on the method of fastening the waistband—button and buttonhole, snaps or hook and eye. If a buttonhole is to be used, make it before attaching the waistband.

18. Attach the waistband.

19. Mark and make the hem.

THE WAISTBAND

Classic vs. unorthodox approach

The classic way to finish the waist of a skirt is with a band of self-fabric. Unorthodox finishes can be a lot more fun, though. Consider the decorative possibilities of a printed, plaid, striped, or checked waistband; of ribbon—grosgrain, satin, or velvet (Fig.

164a); a contrasting color or texture—like suede or braid. Sometimes no waistband at all is more consistent with a design—that is,
no visible waistband. This sleight-of-hand can be accomplished by
an inside waistband of French belting or ribbon (Fig. 164b).

Fig. 164

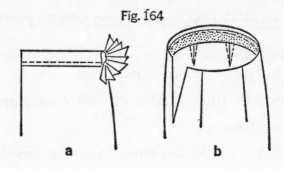

a   b

Grain makes the difference

The waistband is usually cut on the lengthwise grain of the fabric
so that the grain of the band matches the grain of the skirt. If
matching stripes, plaids, directional weaves, or printed motifs become too much of a problem, cut the waistband on the bias. If no
matching is involved, the waistband can with advantage (less stretch)
be cut on the crosswise grain. If you do this you may even plan to
use the selvage for the finished edge. If the selvage happens to be
a handsome one (and sometimes selvages are) it can be used as a
decorative finish for the waistband. Apply this type of band like the
topstitched band (Fig. 167).

When it comes to fit, bias waistbands are best of all. Their "give"
makes them settle very comfortably into the waist. However, in
calculating the length of the waistband you must keep in mind this
stretch quality of the bias. The heavier the fabric, the wider the
sweep of the skirt, the more pull (therefore stretch) on the band.
Subtract 1″ to 2″ from your waist measurement, depending on the
weight of the fabric and the width of the skirt at the hem.

To determine the length of on-grain waistbands

Take a snug waist measurement and add ½″ to 1″ for ease,
depending on personal preference. Or, take your waist measurement

while seated; this automatically adds the necessary ease in a comfortable amount.

To this measurement add 1¼" for two seam allowances and 1½" for a closing—either an extension or an underlay. Decide which will be more attractive or more comfortable for a particular skirt.

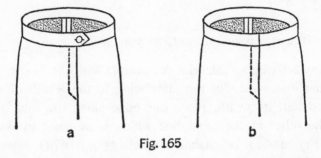

Fig. 165

Extension closing (Fig. 165a)

In this closing, the 1½" extends beyond the side seam line of the skirt and laps over the other end of the band that is flush with the skirt seam. The band is fastened with a buttonhole and button. The buttonhole is made before the waistband is stitched to the skirt.

Underlay closing (Fig. 165b)

In this closing, the upper band ends flush with the seam line while the 1½" closing extension is hidden beneath it. This waistband may also close with a buttonhole and button but presents a trimmer appearance if closed with snaps—large or small, covered or uncovered—or with hooks and eyes. The latter are not as satisfactory; they always seem to get mashed or pulled out of shape in cleaning.

To determine the width of the waistband

A narrow waistband—¾" to 1¼", hugs the indentation of the waist. A wider waistband requires some shaping to conform to the curve of the waist.

Cut the waistband twice the desired width plus two seam allowances. This double width produces a bulky waistband in heavy fabric. For such materials it is advisable to cut the waistband to one width only (plus seam allowances) and face the underside with some lightweight material—lining, grosgrain ribbon, French belting. The last two have the added advantage of staying the length and stiffening the band.

Interface the waistband or not, as you prefer

Use any interfacing material compatible with the fabric. Eliminate all seam allowances. Cut the interfacing to the length of the waistband and half its width. Place one edge along the fold line of the band, the other at the seam line which joins band to skirt. Catch stitch (Fig. 166a) or machine stitch (Fig. 167a) interfacing to the underband, that is, the part of the waistband which will be next to the body.

Often an extra layer of self-fabric makes a very satisfactory interfacing (remember the double-fold hem?). Cut the waistband three times its finished width plus one seam allowance. Mark off the seam allowance. Fold the remaining width in thirds. Press. With right sides together, stitch the skirt and waistband along the seam line. Clip the seam allowances, grade, and press into the band. Hem the folded lower edge of the band to the inside of the skirt at the seam line.

Locate the waistline

It is extremely important that the waistband fit right in the hollow of the waist. Too tight and the band hikes up until it finds some place where it does fit. This means a displacement of darts and shaping seams with inevitable wrinkling across the back and the abdomen. Too loose and the skirt rides the hips cowboy fashion— also displacing the shaping seams and darts—and giving a baggy look to the skirt.

For a well-set waistband: try on the skirt and close the placket; tie a string around the waist; pin along the bottom of the string; remove the skirt and replace the pins with basting. The basting is the stitching line to which the waistband is attached.

An easy method for attaching the waistband to the skirt (Fig. 166)

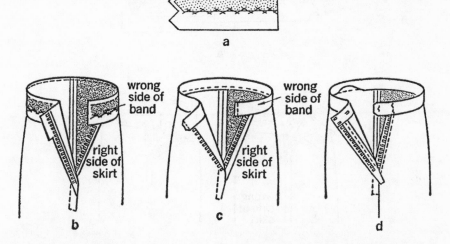

Fig. 166

1. With right sides together, pin the waistband to the skirt, allowing the underlay or the extension and the seam allowances to extend beyond the finished edge of the opening (Fig. 166b).

2. Stitch the band to the skirt (Fig. 166b). Include the lining or backing when present. Grade and clip the seam allowances—the waistline is a slight curve.

3. Press the seam allowances open first, then into the band.

4. With right sides together, fold the band in half lengthwise. Stitch across each end (Fig. 166c).

5. Press the seam allowances open, using the point presser to get into the corners of the band. Grade the seam allowances and free the corners of bulk.

6. Turn the band to the right side. Fold in half lengthwise along the fold line. Make sure that the width is even from the seam to the fold along the entire length.

7. Press the fold line and the ends of the band, rolling the seams to the underside.

8. Turn under the seam allowance of the loose edge of the waistband and hem it to the skirt along the stitching line (Fig. 166d).

9. Finish with hooks and eyes, snaps, or a button.

How to make a topstitched waistband (Fig. 167)

Fig. 167

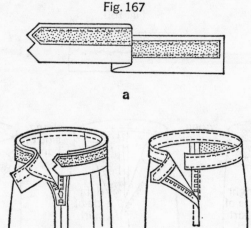

a

b   wrong side of skirt

c

1. Stitch the right side of the skirt band to the wrong side of the skirt (Fig. 167b). Grade and clip the seam allowances.

2. With right sides together, fold the waistband in half lengthwise. Stitch across the ends. Press and grade the seam allowances; clip across the corner.

3. Turn the band to the right side. Press.

4. Turn under the seam allowance of the loose edge. Press. Lap and pin the folded edge over the right side of the skirt, covering the seam line.

5. Pin or baste to position. Topstitch (Fig. 167c).

6. Sew on fastenings.

To make an inside waistband

1. Carefully mark the waistline of the skirt. The band is the exact length of the waistline measurement plus seam allowances at each end.

2. If grosgrain ribbon is used, steam it into a slight curve (ease the inside curve, stretch the outside curve).

3. Turn under the seam allowances of both ends. Stitch.

4. Lap the right side of the ribbon over the right side of the skirt slightly above the waistline marking. This provides an allowance for rolling the seam to the underside. Stitch.

5. Trim and clip the seam allowance under the ribbon to permit an easy and flat turning.

6. Turn the waistband to the inside of the skirt. Roll the seam to the underside. Press to position.

7. Tack the band securely to all seams and darts on the inside for a truly invisible band. Or, if stitching is consistent with the design, topstitch the waistline close to the turn, being sure to include the ribbon.

8. Fasten the waistband on the inside with hooks and eyes (Fig. 168).

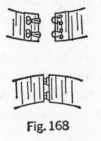

Fig. 168

HOW TO LINE A SKIRT

Most skirts are lined these days. They hang better, look better, and are less apt to wrinkle when they are fully lined. Even half a lining is better than no lining. You can make your first skirt or two without lining to simplify the learning process. After that, think of the lining as an integral part of the construction.

Lining used as a coverup—a fully lined skirt

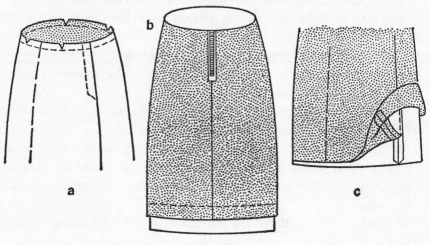

Fig. 169

1. Complete the skirt except for the waistband and the hem.

2. Complete the lining as if it were a half slip. Leave the placket open.

3. Slip the skirt over the lining with the wrong sides together. Pin to position at the waistline, matching the center front and back, all seams, all darts, and the placket opening.

4. Baste the skirt and lining together across the waistline, easing as necessary (Fig. 169a).

5. Fold under the seam allowance of the lining against the zipper tape. Hem (Fig. 169b).

6. Stitch the waistband to both skirt and lining.

7. Loosely and permanently baste the seam allowances of skirt and lining to within 6″ of the hem (Fig. 169c).

8. Turn up the hem in the skirt and the lining separately. Use an appropriate finish for each.

Lining used as a stay

1. Cut the skirt lining from the skirt pattern to either mid-thigh or full length. Do not include any pleats which may be in the pattern. To eliminate the entire pleat, fold back the pattern on the fold line (Fig. 170a); or, cut the lining off at the fold line of a kick pleat (Fig. 170b); or, at the top of a pleat (Fig. 170c); or, leave a slit in the lining instead of a pleat to permit the same freedom of movement as the pleat in the skirt gives (Fig. 170d).

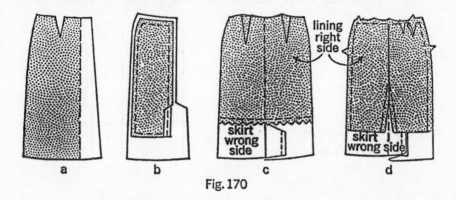

Fig. 170

2. Mark and stitch the darts in the outer fabric. Mark and stitch the darts in the lining. If the skirt has shaping seams instead of darts, join all sections that produce the front and back units in both outer fabric and lining.

3. Press all darts and seams.

4. Place the lining over the tailor's ham wrong side up. Place the skirt over the lining right side up. Match and pin the centers first; tailor baste. Smooth the skirt and lining toward the outside edges; tailor baste.

5. When all units are completely tailor basted, treat them as if they were one fabric and complete the skirt.

ON-THE-MOVE SKIRTS

Slim skirts are trim skirts but swinging skirts lend grace to movement. With one pleat, two pleats, or a round of pleats, skirts are on the move.

You will certainly want to know how to handle pleats in your sewing. Careful marking, plenty of material, and a little time are what's needed to make pleats.

Pleat meets

It takes pairs of markings to make each pleat—one for the fold of the pleat, the other the line to which it is brought.

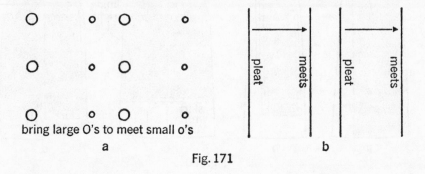

bring large O's to meet small o's

a   b

Fig. 171

When the pattern says, "Bring large O's to meet small o's," make tailor's tacks through the large and small perforations (Fig. 171a).

When the pattern says of two printed lines, "Pleat meets," the marking may be done with basting or with tailor's tacks (Fig. 171b).

In either case the markings are easier to pair off if the line indicating the fold is done in a different color thread from the line to which the pleat is brought. Read the pattern carefully for the direction of the pleat. Some patterns have arrows which tell this at a glance (Fig. 171b).

Meet the pleat

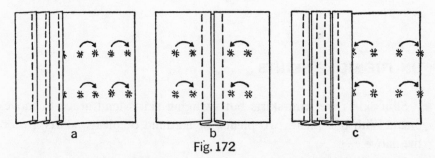

a   b   c

Fig. 172

When even pleats of any size are folded so they all go in one direction, they are called *knife pleats* (Fig. 172a).

When the folds of two equal side pleats meet at the center on the right side, the pleat is called an *inverted pleat* (Fig. 172b).

A *box pleat* (Fig. 172c) is just the reverse of the inverted pleat. The folds turn in opposite directions on the right side and meet at the center on the wrong side.

All of the above are easy enough for any sewer to make. The following pleats are always machine-made in special shops.

Accordion pleats are pleats which overlap one another when closed and stand out when worn (just like an accordion). They are even top and bottom.

Sunburst pleats are formed like accordion pleats except that they are narrow at the top and fan out into wider pleats as they reach the bottom.

Any seaming necessary for additional length of cloth is always concealed in the depth of a pleat.

How to lay in pleats

Pleats may be laid in on the ironing board and pressed to position (Fig. 173).

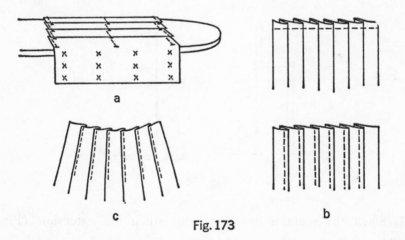

Fig. 173

1. Pin the pleats at top, bottom, and at sufficient intervals between (Fig. 173a). Pins are best placed at right angles to the fold.

2. Press lightly, removing the pins as you reach the area to be pressed. Replace them when the pressing is done. In a skirt, this pressing is done to within 6″ of the lower edge. When the hem is

set and stitched, fold the pleats once more to position and complete
the pressing. For further information on pressing pleats, see page 188.

3. Baste the pleats firmly to position—down each pleat, across
the top (Fig. 173b), or both. Make sure the basting goes through
each pleat.

To pleat a skirt that is fitted from waist to hips: taper the pleats
evenly and proportionately at the waistline (Fig. 173c).

Walking room

To provide walking room in an otherwise slim skirt, the designer
may plan a pleat at the lower edge of the skirt. This is often on a
seam line.

How to make a side pleat (kick pleat) formed by an extension (Fig.
174).

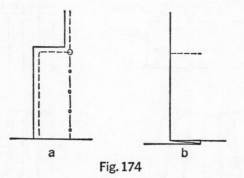

a   b

Fig. 174

1. Stitch the seam above the pleat; stitch the extension (Fig.
174a).

2. Clip at the inside corner (O) of the extension (Fig. 174a).

3. Press the seam allowance open above the extension. Pin the
pleat to position.

4. On the right side: stitch across the top to hold the pleat in
place (Fig. 174b).

How to make an inverted pleat with an underlay (Fig. 175)

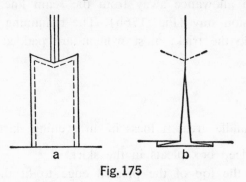

Fig. 175

1. Stitch above the extension. Clip at the corner of the extension.

2. Press the seam allowance open above the extension.

3. Fold the extension back on both sides. Press.

4. Pin the raw edges of the extension to the raw edges of the underlay (Fig. 175a). Stitch down each side. Pin or baste the inverted pleat to position.

5. On the right side: stitch across the top of the pleat either side of the seam line (Fig. 175b).

How to make a pleat from a waist-to-hem extension (Fig. 176)

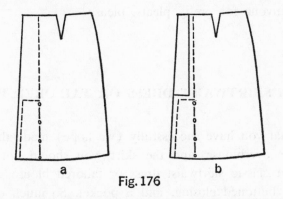

Fig. 176

1. Stitch the seam of the skirt above the pleat and across the extension (Fig. 176a), where indicated on the pattern. Below this cross stitching the extension becomes the pleat. Above this cross stitching, the extension acts as a stay to hold the pleat in place *without* outside stitching.

2. A seam allowance away from the seam line, trim one layer of the extension stay (Fig. 176b). The remaining layer of stay is enough to do the trick; most women are padded enough in this area already.

Dancing room

How to handle great fullness in an evening skirt:

1. Make deep box pleats in the skirt.
2. Gather the top of the pleated edge to fit the waistline.

Plan for making a pleated skirt or a skirt with pleats

Follow Steps 1 to 10 for making the shift dress, page 199.

Continue as follows:

11. Make the pleats as directed in the pattern.
12. Stitch all darts and seams.
13. Insert the zipper.
14. Attach the waistband.
15. Mark and make the hem.
16. Touch up pressing of pleats and hem.

Now, anyone for pretty pleats, please?

MAKE A SHIRTWAIST DRESS OR TAILORED BLOUSE

Now that you have successfully (we hope) made the shift dress, jumper or overblouse, and the skirt, you should not find it hard to make a classic shirtwaist dress or tailored blouse with a collar, sleeves, a buttoned closing, and a pocket. So much of the sewing language and so many of the sewing procedures will be familiar to you.

New information: how to make bound buttonholes, how to sew on buttons, snaps, and hooks and eyes; how to make a looped closing; how to work eyelets and frogs; how to make and attach the collar; how to make and set a sleeve; how to make and attach the cuffs or sleeve band; how to handle a kimono sleeve and its gusset; how to make a pocket; how to make a belt; how to tape the waistline; how to join bodice to skirt.

By the time you've acquired all these sewing skills you will have learned the basic sewing techniques.

This is the *plan of work* for the shirtwaist dress or the tailored blouse.

Steps 1 to 13 are the same as for the shift dress, page 199.

Continue as follows:

The bodice

14. Stitch all darts and seams which complete each unit of the outer fabric.

15. Stitch all darts and seams which complete each unit of the underlining or lining when used. (You may omit these in your first ventures.)

16. Press each unit of the outer fabric and the underpinnings (when used).

17. Decide how and when to apply the interfacing, lining, or underlining when used.

18. Make the bound buttonholes on the bodice right front. Machine-made or hand-worked buttonholes are made after the garment is finished.

19. Make and apply the pocket.

20. Stitch the shoulder seams and the side seams. Leave the placket open on the left side seam.

21. Complete the collar unit.

22. Complete the bodice facing.

23. Attach the collar and the facing to the bodice.

24. Finish the underside of the buttonholes.

25. Make and set the sleeves. Attach the cuffs.

26. Establish the waistline.

The skirt

27. Stitch and press all units of the skirt; do the same for the lining or underlining when used.

28. Join all units which complete the skirt. Leave a placket opening on the left side seam.

29. Establish the waistline on the skirt and tape it.

The dress

30. Join the skirt to the bodice. Clip the seam allowance so there is no strain. Press the seam.

31. Sew in the underarm dress zipper.

32. Mark and make the hem.

33. Sew on the buttons, hooks and eyes, or snaps.

34. Buy, make, or have made the belt.

35. Add any finishing touches.

Obviously no one sequence of steps or set of directions can do for every garment even of the same type. Procedures differ as style details differ. The above plan is a simple, workable one to be used with your pattern instructions. It follows a logical, steady buildup based on the unit system just as most patterns do.

Understanding this should remove the aura of mystery and magic that surrounds the printed set of directions in the pattern. Knowing this, you will not need to be so glued to that instruction sheet. You will develop an independence in your work.

BOUND-TO-BE-GOOD BUTTONHOLES

Delightful as it may be to zip into a dress, there are times—and styles—that call for other types of closing. Probably the most familiar is the button and buttonhole.

Buttons often "make" a dress. They may be treasured or trifles, beauties or the kind that take a beating, used sparingly or in groupings. While machine-made buttonholes are acceptable and perhaps even preferable on wash-and-wear clothing, all good clothing deserves beautifully bound buttonholes.

Many a veteran sewer has been known to blanch at the thought of making bound buttonholes. You may even have heard dour tales of buttonhole fiascoes. In all fairness, the fault was not so much with the sewers as with the earlier techniques of buttonhole making. Present methods produce foolproof, successful buttonholes. When you learn this new way from the start you will never be fearful.

How to make the bound buttonhole (Technically, it is really a piped buttonhole, but why get into semantics? Sewers, professional as well as amateur, always refer to this type of buttonhole as "bound.")

Some suggestions before you begin

The buttonhole is always made through the right side of the garment *before* it is joined to the facing.

An area to be slashed needs reinforcement. Therefore, the bound buttonhole is always made *through both outer fabric and interfacing*.

Make the buttonhole fit the button rather than the marking on the pattern. It should be long enough so the button slides through easily—at least ⅛" ease (Fig. 177a). Make a test slash to be sure. Allow for the fact that the buttonhole tends to be somewhat smaller when completed than the original slash. The rule for "bumpy" buttons is length plus height equals size of buttonhole. An easy way to determine this is to wrap a strip of paper around the button at its widest part (Fig. 177b). (A very narrow tape measure would be even better.) Half this measurement is the correct size for the buttonhole.

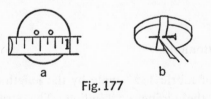

a   b

Fig. 177

It is a good idea to make a test buttonhole through an extra piece of the fabric and the interfacing of the garment. This gives an idea of how the fabric handles, how the buttonhole works up, and if the size is right.

The button you select should be as large in diameter as the width of the opening extension, that is, the width from the center front to the finished front edge (Fig. 178a). When buttoned, there should be half a button's width between the rim of the button and the finished edge of the garment (Fig. 178b). You may use a slightly smaller button in the same space. The only time you can use a larger button is when you observe this rule: the distance from center front to finished edge equals half a button's width plus ½″ (Fig. 178c).

If the button is too large for this space or placed too close to the edge, it will spill over the edge. Many an otherwise beautiful garment is spoiled by this very thing.

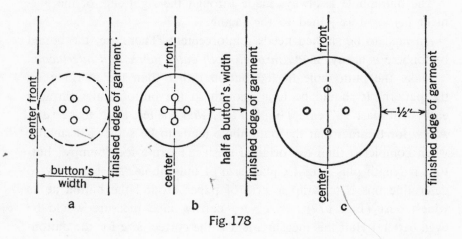

Fig. 178

To make the buttonhole

1. Cut a strip of fabric 1½″ wide by the length of the buttonhole plus 1″. This is the piping or binding. The straight of goods is generally used. If matching the stripes, plaids, or checks of the piping to those of the garment presents too much difficulty, cut the piping on the bias. This may be even prettier.

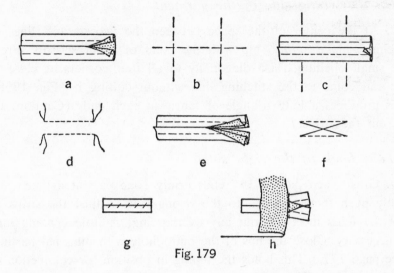

Fig. 179

2. Fold the strip lengthwise into three equal ½″ sections, right side outside. Press.

3. Stitch ⅛″ in from both folds (Fig. 179a).

On the right side of the garment

4. Mark the position and size of the buttonholes with guide basting. Mark the slash line or opening, mark the beginning and the end (Fig. 179b).

5. Place the folded strip, face down, on the marking, centering the strip on the slash line.

6. Stitch the piping to the garment directly over the previous stitching. Start and stop at the vertical basting (Fig. 179c). *Do not stitch across the ends.* On the wrong side this will appear as two parallel lines of machine stitching (Fig. 179d). Pull all four sets of thread ends through to the wrong side. For perfect corners each pair of threads must end exactly at the marking and directly opposite another pair. Tie each pair of threads. (Back-and-forth stitching is too inaccurate.)

7. Cut the strip into two pieces straight through the center (Fig. 179e). (Caution: do not cut the garment.)

On the wrong side of the garment

8. At the center of the space between the two parallel lines of stitching, make a *tiny* snip with the point of small scissors. From this small opening, slash diagonally to all four corners as close as you can come to the stitching line without cutting it (Fig. 179f). This produces a long triangle of fabric at each end. (Caution: do not cut the strips.)

Turn back to the right side

9. Grasp each pair of ½″ ends firmly (one pair at a time) and gently push them through to the wrong side. Adjust the strips so that the folds meet without any overlapping. A little coaxing may be necessary. Close the lips of the buttonhole with diagonal basting. (See page 177.) This holds the piping in position for completion of the buttonhole (Fig. 179g).

Turn back to the wrong side, once more

10. Fold back the garment over the buttonhole so you can see the long triangles as they lie against the strips. These must be fastened by machine stitching across the ends to complete the buttonhole. Stitch close to the fold but not over it (Fig. 179h). Stitching over it produces an unsightly pleat or dart on the right side. Stitching too far away from the fold leaves a hole at each end.

It truly doesn't take too much to make beautiful bound button-holes—just careful marking, precision sewing, judicious cutting, and lots of time. That's all!

There are variations of this method but in principle they are all the same. Once you've mastered this easy method, you will be able to do any of the others that call for a slightly more complex technique.

To finish the buttonhole on the underside

The opening of the buttonhole is made through the outer fabric and the interfacing. The facing on the underside also needs an opening or the button never could get through. There are several ways in which this can be done.

Use Method I for firm fabrics

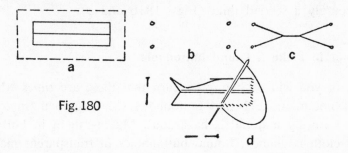

Fig. 180

1. Pin or baste around each buttonhole to keep the facing in place (Fig. 180a).

2. Push a pin through each corner of the buttonhole so the point emerges on the facing. This shows exactly the size of the buttonhole (Fig. 180b). The opening on the facing must be identical.

3. Cut the facing. Make a long slash through the center and short slashes diagonally to each corner of the markings (Fig. 180c). This is the exact opposite of the slashing done for the buttonhole, itself.

4. Turn under each of the four little facing flaps until the resulting rectangular opening exposes the lips of the buttonhole.

5. Hem neatly and securely to position (Fig. 180d).

Method II for fabrics that ravel easily

Fig. 181

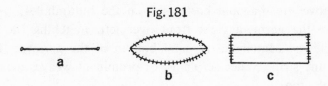

1. Push a pin through each end of the buttonhole opening (Fig. 181a).

2. Slash the facing from one pin to the other.

3. Quickly turn under the raw edges of the facing to form an ellipse (Fig. 181b). In some fabrics you may even be able to push the ends of the slash into a rectangle with the point of the needle (Fig. 181c).

4. Hem quickly and tentatively to position to prevent raveling. Hem securely a second time (Figs. 181b and c).

When not to make a bound buttonhole

Some of you will be happy to learn that there are times when it is better not to make bound buttonholes. Making them in loosely woven or ravelly material is hazardous. Making them in knits and stretchy cloth is chancy. Bound buttonholes in transparent material reveal all the inner workings. Jeweled or rough-surfaced buttons often damage the material as they pass through a buttonhole or may, in turn, be damaged by it.

You may fake a buttoned closing by sewing a button to the right side of the garment and a snap directly beneath the button on the underside. Fakes generally look like what they are and if you object to this try another means of closing—loops, silk-covered snaps, outsize hooks and eyes, buckles and bows, eyelets and studs, braid frogs—and there are always zippers.

AND SEW ON—THE BUTTON

Buttons are sewn to the left front directly on the center front line.

1. Remove the diagonal bastings from the buttonholes.

2. Close the garment right front over left, matching the center front markings. Match the top and bottom of the garment. Pin. If there are any stripes, checks, plaids, or prominent weaves make sure they match, too.

3. Using a safety pin (this won't fall out as a straight pin may), pin through the opening of the first buttonhole directly on the center line where the button is to be located. Close the safety pin. Unbutton the pin.

4. Sew on the button in the following way:

Use a single thread of matching color. Knot the end. Take several tiny over-and-over stitches where the button is to be sewn. Cut away the knot.

If the button has a shank (Fig. 182a) sew through the loop, taking enough stitches to fasten the button firmly. How many stitches depends on the thickness of the thread, the kind of fabric, and the size of the shank. Use your judgment. Fasten at the base of the shank with several over-and-over stitches.

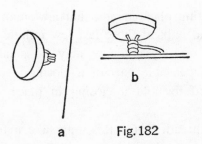

b

a   Fig. 182

If the button has no shank, you must create one of thread. The shank is the bridge between the right and left front. It should be as long as the several thicknesses of fabric are thick—outer fabric, interfacing, facing. The shank floats the button on the surface of the right front. If there were no shank, the garment would bunch rather than button.

To create the shank: Fasten the thread as above, hold the garment over the forefinger, stitch alternately through the eyes of the button and through the fabric. Keep the stitches loose and as long as you determine necessary. Make enough stitches to fasten the button securely. This depends on the eyes of the button, the thickness of the thread, and the character of the fabric. When the stitching is completed, wind the thread around and around the loose stitches to form the shank (Fig. 182b). Finish with tiny over-and-over stitches at the base of the shank.

5. When the first button is stitched on, button the garment. Pin it closed below to locate the correct position of the next button. The original pattern location may or may not be right by this time.

6. Sew on the second button. Repeat the procedure for each remaining button.

SNAPPY SNAPS

It is a fascinating phenomenon that a woman can work for days at her sewing and balk at those last few minutes it takes to sew on snaps or hooks and eyes. These may be small—and pesky—but they are an indispensable part of a closing.

Snaps are used to hold a closing in place when there is little strain.

Use a single thread. While this may take a few more stitches to anchor the snap securely, it does avoid the tangling and knotting of thread.

Start with a knotted thread but conceal it. Or start with several over-and-over stitches in a spot that will be covered by the snap.

Sew the ball first. Use overhand stitches through the small holes at the edge. Carry the thread under the snap to the next hole (Fig. 184a). Be careful that no stitches come through to the right side.

Press the ball against the opposite edge for an accurate location of the center of the socket. Sometimes chalking the ball is a help. Fasten the thread at this marking to conceal it under the socket.

Stitch the socket in the same way as the ball.

Covered snaps: a custom touch

If a snap is necessary in a place where it will be exposed at some time in wearing, the metal variety can be an eyesore. A camouflaged snap will merge into the background. Lining that matches the fabric is great for this purpose. Cover the snap with it.

Fig. 183

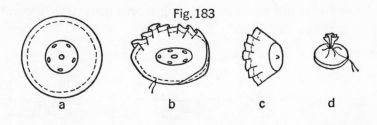

a   b   c   d

Here's how to cover a snap

1. Use metal snaps.

2. Cut two circles of matching lining fabric or self-fabric if it is not too thick. Make them slightly more than twice the diameter of the snap (Fig. 183a).

3. Gather the outer edges of each circle (Fig. 183b).

4. Pierce a tiny hole directly in the center of the circle. Force the ball through it (Fig. 183c).

5. Draw up the gathering until it fits taut over the snap. Fasten with stitches through the gathering (Fig. 183d).

6. Trim away the excess fabric.

7. Cover the socket with the second circle. Draw up the thread. Fasten.

8. Snap the ball and socket together. The exposed ball will create the hole in the socket as it is forced down.

9. Attach to the garment in the same way as metal snaps.

AND HOOKS AND EYES

Hooks and eyes are used for a closing where there is considerable strain. Be sure to fasten them securely.

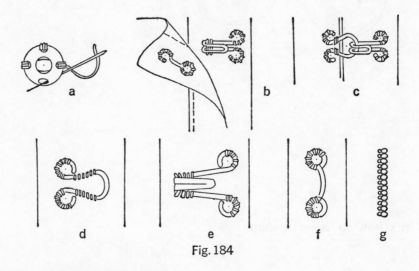

Fig. 184

1. Mark the position for the hook and eye carefully. Use straight eyes where the edges overlap (Fig. 184b). Use round eyes where edges meet (Fig. 184c). Notice that the round eye is extended slightly beyond the edge for a true closing.

2. Using overhand stitches and a single thread, sew through the loops and around the bill of the hook (Figs. 184d and e). Be sure the stitches do not come through to the right side.

3. Sew the eye through the loops. The curve of the bar is toward the outer edge of the closing (Fig. 184f). A custom touch for an eye in an exposed location is one made of thread (Fig. 184g). To make this embroidered bar: take two or three stitches directly over each other the length of the bar. Keep the stitches taut. Bring the needle up at one end. Work blanket stitches (see page 179) the entire length of the bar. Fasten at the other end with tiny over-and-over stitches.

THE LOOP-AND-BUTTON CLOSING

A charming, much-in-vogue closing is the loop and button.
The loop may be made of braid or fabric; it may be firm or soft.
This is the way to make a *firm loop* of self-fabric.

1. Cut a 1″ strip of bias. (Remember that all joinings are on the
straight of goods. Trim the seam allowances to ⅛″ and press them
in the direction of the pull.)

2. Cut a length of ⅛″ cable cord or firm string twice as long
as the bias strip.

3. Midway through the cord, fold the bias strip over it, right side
against the cord, wrong side out.

4. Machine stitch or tack across the bias strip at the middle of the
cord (Fig. 185a). Using a cording foot, stitch close to the cord but
leave a little room for the seam allowance when turned (Fig. 185a).
Make the beginning and end a little wider so the turning will be
easier. Note: when stitching bias, remember to loosen the tension and
use smaller stitches so there is more thread to accommodate to the
bias stretch. Also, stretch the bias a little as you stitch to provide
more elasticity.

5. Trim the seam allowances to ⅛″.

6. Reverse the bias over the other end of the cord (Fig. 185b).
Smooth the bias over the cord. The right side is now out and the
seam hidden. Cut away the unnecessary cord.

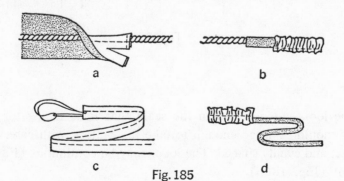

a   b

c   d
Fig. 185

For a *soft loop,* don't use the cord.

1. Make a 1″ bias strip.

2. Fold the strip with the right sides inside. Stitch to the desired width of the tubing. Make the end and beginning of the strip a little wider for easing turning.

3. Trim the seam allowance to a width a little wider than the finished tube. The seam allowance is used to pad the tube in place of cording. A thin fabric requires larger seam allowances to fill the tube; heavy fabrics need smaller seam allowances.

4. Turn the tubing to the right side. Fasten a blunt needle and buttonhole twist to one end. Push the needle through the tubing head first (Fig. 185c). The thread and tubing following through to the right side (Fig. 185d).

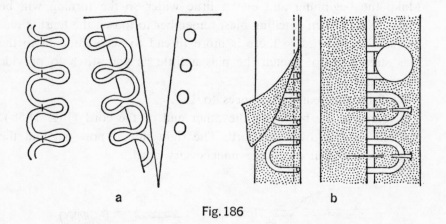

a   b

Fig. 186

The loops are inserted in the seam that joins facing to garment. They should be large enough to take the buttons with ease, identical in size, and evenly spaced. The loops may be continuous (Fig. 186a), or cut (Fig. 186b).

FANCIFUL FROGS

If you can make tubing, you can make frogs.

Twist the tubing into fanciful shapes. Fasten with small stitches to the wrong side at the crossings of the tubing to hold the design in place (Fig. 187a). Keep one loop free for buttoning. Stitch a button to the other loop (Fig. 187b). Place the buttoned frogs in position on both sides of the closing. Sew to the garment with small stitches on the underside.

Fig. 187

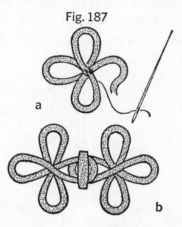

EMBROIDERED EYELETS — EYE OPENERS

If you are the proud owner of beautiful studs, here is still another lovely closing—embroidered eyelets.

1. Pin right and left sides of the garment closed on the center line.

2. Punch a hole through both at the same time. Use a stiletto, a darning needle, an orange stick, or any similar sharp tool that won't injure the fabric. Unpin the garment.

3. Overcast each eyelet to hold the edges of outer fabric and facing together. Work the eyelet with a blanket stitch, a buttonhole stitch or just a plain satin stitch (Fig. 213c). (See page 179 for stitches).

You may need to insert the stiletto from time to time to keep the eyeles open and to make sure they are the right size. Fabric has a tendency to creep back to cover the hole.

This is a particularly good idea for washable blouses. No loss or mangling of buttons in washing. Pressing the flat, buttonless surface is easy.

FLATTERING FRAME FOR THE FACE — THE COLLAR

There's no doubt about it! A collar is certainly a flattering frame for a face (be it eight or eighty). Fortunately there is a collar for every shape, size, and type of face. Little ones, big ones, tailored ones, frilly ones, dramatic ones, and modest ones—take your choice.

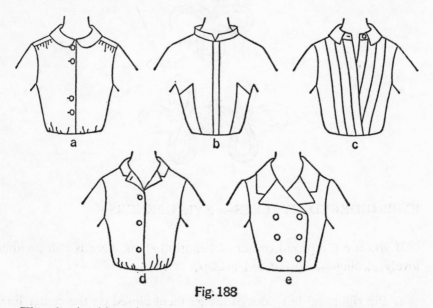

Fig. 188

The classic shirtwaist dress usually has a Peter Pan collar or some variation thereof (Fig. 188a), a band collar (Fig. 188b), or a combination of the two (Fig. 188c), a convertible collar (Fig. 188d), or a notched collar (Fig. 188e).

The method of making and attaching these collars is much the same.

When the collar and its facing are cut separately

1. Cut the collar (upper collar), facing (undercollar), and inter-facing. The interfacing is generally cut from the undercollar pattern.

2. Trim off the corner of the interfacing to about ¼″ beyond the seam line (Fig. 189a). This eliminates bulk at the point of the collar when it is turned. (Treat an interfacing at any corner in the same way—that is, cuffs, lapels, extensions, tabs, welts, etc.)

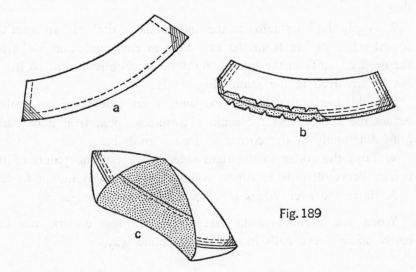

Fig. 189

3. Apply the interfacing to the collar rather than the collar facing. This places the interfacing in such position that when stitched and turned, the seam allowances will not show.

4. Stitch the collar and interfacing to the facing, leaving the neck edge open. Press the seam allowances open and grade them. Free the corners of bulk. Notch the outside curved edge (Fig. 189b).

5. Turn the collar to the right side. Carefully work the corner out, pushing up gently from the inside. Don't use a sharp instrument; don't push too hard.

6. Press all outside edges, rolling the seam to the underside. Understitch the facing to the seam allowances. End the stitching 1″ each side of a corner (Fig. 189c).

7. Baste the neck edges together ½″ from the neck edge.

When the collar and its facing are cut all-in-one

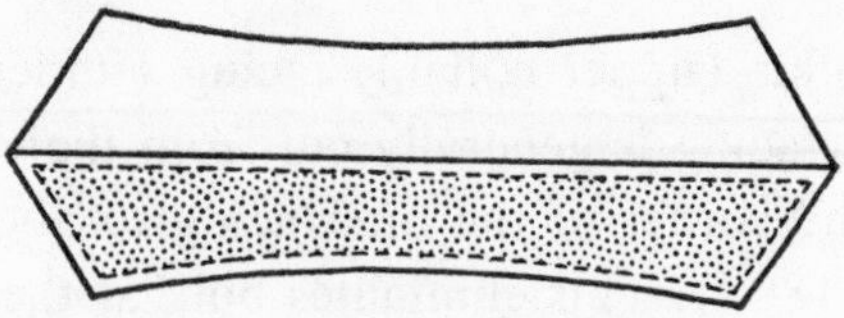

Fig. 190

1. Cut the interfacing from the undercollar pattern to the fold line.

2. Apply the interfacing to the undercollar. Stitch ⅛″ in from the folded edge, ¾″ in from the raw edge at each end, and ½″ from the neck edge. Trim the interfacing close to each seam line so it will not be involved in the seam (Fig. 190).

3. Fold the collar lengthwise with right sides together. Stitch across the ends. Press the seam allowances open, trim and grade. Snip diagonally at the corner to free it of bulk.

4. Turn the collar to the right side. Work out the points of the collar. Press all outside edges, rolling the seams to the underside.

5. Baste the neck edges together ½″ from the edge.

When you know how to make both of these collars, you can easily make sleeve cuffs in exactly the same way.

How to attach the collar to the bodice

Stitch the back neck facing to the front facing at the shoulders. Be sure to make the necessary adjustments for fit. Stitch the front facing to the front edge of the bodice when necessary. Finish all the outside edges of the facings.

Pin and baste the completed collar to the bodice neckline, matching center backs, notches, and the point at which the collar joins the front neck edge. To hold the collar securely in place at this point, back stitch or machine stitch for ½″.

Fold the facings back against the bodice along the front fold line (or seam) so that the right sides of bodice and facing are together. At the neck edge the collar is sandwiched between the two (Fig. 191a). Match all notches and shoulder seams. Ease, stretch, and clip as necessary. Pin and baste to position.

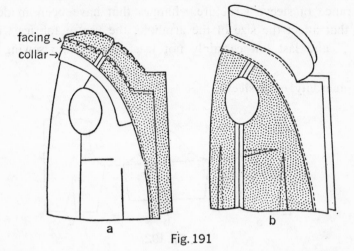

facing →
collar →

a   b
Fig. 191

With the garment side on top, stitch through all layers in one continuous seam which joins collar and facing to the bodice at the same time.

Understitch the facing at the neck edge (Fig. 191b). Turn the facing to the inside of the bodice (Fig. 191b). Trim, grade, and clip as necessary to make it lie flat. Press and pin to position. Tack the facing at the shoulder seam.

HOW TO SET AND SEW THE SLEEVE

Fashion has been kind in recent years to beginning sewers. It has given us the sleeveless shift dress. In addition to its fashion appeal is the appeal of easy construction.

Many not-so-new sewers as well as beginning sewers do their utmost to postpone (if not altogether to avoid) the selection of a set-in sleeve with all the problems they think it presents. A great and popular dodge is limiting the choice of patterns to those with kimono sleeves. But after all, how many sleeveless or kimono-sleeved dresses can a wardrobe sustain? If the truth must be known, there are problems with kimono sleeves, too. Ask anyone who has tried unsuccessfully to put in a gusset.

Setting and stitching the sleeve is not the easiest operation in sewing. It has been made more difficult by the following factors:

ignorance of sleeve structure, changes that have been made in fitting that affect the size of the armhole, the use of fabrics with little "give," and last but certainly not least, inadequate sewing advice.

The anatomy of a sleeve

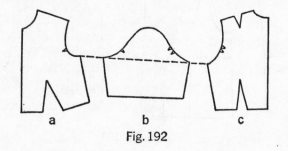

a   b   c

Fig. 192

Examine the pattern above (Fig. 192). The part of the sleeve above the broken line is called the sleeve cap. The sleeve cap is as long as the front and back armholes combined plus 1″ to 1½″ for ease. The shape of the front armhole is different than the back armhole. It is shorter and the curve deeper (Fig. 192a). The back armhole is longer and the curve shallower (Fig. 192c). The sleeve cap is drafted to fit each of these lengths and curves (Fig. 192b).

Make this simple test and you will see this difference (Fig. 193).

Fig. 193

If you are ever in doubt as to which side of a sleeve is front and which back, fold the sleeve in half lengthwise. The front cap is always deeper. (In a below-elbow-length sleeve, there is another way to tell front from back. The elbow darts or gathers are *always in back*.)

On both sleeve cap and armhole you will find matching notches to aid in setting the sleeve. The curve of the sleeve cap that arches over the shoulder from the front notch to the back notch contains the ease. The underarm curve that swings from front notch to back notch is exactly the same in length for sleeve and bodice. Notches are placed on the sleeve cap at those points where the curve of the cap changes direction. This corresponds to the creases where arm and body meet. The fact that bodies differ in measurement from this point to the shoulder while patterns have standard caps accounts for many ill-fitting sleeves.

No other will do

A sleeve cap is designed for a particular armhole. It will fit no other. Where changes that affect the armhole have been made in the fitting (shoulder seams or side seams, chest or shoulder blade areas) you must re-establish the original armhole.

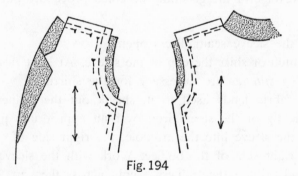

Fig. 194

Using the original pattern for the sleeve, match the front, then the back in the following manner:

Lay the shoulder seam of the pattern along the shoulder seam of the garment. Set the armhole seam of the pattern at that point on the shoulder where you have decided it will look well on you. Pin securely.

Let the underarm of the pattern fall as much below the armhole of the garment as is necessary for the pattern to lie flat while touching the side seam. Pin securely.

Using the pattern as a guide, cut a new armhole.

In Fig. 194 the shaded part represents a fitted garment with shortened armhole that needs to be recut to size. The original pattern is superimposed for cutting.

It's ease that does it

A sleeve cap must have ease to accommodate the roundness of the upper arm. Ease also permits the arm to move without strain or restraint. Were it eliminated, the sleeve would bind and wrinkle. Since the curve of the cap creates a bias line, it is comparatively simple to ease the cap into the armhole in most fabrics. There are some, however, that hardly "budge"—pique, ottoman, taffeta, to name a few. With these fabrics, easing is almost impossible.

There are two possible solutions: (1), eliminate some of the ease in the cap (a risky business unless one has studied her figure requirements very carefully and in addition knows something of pattern alteration); (2), set the sleeve by the method described below. This is the reverse of the generally accepted procedure but it works beautifully.

1. Stitch the sleeve seam. Press open.

2. Ease-stitch or shirr the cap of the sleeve. At least *two rows of tiny gathering stitches* are necessary for the shirring.

3. If the fabric lends itself to it, shrink out the fullness at the cap with the tip of the steam iron over an appropriate press pad.

4. Insert the sleeve into the armhole, the right side of the sleeve against the right side of the bodice. Work with the sleeve side up so you can distribute the fullness evenly across the cap. Hold the sleeve in an outside curve as it will appear when worn (Fig. 195a).

5. Start the matching *at the shoulder*. Match the shoulder seam of the garment with the shoulder marking of the sleeve cap. If, in fitting, the shoulder seam has been brought forward or backward, then the shoulder marking of the sleeve cap must be changed accordingly.

6. Starting at the shoulder and working down, gently distribute the fullness across the cap. Pin the cap down to the notches. Do not pin the underarm yet (Fig. 195b).

7. Try on the garment to check the set of the sleeve. Check the vertical and horizontal grains. Examine the distribution of the ease—front and back. Note any adjustments that need to be made. Remove the garment, make the needed changes, try on again.

8. Finish setting the sleeve. Let the sleeve underarm drop on the

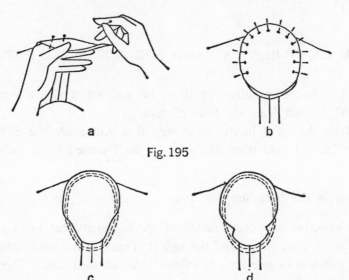

Fig. 195

bodice. This may be as much as ¾" but no more. Match the underarm seams of the sleeve and garment. Pin securely. Baste, if you
like, though pinning should be sufficient.

9. Using the underarm of the sleeve as a guide, trim away the
garment to match the underarm curve of the sleeve.

10. Stitch the sleeve into the armhole. Work with the sleeve up
so you can continue to control the ease. Start at the underarm seam
and stitch until you return to the starting point. Examine the stitching line from the bodice side. If the line is somewhat wavering,
make a second line of stitching close to the first. For this second
stitching, work with the garment up; it is easier to see how to correct
the stitching. The two lines of stitching also reinforce the underarm,
which is subjected to considerable stress (Fig. 195c).

11. The sleeve is meant to fit at the armhole seam and not at the
shorter raw edge of the seam allowance. Clip the seam allowances at
the notches. Clip the underarm seam allowances every ½" or so to
release the strain. Or, since there are two rows of stitching, you can
safely trim the underarm seam allowance close to the underarm
seam (Fig. 195d). Press the seam allowance of the cap into the
sleeve to serve as support.

If you can set and stitch a sleeve properly you are well on your
way to being an expert sewer.

YOU CAN'T BEAT A BAND FOR A SLEEVE FINISH

What would a shirtwaist dress be without a sleeve band for a finish? It completes the tailored look.

Make the band in the same way that you made the collar. (See page 258.) Leave open the edge to be fastened to the sleeve.

Room at the bottom

A long, tailored sleeve needs an opening at the band or cuff so you can easily slide your hand through it. This is provided by the pattern in a position in line with the little finger of your hand. The opening is handled in one of two ways.

A faced opening

1. Cut a straight strip of self-fabric for a facing (Fig. 196a).

2. Place the facing, centered, over the slash line, right sides together. Baste to position.

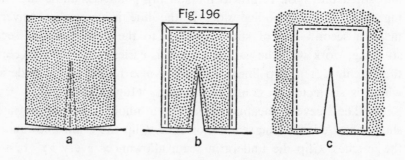

Fig. 196

a   b   c

3. Stitch along one side of the marking starting ¼″ from it, taper to almost nothing at the point, take one stitch across the point, then down the other side in the same way as the first side (Fig. 196a).

4. Slash between the stitching (Fig. 196b).

5. Turn the outside edges of the facing to the wrong side. Edge stitch (Fig. 196b).

6. Turn the facing to the inside. Tack at each corner (Fig. 196c).

A continuous lap

1. Cut a strip of self-fabric twice the length of the opening by 1½″ or 1¾″ wide.

2. Stay stitch the slash. Slash between the lines of stay stitching (Fig. 197a).

3. With right sides together, stitch the strip of self-fabric (lap) to the opening taking ¼″ seam allowance on the lap, ¼″ tapered to nothing on the sleeve opening (Fig. 197b).

4. Turn under ¼″ seam allowance on the free edge of the lap. Bring the fold to the stitching line. Hem (Fig. 197c).

5. Turn in the fold on the front edge of the sleeve and press. The lap forms an extension on the back edge of the sleeve (Fig. 197d).

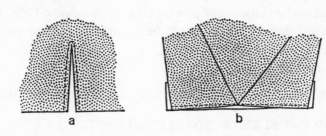

Fig. 197

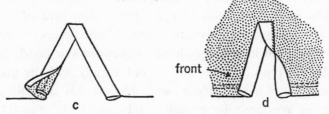

How to attach the sleeve band to the sleeve

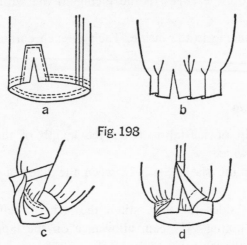

Fig. 198

1. Either gather the wrist edge of the sleeve (Fig. 198a) or pleat it (Fig. 198b).

2. Make a bound buttonhole in the sleeve band; hand-worked or machine-made buttonholes can be done when the sleeve is finished.

3. Complete the band, leaving open the edge to be attached to the sleeve.

4. With right sides together, seam one side of the open edge of the sleeve band to the gathered or pleated edge of the sleeve (Fig. 198c).

5. Turn under the free edge of the band and hem to the inside stitching line (Fig. 198d).

6. Sew on the button.

You can't beat that for an easy, pretty sleeve finish, can you?

THE KIMONO SLEEVE AND ITS GUSSET

It is no wonder the kimono sleeve has long been a favorite. It is easy to wear, easy to fit, easy to sew. There is only one troublesome little detail—the gusset—and that is easily taken care of.

A gusset is a hinge that permits a fitted kimono sleeve freedom of movement. Without it we might have to abandon our dearly beloved kimono sleeve or go back to the ancient variety with its great un-fitted depth. Even the Japanese, who devised this delightful garb, now work in Western-type clothing and save their graceful deep-sleeved kimonos for dress and ceremonial occasions.

It's easy enough to sew the gusset if you do it by hand. (In sewing, this is always a good rule to follow: if it's too difficult to do it by machine, do it by hand. Custom dressmakers have raised this axiom to a fine art. So much of fine dressmaking is done by hand.)

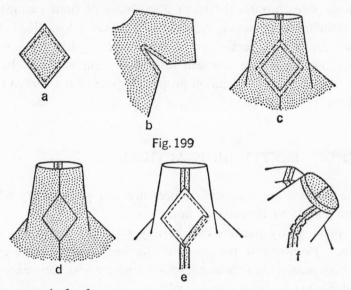

Fig. 199

How to stitch the gusset

1. On the gusset: mark the seam line with guide basting (Fig. 199a).

2. On the garment: stay stitch the opening as marked on the pattern; reinforce the point with tiny machine stitches or a small square of seam binding. Slash on the slash line (Fig. 199b).

3. Turn under the seam allowance of the slashed opening along the line of stay stitching, rolling it slightly to the underside.

4. Lap the folded edge of the slash over the right side of the gusset, bringing the fold to the guide basting. Pin or baste to position (Fig. 199c).

5. Using a single strand of thread and a ⌗10 crewel needle, slip stitch the fold to the gusset. Reinforce the points with tiny whipping stitches (Fig. 199d). (See page 179.)

Slip stitching is really strong enough if the stitches are small enough. For athletic types and doubting Thomasinas: make a second row of slip stitching. Or, using the slip stitching as a guide, machine stitch right over it (Fig. 199e).

If you insist on machine stitching, don't attempt to stitch all four sides in one continuous line. Stitch one side at a time, break the thread at each corner, tie the ends, begin the next row of stitching where the previous one ended. Machine stitching is always done on the wrong side through the seam allowances of both garment and gusset. Stitching a gusset on the right side makes it look like a patch.

There are a few semi-fitted kimono sleeves that do not need gussets. Just make sure you can raise your arm in them. In these sleeves, fit and action depend on proper clipping of the curved underarm seam (Fig. 199f).

POCKETS — PRETTY OR PRACTICAL

Some pockets are practical. Others are just plain pretty whether they are meant to be used or not.

Just plain pretty pockets can be any size, any style, any shape, any place. No-nonsense pockets, built for use, must be large enough to get your hands into them and placed where you can reach them without having to be a contortionist.

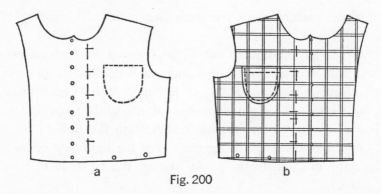

a   Fig. 200   b

Seam, slash, or surface—the place for pockets

The patch pocket is a surface pocket. It is made and applied to the right side of the garment. It is a very easy one for beginners.

1. Mark the position of the pocket carefully on the right side of the garment with tailor's tacks or basting (Fig. 200a). If striped, checked, or plaid material is used, be sure to match the pocket to the garment (Fig. 200b).

2. Mark the pocket carefully—seam allowances, fold line for hem facing (Fig. 201a).

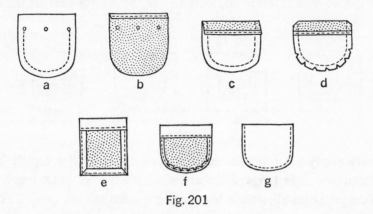

Fig. 201

3. Turn under ¼″ at the top of the pocket to the wrong side. Press and edge stitch (Fig. 201b).

4. Turn the hem to the outside of the pocket along the fold line. Pin or baste to position (Fig. 201c).

5. Stitch on the seam line around the entire pocket, catching in the hem facing (Fig. 201c). This line of stitching makes it easier to turn the seam allowance under to form the patch.

6. Trim the seam allowance. Make a diagonal slash across the seam allowance at each corner. If the pocket is round, notch the seam allowances on the curve (Fig. 201d). If the pocket is square, miter the corners (Fig. 201e).

7. Press open the seam allowances of the hem on the point presser. Grade.

8. Turn the hem to the wrong side of the pocket, working out the corners carefully. Turn under the remaining seam allowances, rolling the stitching line to the wrong side (Fig. 201f). Press.

9. Fasten the hem in place either by topstitching or by tiny hemming stitches (Fig. 201e)—whichever is consistent with the design.

10. Pin the pocket to position on the right side of the garment. Place pins at right angles to the edge. Baste if necessary.

11. If machine stitching is consistent with the design of the garment, topstitch the pocket to the garment close to and an even distance in from the edge (Fig. 201g).

If the design looks better without stitching that shows, slip stitch the pocket to the garment. Make the stitches a tiny bit in from and under the edge. Reinforce the corners on the wrong side with over-and-over stitches.

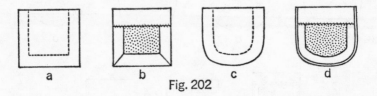

a   b   c   d

Fig. 202

A very pretty patch pocket can be made by decorative topstitching away from the edge (Figs. 202a and c). This type of pocket needs a much deeper seam allowance for a straight-sided pocket (Fig. 202b), and a facing for a curved pocket (Fig. 202d).

A set-in-a-seam pocket has the virtue of being inconspicuous. This pocket may be placed anywhere there is a seam.

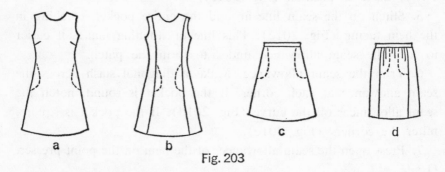

a   b   c   d

Fig. 203

The broken lines in Fig. 203a show the position of the pocket in the side seam of a dress. Fig. 203b shows the pocket in a front style line of a dress. It may appear in the same positions in a skirt (Figs. 203c and d). Even if the pattern doesn't contain a pocket, you may easily add one in any convenient seam.

This pocket consists of two pouch-shaped pieces of self-fabric or lining. The opening of the pocket should be large enough to get your hand into it easily; the pouch should be deep enough to let your hand settle comfortably.

Here is an easy way to set this pocket into the seam.

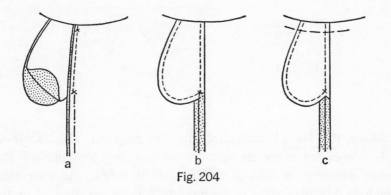

Fig. 204

1. With right sides together, stitch the straight edges of the pocket to the garment, matching the markings for the opening. Use only ⅜" of the ⅝" seam allowance designated in the pattern. This will provide ¼" for rolling the seam to the underside (Fig. 204a).

2. With right sides together, stitch the seams of the garment below and/or above the pocket. Take the regulation ⅝" seam allowance (Fig. 204a).

3. Clip the seam allowance of the garment at the place where the pocket joins it.

4. Press the garment seam allowances open. Press the pocket to the front along the original seam line. Be sure to roll the seam to the underside to conceal it (Fig. 204b).

5. Stitch the pocket sections together with the regulation ⅝" seam allowance (Fig. 204b).

In a skirt, baste the top edge of the pocket to the waistline (Fig. 204c). Stitch the top of the pocket into the waistband seam.

The bound pocket is set in a slash. If you've learned to make a beautiful bound buttonhole you can easily convert it into a bound pocket (Fig. 205a).

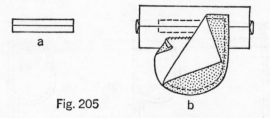

Fig. 205   b

1. Make the bound buttonhole in the garment. The piping is usually deeper for a pocket than for an ordinary buttonhole. (Remember: whenever a slash is to be made in fabric, the area must be reinforced with a strip of lightweight interfacing applied to the underside.)

2. Cut two pieces of self-fabric or lining for the pouch of the pocket. Make them as wide as the opening of the buttonhole and deep enough to get your hand into the pocket comfortably. Add seam allowances.

3. Stitch the underpocket to the upper binding with backstitching. Hem the upper pocket to the under binding (Fig. 205b). (The under pocket is the part against the body; the upper pocket is the part against the outer fabric.)

4. Stitch the upper and under pockets together by machine.

The fake welt or flap used decoratively though deceptively

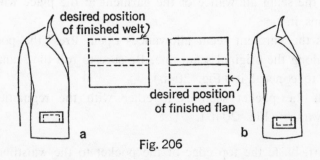

desired position of finished welt

desired position of finished flap

a   Fig. 206   b

1. Mark the position of the finished welt on the garment (Figs. 206a and b).

2. Cut a strip of fabric the length of the welt by twice its width plus ¼" seam allowances.

3. Fold the welt in half lengthwise, right sides together. Stitch across the ends.

4. Press the seam allowances open on the point presser, clip diagonally across the corner. Grade.

5. Turn to the right side, working out the corners carefully.

6. Press, rolling the seam to the underside.

7. Stitch across the open edge of the welt.

8. Pin the completed welt on the right side of the garment just opposite to the way it will look in the finished garment.

For instance: a welt that will eventually turn up to simulate a welt pocket is placed "head down" below the marking (Fig. 206a); a welt that will turn down as a flap is placed "head up" above the marking (Fig. 206b). The broken lines in the illustration show the desired position on the garment; the solid lines show the pinned position of the welt.

9. Match the seam line of the welt to the line that marks its position on the garment.

10. Stitch the welt to the garment. Trim the seam allowance close to the stitching (Fig. 207a).

11. Turn and press to position.

If you wish *to make an honest pocket out of this outright fake* follow Steps 1 to 10 and continue as follows:

11. Cut the pocket of self-fabric or lining. Make it equal in width to the welt (or flap) and twice the depth of the pocket plus seam allowances. Mark the opening slash.

12. Place the pocket over the welt, right sides together. Set the slash line of the pocket ⅛" below the line of machine stitching on the welt. Baste to position (Fig. 207b).

13. Turn to the wrong side. Stitch a rectangle for the opening. Make the first side directly over the line of machine stitching that fastens welt to garment, the second parallel to it and ¼" below it. *Start and stop the stitching two or three stitches in from each end.*

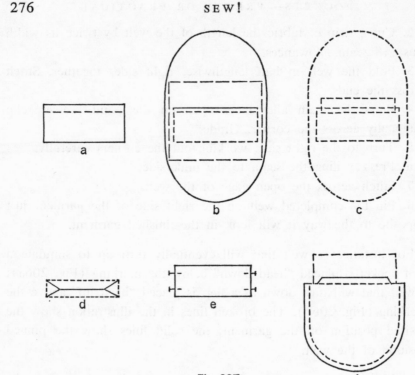

Fig. 207

Stitch across the ends. This will make the opening of the pocket slightly smaller than the welt so that when the welt is turned to its final position it will completely conceal the opening (Fig. 207c). (If you wind up with holes at each end, your stitched rectangle is too large.)

14. Slash through the center of the rectangle to within ¼" of the ends. Clip diagonally to the corners (Fig. 207d).

15. Turn the pocket to the wrong side by slipping it through the opening. The welt or flap will automatically assume its proper position on the right side. Pin in place (Fig. 207e).

16. Turn to the wrong side. Stitch the upper and under pockets together. You will notice that the upper pocket is slightly longer than the under pocket because of the ¼" depth of the stitched rectangle (Fig. 207f). Trim it to match the under pocket.

17. On the right side, slip stitch the ends of the welt to the garment. To hold a flap in position, either slip stitch ½" down from the top on each side or machine stitch across the flap ½" down from the top edge.

TO BELT OR NOT TO BELT

How to hide or disguise a waistline seam? Somehow, unlike any other seam, this particular one when exposed and unadorned makes a dress look unfinished.

Sometimes just topstitching (Fig. 208a) or piping (Fig. 208b) adds just the right finishing touch. Most often it is a belt that encircles the seam at the waistline (Fig. 208c).

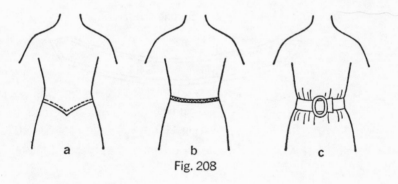

Fig. 208

If it is a belt you decide on, there are limitless varieties: ties, strings, braids, ribbon, leather, suede, fur, studded, beaded, jeweled, buttoned, buckled, bowed, straight, shaped, contoured—just about anything your fancy can devise and your waistline take. Whatever it is—it is always an attention-getting accessory. Let the experts make it, or learn to make it expertly yourself.

A turned belt of self-fabric is the simplest kind of belt to make.

1. On the lengthwise grain, cut a strip of self-fabric of sufficient length and twice the width of the finished belt. Add seam allowances (Fig. 209a). A shaped belt takes two similar pieces (Fig. 209b).

2. If the belt is to tie, then both ends must have the same finished look. Fold the band lengthwise with the right sides inside. Stitch across both ends and along the long edge, leaving an opening for turning on the long edge. Press the seam open, grade, free corners of bulk. Turn to the right side. Slip stitch the opening.

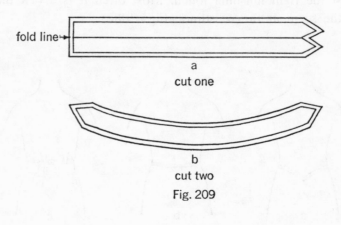

fold line→

a

cut one

b

cut two

Fig. 209

If the belt is to be buckled, stitch all sides except the end to which the buckle is to be attached. Press the seam open, grade, etc., turn through the open end.

To stiffen a washable belt, use a washable interfacing like muslin, cotton belting, or an extra layer of self-fabric.

To stiffen a non-washable belt, use any interfacing material that will make the belt stiff enough for the design or to your taste.

If the fabric is bulky or heavy, use French belting or ribbon for a facing just as you did for the waistband.

A stiffened belt is built over the interfacing

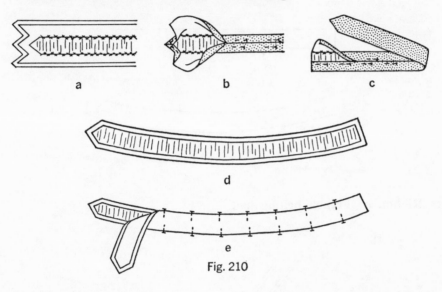

Fig. 210

1. Cut one thickness of interfacing without seam allowances to the shape, length, and width of the belt.

2. Pin the interfacing to position on the wrong side of the belt (Fig. 210a).

3. *For a straight belt:* catch stitch the interfacing to the belt, making sure that no stitches show on the right side. Fold the facing to position on the underside of the belt. Turn under the seam allowances and pin so the folds meet at the center (Fig. 210b). Slip stitch the seam (Fig. 210c).

For a contour belt: Turn the seam allowances down over the interfacing. Catch stitch, making sure the stitches do not come through to the right side (Fig. 210d). Turn under the seam allowances of the facing; press. Pin carefully over the interfaced belt (Fig. 210e), and slip stitch.

All pinning and stitching must be done very carefully to preserve the grain. Off-grain pulling and wrinkling disfigure a belt. Top-stitching when the belt is completed adds firmness.

A straight belt (Fig. 211a) may be shaped to fit the waistline better by steam pressing in a slight curve (Fig. 211b).

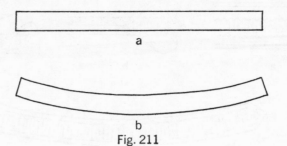

a

b

Fig. 211

Ribbon or French belting belt

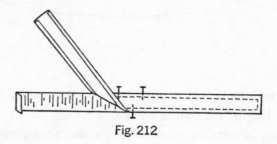

Fig. 212

1. Cut the belt to the desired width and length plus seam allowances.

2. Turn under all seam allowances of the fabric. Press to position.

3. Turn under the ends of the ribbon.

4. Pin the ribbon to the fabric on all edges (Fig. 212).

5. Stitch.

A buckled belt

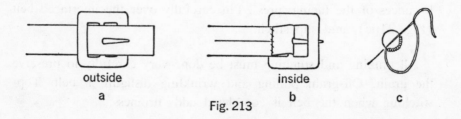

outside

inside

a

Fig. 213

b

c

When a buckle is to be used for fastening a belt, the finished width of the belt must fit the inside measurement of the buckle. Allow 1″ additional length for turning the belt back after the buckle is inserted.

1. Pierce the belt for the prong of the buckle 1″ from one end. Enlarge the opening with the point of scissors to fit the prong (Fig. 213a). Work the opening as an eyelet.

2. Insert the prong, pull the end to the underside. Stitch either by hand or by machine (Fig. 213b).

3. Try on the belt. Mark the position for an eyelet. Pierce and work the first eyelet (Fig. 213c). Make second and third eyelets 1″ either side of the first for variations in waist measurements. For eyelets, use any thread that matches in color.

A belt must know its place

A belt may be completely separate from a dress or it may be held in place by thread or carrier.

A French tack (sometimes called a swing tack or a suspension tack) holds a belt in place invisibly (Fig. 214a). Take a tiny stitch on the side seam of the dress at the waistline, then another directly opposite on the facing at the center of the belt. Pull up the thread

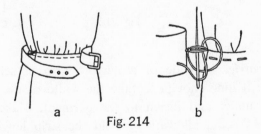

a   Fig. 214   b

to about ¼″ or ⅜″. Repeat, making several such stitches. Work blanket stitches (see page 179) over the threads (Fig. 214b).

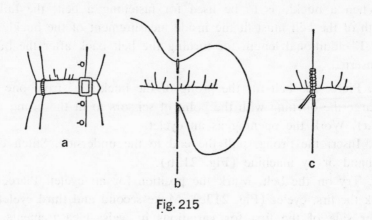

Fig. 215

A thread loop carrier visibly holds the belt in place (Fig. 215a). Make the carrier slightly longer than the belt and placed so that the belt is centered over the waistline. Several strands of thread go through the fabric at the side seam (Fig. 215b). Work with blanket stitches like the French tack (Fig. 215c).

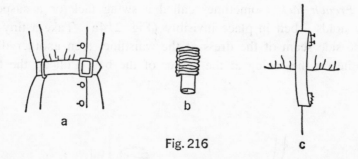

Fig. 216

A fabric carrier is made of a narrow strip of self-fabric (Fig. 216a). Make it long enough to take the width of the belt plus two ends to turn under and fasten to the garment. Make it twice the width plus ¼" seam allowances. Fold the strip lengthwise, stitch, and turn to the right side like *tubing* (Fig. 216b). (See page 255.) Place the carrier on the side seam over the waistline so the belt will be centered. Turn under the ends and whip stitch to the dress (Fig. 216c).

MORE THAN MEETS THE EYE

Inside as well as outside the waistline shapes up to its potential—but it needs a slight assist from the sewer.

Tape shape

For a trim waistline in a dress with a waistline seam, stay the seam with cotton or rayon tape. This insures that the waistline will remain the correct measurement. The tape is applied to the inside of the skirt before it is joined to the bodice.

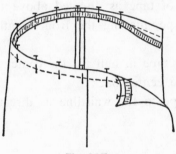

Fig. 217

If the dress has a center back opening:

1. Cut a length of tape equal to your waist measurement plus ½" ease plus two seam allowances.

2. Fold the tape in half and mark the center with a pin or a loop of thread.

3. Pin the center of the tape to the center front of the skirt. Pin the ends of the tape to the center back opening with raw edges matching.

4. Pin the rest of the tape to the skirt at intervals evenly on both sides (Fig. 217). Remember that the front of the skirt is always wider than the back (about 1") so the side seams are not really at the quarter mark. Make the front tape ½" longer than the back tape on both sides.

5. Baste stitch the lower edge of the tape to the seam line of the skirt.

6. Join the bodice and the skirt stitching through the lower edge of the tape. Clip the seam allowances.

7. Stitch the upper edge of the tape to the seam allowances.

8. Trim the remainder of the seam allowances of skirt and bodice close to the upper tape stitching line. Press the tape and seam allowances up into the bodice.

If the dress has a side opening:

1. Cut a length of tape as directed above (Step 1).

2. Section the tape, making the front length 1″ wider than the back.

3. Fold the front tape in half for the center front. Fold the back tape in half for the center back.

4. Attach the tape to the waistline as directed above.

Final touch

For a trim waistline in a fitted dress that has no waistline seam, use 1″ grosgrain ribbon. (Paris uses stiff belting.) The ribbon is applied to the inside of the dress after it is completed.

1. Cut the ribbon to your waist measurement plus seam allowances—no ease. This should fit snugly.

2. Turn back the ends and sew on hooks and eyes.

3. Section the ribbon for center front, center back, side seams in the same way as directed for the tape.

4. Pin the ribbon at the waistline at center front, center back, all seams and all darts.

5. Tack the ribbon to all seams and darts. Leave the ribbon unfastened several inches either side of the opening (Fig. 218a). (Fasten the ribbon before fastening the dress.)

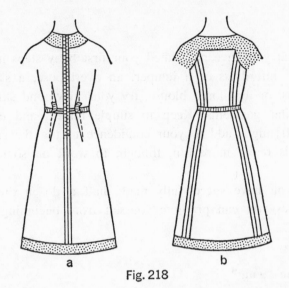

Fig. 218

This inside ribbon stay not only shapes the waistline as intended by the design, it reduces the strain on the zippered closing. If this seems desirable to you, apply grosgrain ribbon in the same way to a dress that does have a waistline seam (Fig. 218b). Omit the tape, press the waistline seam allowances open, and apply the ribbon.

An inside ribbon band is truly a fitting, concluding couture touch.

BEGINNER'S LUCK?

Anyone who has come *this* far in this book knows there is no such thing as beginner's luck. She is only too aware of the thought, the planning, the skill, the patience, the time, the work that go into making any beautiful garment. (Who would want any other kind?) The same considerations would hold for a professional: there are not two sets of rules—one for home sewers and one for professionals. The difference between the two is largely one of degree rather than of kind—the degree of knowledge, the degree of experience, the degree of dedication.

Baby steps

Now that you have negotiated your first baby steps in sewing by making a shift dress or a jumper, an overblouse, a skirt, a shirt-waist dress, or a tailored blouse, try your newfound skill on a few more similar garments. Keep to simple fabrics and easy-to-make patterns. It might add to your confidence to use the same pattern again. It is really more fun, though, to work on something a bit different.

When you have successfully made half a dozen dresses, skirts, and blouses you can promote yourself from beginning to average sewer.

One of the "gang"

During your "average" sewer days make the following:

a wool dress with any of the style details you have already learned how to handle; this will give you some experience in stitching and pressing wool

a dress with different styling but still not too intricate—a different neckline, different sleeves, different skirt; make this of any fiber but silk or synthetic

a detailed skirt—one that has pockets, pleats, insets; use any fiber but silk

a detailed blouse of any fiber but silk—one that has a yoke, tucks, or scallops, an interesting neckline or collar

a one-piece dress—of silk (at last!)

a two-piece dress of any fiber

When you are proud to announce to a flabbergasted group of admiring friends, "I made this myself," you can consider yourself graduated from average to advanced sewer.

Take a giant step

Now take a giant step!

Choose a problem fabric like velvet, a knit, lace, chiffon, stripes, plaids, checks, diagonals, any of the foreign beauties or man-made wonders. Buy a length of expensive cloth and a designer pattern.

Don't wait too long before you try your hand at tailoring a coat or suit. You will find that many of the tailoring techniques are important to your fine dressmaking.

Keep studying, keep reading, keep observing, keep experimenting! When you've done all this—anything can be yours for the making.

Those who continue as confirmed sewers will be rewarded not only with handsome clothes but with all the aesthetic pleasures which are an integral part of the creative process of producing them —the excitement at the inception of an idea, the soaring imagination set in motion by a length of cloth or an intriguing line, the satisfaction of fitting together all those baffling little pieces of pattern, the sensual pleasure in the "look" and the "hand" of the material, the delight in seeing a thing of beauty emerge.

It is the author's sincere hope that the making of your clothes will *always* be as much pleasure as the wearing of them.

ADELE POLLOCK MARGOLIS

Philadelphia, Pennsylvania
October 7, 1965

INDEX